Passport of Faith

PASSPORT of FAITH

A Christian's Encounter with World Religions

by PATRICK NACHTIGALL

Warner Press
ANDERSON, INDIANA

Copyright © 2006 by Patrick Nachtigall. All rights reserved. No part of this publication may be reproduced, stored in a retrieval system, or transmitted in any form or by any means—electronic, mechanical, photocopy, recording or any other—except for brief quotations in printed reviews, without prior written permission of the publisher. For this and all other editorial matters, please contact:

 Coordinator of Communications and Publishing
Church of God Ministries, Inc.
PO Box 2420
Anderson, IN 46018-2420
1-800-848-2464
www.chog.org

To purchase additional copies of this book, to inquire about distribution and for all other sales-related matters, please contact:

Warner Press, Inc.
PO Box 2499
Anderson, IN 46018-9988
1-877-346-3974
www.warnerpress.com

All Scripture quotations, unless otherwise indicated, are taken from the *New King James Version*. Copyright © 1982 by Thomas Nelson, Inc. Used by permission. All rights reserved.

All Scripture quotations marked NIV are taken from the *Holy Bible, New International Version*®. NIV®. Copyright © 1973, 1978, 1984 by International Bible Society. Used by permission of Zondervan. All rights reserved.

Cover and text design by Carolyn Kuchar
Edited by Stephen R. Lewis

ISBN-13: 978-1-59317-130-8
ISBN-10: 1-59317-130-7

Printed in the United States of America.
06 07 08 09 10 /EP/ 10 9 8 7 6 5 4 3 2 1

*This book is dedicated to my greatest mentor, my mother.
Not a day goes by that I don't think of you.*

*W. Jene Nachtigall
1937–1991*

Contents

Acknowledgements ix

Introduction 1

1. **A Godless Paradise**
   Atheism in Cuba 15

2. **Losing Stock in the Sun Goddess**
   Shinto in Japan 49

3. **Taming the Tigers**
   Hinduism in Sri Lanka and Singapore 79

4. **The Meaning of Nothing**
   Buddhism in South Korea and Thailand 113

5. **The Rules for Long Life**
   Confucianism and Taoism in China 143

6. **Scattered Sheep**
   Judaism in Israel 175

7. **Searching for Osama**
   Islam in Morocco and Egypt 205

Appendix 1
   Globalization and Counteraction 247

Appendix 2
   7 Commitments to Help Us
   Become Global Christians 279

Bibliography 311

Acknowledgements

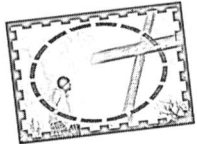

In 1970, I was a dying baby in an orphanage in Costa Rica, but by the grace of God, a family of missionaries found me, adopted me, and saved my life. I would first like to thank God for the miracle of my physical and spiritual salvation and for allowing me the privilege of both serving him in ministry and having the opportunity to travel around this beautiful world he created.

The following people are so deserving of appreciation:

In Anderson, I would like to thank Dr. Robert Edwards, director of Global Missions, for supporting this project since we first talked about it in Chiang Mai, Thailand, as well as Sharon Skaggs for working tirelessly on the behalf of us missionaries. A special thanks to all in the Communications and Publishing department at Church of God Ministries, especially Joe Allison and Stephen Lewis for making the book better. I would also like to thank those faculty members of Anderson University who supported me. Dr. Fred Shively and Rev. Don Collins deserve special recognition for their encouragement to me at pivotal points in my life. Dr. Don Johnson is not only an inspiration but loves the world's cultural diversity as much as I do. I'd also like to thank all my great friends on staff at Global Missions.

In Connecticut, a special thanks to those members of the Yale University faculty who encouraged me, as well as to Rev. Kermit and Susi Morrison of New Haven, who are an example to me of everything professional ministers should be. I would like to thank the congregation of St. Andrew's United Methodist Church for accepting Jamie and me and giving us a home.

In Costa Rica, I would like to thank the Cajina family for their love, Julia and the Monge family, and my father, Harry Nachtigall, who inspired me to become a missionary and who was not just my father but my friend—a reflection of our holy Father.

In New Hampshire, I also must recognize Dean Abbott, who has been my fellow pilgrim in the journey that is the Christian faith. We have gone through so much together since we first met as angry, disillusioned teenagers, but we have encouraged each other to stay faithful in the Lord and to mature. I can't imagine being who I am today without his strong influence in my life.

In New Zealand, I would like to recognize Chad Davenport, my fellow Gen-X missionary, whose work in the field encourages me and who has known about this book longer than anyone.

In Oregon, a special thank you to everyone at the Association of the Churches of God in Oregon and Southwest Washington for supporting me and granting me my ordination. At the state office, I must especially thank Julie Gregory

Acknowlegements

for her unwavering support and Bill and Honerrhea Martin, with whom Jamie and I have been able to share both our joys and struggles. I would like to thank Rev. Gale and Marilyn Hency for decades of encouragement; Rev. Bruce Hazel and my family at the Tigard Church of God in Tigard for helping to raise me; my sister Marcel, whose petition for a new baby brother won my parents over and gave me an incredible new life; and Daniel, Daniella and Marcellina as well. Special recognition goes to my best friends: Greg Dorr, Mike Russell, Alan Ryman, and Scott Stine. You are my brothers forever. Greg Dorr deserves special recognition for the many hours that he spent reviewing portions of this manuscript and assisting me with his excellent suggestions. Mike Russell also took time away from his busy schedule to offer invaluable input. Both of them are superb writers; I stand in awe of their abilities.

In Hong Kong, I want to thank our leaders Edmund Leung and Lisa Sin, who have been so supportive of our ministry. Working with them has been a dream come true. I especially value Edmund's friendship as we have partnered together for God's kingdom here in Hong Kong as well as watching crucial soccer matches together. *Dojeh-sai* to my Hong Kong Church of God brothers and sisters, whom Jamie and I absolutely adore! They inspire me more than I can say; it has been a true joy growing up in the Lord together as family.

Last, but certainly not least, I would like to give a very special thanks to my wife Jamie and my son Marco (named after Marco Polo, the great traveler who helped to bridge the gap between East and West).

Every day, Jamie, I love you more, and every year, I am more in awe of your seemingly effortless ability to be great at everything. You are a wonderful wife and mother, and you are my best friend. Thank you for doing the millions of unrecognized things that make our ministry possible, as well as your constant support of me. This book would not have been written without you. You are my best travel partner in more ways than one. When I asked you to marry me on that narrow, wooden, suspension bridge high above a Canadian gorge, I told you that our life together in ministry would be just as precarious as crossing that bridge but that we would survive if we hung on to each other and God. Thank you for hanging on and for making the adventure worthwhile.

Marco Nachtigall, you are my son in whom I am very proud. You inspire me to be a better man, and I pray that I will always be able to give you all the love, hope, and grace that your beautiful heart deserves. I'll love you forever. May the wind of the Holy Spirit always be at your back as you walk down Christ's narrow road on travels of your very own.

Introduction

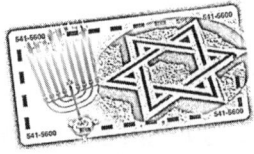

My command is this: Love each other as I have loved you.
—John 15:12 NIV

In his 1993 article in *Foreign Affairs*, "The Clash of Civilizations," and in the book that followed, Samuel P. Huntington argued that the new order created by the end of the Cold War is not a safe one. Many believed that an age of peace was possible now that the Soviet Union and her satellites had abandoned totalitarianism, having succumbed to democracy. Huntington, a Harvard political scientist, believed, however, that a fault line still existed, one based on culture and religion rather than ideology. He warned that globalization would not lead to worldwide homogeny; instead, the world's local cultures would reassert themselves. He predicted a backlash against the "victory" of the West in the Cold War.

Many were outraged by Huntington's arguments, which raised the possibility of the West finding itself in a massive conflict with Islamic and East Asian civilizations. The book predicted a coming clash between "the West and the Rest:"

Passport of Faith

societies based in Judeo-Christianity (Europe, the Americas, Oceania) versus societies grounded in Islam and other East Asian faiths. The book was roundly criticized for being too simplistic and for propagating the idea that hostility between civilizations was inevitable and that the West would need to assert itself more forcefully in the future. It was a very politically incorrect book in a very politically correct era. While there is room for criticism of some of Huntington's ideas, the geopolitical events of the last ten years have made it abundantly clear that his thesis has significant merit. This era, though different from the cold war era, is indeed one of conflict, as evidenced by the crisis in the Balkans; the genocide in Darfur, Sudan; local wars along religious fault lines; the rise of transnational terrorism; the spread of Islamic militancy; the Pentagon's restructuring for asymmetrical warfare; the proliferation of weapons of mass destruction among nonstate actors; and the war on terrorism.

What was especially disturbing to the secular academy at the time was the idea that religion, of all things, could be that important in world affairs. Huntington's colleagues in and around Harvard roundly criticized and scoffed at this suggestion. In the analysis of some of Harvard's brightest minds, religion was simply not a significant factor in global affairs. After all, how could people's private religious beliefs be the defining issue in shaping the new geopolitical world order. September 11, 2001, undoubtedly changed the minds of many who held that opinion.

The events of September 11, 2001, reminded the world that religion is important. The aggressive actions of a group of Islamic martyrs not only altered the world's focus in a single day but also reminded all of us that religion is a fundamental part of our world. Whether we recognize it or not,

Introduction

religion defines who we are, where we are, and why we are here. It is present in all cultures and appears to have been practiced by every civilization throughout history. It has only been in the past three hundred years or so that being nonreligious has become an intellectually viable option; even today, only a small fraction of the world's population denies the existence of the spiritual world.

For the most part, people in cultures throughout the earth are taught that we are more than just physical beings, that there is a spiritual element to our existence, and that it is accessible to ordinary human beings. All of us have seen that spiritual connection has the power to comfort people, transform individuals, and inspire acts of kindness and even terror. Mother Teresa's service to the poor amazes us, as do the inspirational words of Billy Graham. The misguided actions and tragic influence of religious figures like David Koresh in Waco, Jim Jones in Guyana, and the Taliban in Afghanistan have also shocked us. Religion is fundamental to our existence as human beings whether we consider ourselves religious or not.

In the West, when we do admit that religion is important, we often contradict that assertion by claiming that the world's various faiths are not unique. One of the great myths of our time is the idea that all religions are basically the same. I have heard many people comment that the world's religions just take different paths to the same place and that it doesn't matter what you believe as long as you believe in something. Even more disheartening are people who say, "Call him Buddha, Shiva, Christ, Allah—it is all the same God." Nothing could be further from the truth, figuratively and literally.

Passport of Faith

While it is true that all religions have some similar characteristics—deities to worship, scriptures to recite, rituals to practice, and guides or spirits to follow—these are merely superficial similarities. Consider a sports analogy: The New York Yankees and the Los Angeles Lakers both have coaches, trainers, general managers, and players. Both teams wear uniforms and play with a ball in front of large crowds. Clearly these sports teams share some definite similarities. But these similarities are superficial because the Yankees and the Lakers play two entirely different sports. Baseball and basketball are fundamentally different, and those differences become obvious very quickly to the observant spectator watching the teams play their respective sports.

Religion is the same way. Anyone who seriously explores the fundamental beliefs of different religions quickly discovers that they are not even playing the same sport. The goal of the game is completely different, and there are different expectations of the players. Some religions have a general manager directing the team, for instance, the monotheistic religions of Islam, Judaism, and Christianity. Others, such as Shinto and Hinduism, insist that everyone and everything is the general manager; others, such as Zen Buddhism, insist that there is no such thing as a general manager, a team, or even a ball park. These are big differences!

It is often said that the believers of the three great monotheistic faiths—Jews, Muslims, and Christians—all worship the same God, the God of Abraham, who is credited with being the founder of monotheism. But believers of these respective faiths would disagree. While it is true that all three faiths trace their origin back to Abraham, the Jews and the Muslims would certainly object to the Christian's "paganized polytheistic" triune God; Christians might question

Introduction

the God of the Quran, describing him as angry and completely removed from his people. Jews, as we all are painfully aware, have enormous disagreements with Muslims; nor do they believe that Jesus of Nazareth is their messiah. By no means do these three faiths agree about who the God of Abraham is. To say that Islam, Judaism, and Christianity are all basically the same is not only ignorant but downright disrespectful. Yet these three faiths are closer to each other than many others. It is worth repeating: the differences between the world's religions are great.

Mass media, travel, and modern migration patterns are teaching us more about the complexities and differences of the world's cultures each day. Religion is often a volatile issue; it is tempting to try to diffuse the tension by claiming that all religions are the same or, worse yet, to say that religion is just a source of problems for the world and we would be better off without their presence. John Lennon sang, "Imagine there's no heaven…No religion too."[1] It sounds nice in theory, but not only is it impossible, it would be catastrophic.

Some, like Lennon, choose to focus on the wars and conflicts based in religion, suggesting that religion is nothing more than a weapon used to oppress, divide, and conquer. This is not a clever argument. It ignores the many ways that religion subtly influences us in positive ways each day, serving for instance as the underpinning of our civil society and even our economic markets. The United States, whether it is a Christian nation or not, owes an incredible amount of its success to its Judeo-Christian foundations, which have provided the moral framework for "life, liberty, and the pur-

---

1. Lyrics from "Imagine" by John Lennon, © 1971. Administered by EMI Music Publishing Inc.

suit of happiness." Blaming the world's problems on religion because it can cause conflict makes about as much sense as banning soccer because it sometimes leads to rivalries, gang violence, and even war (as it did between Honduras and El Salvador in 1969). Like politics, money, sex, and sports, religion can produce conflict. Suggesting that the world would be better off without these things is a simplistic argument that needs to be abandoned. Without religion and the moral framework it provides, the world would be an even more violent place.

In dismissing religion, we not only sell the world's great religions short, but we also sell *ourselves* short. This is not a viable option for anyone who wants to thoughtfully exist on this planet. It is sad that so many Christians do this by retreating into their own beliefs without learning about other faiths. As Christians, we do ourselves a tremendous injustice by hiding from the world's religions, deeming them unimportant or simply attacking them. There is a better way for us to meet the challenge of other faiths.

Christians should never detach themselves from the world like modern-day gnostics; rather, we should engage culture and allow the world to question our beliefs. If we are confident in the resurrected Christ, we should not fear any challenge to our beliefs; rather, we should invite it. By doing this, we invite God to illuminate our hearts and we invite Christ to reveal himself to others through us. For too long, we Christians have hemmed and hawed, avoided conflict, or stuck our necks in the sand when confronted about our faith's exclusive claims. Some of us have lashed out at nonbelievers for challenging our faith, using Scripture as a weapon, more for self-protection than for revelation. It is

Introduction

my opinion that that we cannot afford to make these mistakes in the emerging new world order.

In a world of globalization and its counteractions, Christianity will be challenged more than ever. Christians will be asked by people in an interconnected world how we can be so arrogant as to believe that Jesus Christ is the only way to salvation. And we will encounter believers of other religions asking why we are not converting to their faith. In some cases, religions may be hijacked to form dangerous ideologies aimed at oppressing and intimidating us. Both moral relativism and absolutism will surround us. Ours will be a world in which the secularizing force of globalization will challenge religion and in which religion will assert itself in counteraction to that secularizing force. At this important juncture in history, Christians must be bold and informed in our faith while at the same time being peaceful, tolerant, and full of *agape*-love for our neighbor.

One of the best ways to see the beauty and uniqueness of the Christian message is to engage the world and discover as much as possible about other faiths. I am convinced that no other religion or philosophical system offers what Jesus Christ offers. At the same time, I value other faiths. They fascinate me because I see in them humanity's pursuit of God and the unending quest to be in touch with the divine. I draw strength in my spiritual life from studying other world religions because as I study them, I see again and again that in Christianity we are being pursued by God! This remarkable revelation of Christianity never ceases to amaze and comfort me. I enjoy seeing the beauty of other religions and learning about their traditions and rituals, but all of them inevitably remind me of how much we need a personal savior and how tremendous it is that God seeks to know us in an intimate way.

Objectives of This Book

In this book, I hope to accomplish five things. ***First, I want to introduce the reader to the basic beliefs of eight different religious worldviews.*** This is by no means a comprehensive survey of world religions, nor is it a scholarly work on comparative religion. Other writers have presented that kind of material far better than I can. Instead, I aim to cover the basics of each of these religious worldviews and provide a starting point for those inclined to explore them further.

For instance, in the first chapter on atheism (which I consider a religious worldview), we will not explore the philosophical arguments against atheism (cosmological, teleological, ontological, moral, transcendental, presuppositional, etc.). Instead, the basic ideas are presented and the focus quickly shifts to how these ideas affect a particular country or countries.

Neither does this book present scriptural arguments to prove that Christianity is right and other faiths are wrong. Once again, there are many books that capably contrast Christian ideas with those of other faiths. The primary focus of this book is neither theology nor apologetics. While I may at times discuss theology or compare Christianity to another worldview, my essential aim is always to introduce the reader to the core beliefs of these religious worldviews and explore how these worldviews have shaped specific countries and how they continue to influence them. I am trying to capture a snapshot—merely a snapshot—of each particular faith as I observed it as a Christian traveler passing through various

Introduction

countries on my own journey of faith. I hope that the reader will be inspired to seek out more information.

Second, I want to demonstrate that religion is extremely important to our world. By focusing on how religious worldviews have affected countries around the world—their people, history, economics, and culture—I hope to show how important religious beliefs are. We are coming out of an era, particularly in the West, in which religion has been marginalized and viewed as nothing more than a private affair. But religion has always had a tremendous impact on our world. We are now entering a new era in which religion will not be as easily ignored, because it will be a primary force of change in this new world.

Third, I want to foster mutual understanding and respect between Christians and non-Christians. There is a very good chance that this global shift will lead us into a prolonged period of heightened religious conflict around the world. Even if a clash of civilizations does not occur as Huntington has suggested, I agree that there will be a backlash against globalization and that religious worldviews and ethnic identity will be at the center of the conflict. Therefore, this book encourages Christians to take the first step toward mutual understanding and respect by learning about other faiths.

I am not suggesting that we water down our faith in order to make it more acceptable to nonbelievers. On the contrary, I think Christianity can stand up to any challenge. I am neither ashamed of the gospel nor worried that it will fail to answer the claims of other faiths. At the same time, however, I believe that the only way to get a proper hearing from nonbelievers is to genuinely examine their faith, thoughtfully and respectfully appraising it.

Passport of Faith

I realize that some Christians believe that all other faiths are demonic and dangerous. While I do not deny that other religions have the power to lead people away from the truth, I believe that the majority of people of other faiths are good, decent people who find comfort in their chosen faith. Often, they have never heard of Christianity and know very little about their own faith. To dismiss dialogue with them about their faith for fear of demonic influence disrespects both the nonbeliever and Jesus Christ himself, who has the power to protect us if we place our faith in him.

Some Christians are vehemently opposed to visiting temples, mosques, and other places of worship because they view these places as home to evil spirits and sacrilege. While I respect their feelings, it is important to nonbelievers—and a sign of respect—that we are willing to appreciate the history, art, and culture of their particular religion, and these things are often best found in places of worship. I do not fear for my spirit in these places because I am quite confident that Jesus Christ abides in me and that my deep desire to connect with a nonbeliever for the purpose of sharing Jesus honors God. God doesn't need my protection, and I need not fear evil spirits.

In this book, you will encounter conversations and experiences with people of different faiths. When sharing Christ with others, we must aim to be friends first. We must also be genuine learners. Agape love—seeking our neighbor's highest good—should be our first priority when dialoguing with a nonbeliever. This means viewing them as human beings, not as enemies of the Christian faith. When we interact with nonbelievers, God is more concerned with our capacity to show agape love to them than about speaking out against their faith. I hope that in this book I model that spirit and

Introduction

that it will encourage you to enter into dialogue with non-believers without being defensive or disrespectful.

Fourth, I want to inspire young people, especially the younger generation within our churches, to consider missions as a career option. While this book is intended to be entertaining and educational, my hope is that it sparks an interest in cross-cultural ministry in the hearts of our young people. The cultures and countries of this world are all diverse and beautiful. This book aims to capture some of that diversity in a fun, engaging way. Traveling far and wide to share the good news has been a wonderful privilege for me. Not many of my generation (Generation X) have chosen pastoral ministry or cross-cultural ministry as a career. I hope that some of the current generation of young people, particularly college students, will read this book and feel inspired to learn more about the tremendous challenges that face all of us and will then commit themselves to taking the gospel into all the nations of the world with faith *and* knowledge complementing each other.

Fifth, I want to share with the non-Christian why I believe in Jesus as my Lord and Savior. I do not do this in an overt way because I am not writing a tract on why people need to accept Jesus Christ. Nor am I sharing a traditional testimony about my life and decision for Christ. (I am too young to write my autobiography, and I doubt that it would be as interesting as the subjects covered in this book.) However, my belief in Christ is evident in what I write. Any astute reader will see that this ultimately serves as a testimony to the power of Jesus Christ.

Passport of Faith

Method of Presentation

By mixing personal stories with more technical information, I hope to create a narrative flow that will keep the reader from getting bored by too many details. For those who want more information, the bibliography will provide a good jumping-off point for more research about the subjects explored in this book.

In each chapter, I focus on a different religious worldview within the context of a specific culture. I spent up to a year or more in some of the countries I write about, while in others I only had a few days in which to make observations. Trying to draw a complete picture of a culture after only a few days of traveling is a hopeless endeavor; this is why I only claim to offer a snapshot of these countries and faiths.

While I am not an expert on all of these different religions and cultures, I am confident that my basic presentation is accurate. I have aimed for "simplicity on the other side of complexity," as C. S. Lewis once said. I am confident that I stay away from simplistic stereotypes and extreme generalizations. At the same time, I'm not afraid to generalize about a culture or country when the facts are quite obvious.

The book begins in Cuba, highlighting atheism as the dominant religious worldview. I consider atheism a faith because it requires a tremendous amount of faith to negate God's existence. Atheism (the belief that there is no God) has become an intellectually viable option in the West, so it is certainly worth discussing. Furthermore, atheism has helped to marginalize religion, particularly in the secular university.

I also treat Confucianism as a faith and include it in this examination of religious worldviews because it is a powerful philosophical belief system that has helped to shape the

Introduction

East Asian worldview. East Asia will play a large role in the geopolitical restructuring of the world, so the religious and philosophical ideas of the East need to be discussed. Furthermore, many Westerners in their religious quests have been drawn to Confucianism and Taoism and view them both as valid religious options. Confucianism has also come to be admired by some in the West who perceive it as having helped build economically productive societies.

The title of this book pays homage to Lester Crose's *Passport to a Reformation*, which chronicles the development of the missionary efforts of the Church of God (Anderson, Indiana). I have had the privilege of visiting over forty countries on five continents around the world as a Church of God missionary kid and now as a missionary myself. The beauty and diversity of this planet reaffirm my Christian faith as well as my appreciation for the world's remarkable diversity.

Samuel P. Huntington was right. Religion will be on center stage in this new era. But Huntington is just tapping into biblical fact. In every day, in every epoch, and at all times, religion is always on center stage, because Jesus Christ is the Alpha and the Omega.

1

A GODLESS PARADISE:
ATHEISM IN CUBA

Words that do not match deeds are unimportant.
—Ernesto (Che) Guevara

In 1991, I smuggled Bibles into Cuba. A friend of ours who worked for a Christian organization specializing in outreach to Communist nations asked my father and me to join a small group posing as tourists in order to deliver Christian materials and make contact with underground Christians in Cuba. We jumped at the chance.

Both my father, Harry Nachtigall, and I had long been interested in Cuba. Dad had expressed admiration for Fidel Castro's longevity and tenacity in the face of tremendous odds, although he did not agree with Castro philosophically, politically, or spiritually. I was intrigued by Castro's intellect and the revolution he had waged alongside Ernesto (Che) Guevarra, the infamous guerilla fighter. Indisputably, Castro was a cruel dictator, and Cuba was a decaying totalitarian state that robbed its people of basic freedoms. Nevertheless, this small island nation had managed to stand up to the United States for over thirty years, and that was of great interest to us both. Getting a firsthand look at one of the last strongholds of communism was an opportunity too good to pass up. Of course, we hoped to deliver some Christian literature as well.

It had only been two years since the Iron Curtain had fallen in Eastern Europe and a mere two months since the Soviet Union had collapsed. Mikhail Gorbachev's policy of *glasnost* had accelerated the collapse of the communist empire, and now President Boris Yeltsin was attempting to salvage the nation of Russia as the USSR quickly disintegrated. Unlike my sister Marcel, who had studied Russian in Moscow and Leningrad, I would never have the opportunity to visit the Soviet Union, the brightest beacon of communism in the world. It was gone. Cuba remained committed to the socialist cause nevertheless and was now within my reach. I was curious to see the effects of socialism on the country and thought it would be fascinating to meet Christians in a nation where the government is staunchly atheistic.

DIFFICULT TIMES

It had been a difficult year for my family. In January, my mother Jene had died of cancer. She was fifty-three years old and had spent most of those years working tirelessly to help other people My mother was a missionary, a registered nurse, and a mental-health worker. She had delivered over two hundred babies in Africa, saved a few people from death, and had been one of the first American health workers to work with AIDS patients. Jene Nachtigall was a phenomenal Christian, possessing a generous spirit and a sharp intellect. She seemed to have a book in her hand at all times, and this rubbed off on me. She felt quite comfortable with nonbelievers and would befriend anyone. People around the world remember my mother as a person who always showed up at the right time—with money, gifts, or a hot meal.

My mother was also very funny. Once, hearing that a friend collected ceramic cows, my mother showed up at the friend's house on her birthday with a live cow in tow. (She had convinced a local farmer to lend her the cow so she could pull off this gag.) She was not above passing notes in church or throwing a bucket of water on a helpless person walking past the deck of our house. Everyone was charmed by my mother, me most of all. She showed me that being a Christian didn't mean having to check your intellect at the door. Nor did it mean having to turn into a bland, humorless person, unable to enjoy life. Most importantly, Mother taught me to appreciate the world. She brought mentally ill people from the local sanitarium to our home for Thanksgiving dinner and would often force me to go with her on drives in the countryside to get close to nature. Life was full of joy and meaning for my mother.

Needless to say, we were all devastated when Mother was struck with breast cancer, which later spread to her lymph nodes and lungs. Throughout her struggle with cancer, however, Mom retained her sense of humor. When she had a mastectomy, she threw a "Farewell Boob" party; each person was expected to bring a gift made out of one cup of a bra. By doing such things, she made a difficult situation bearable for everyone else, even while she was in pain.

This kind of situation, losing the person you love most in the world, often leads people away from faith. How can a loving God let someone as wonderful and full of goodness as my mother die of cancer? This traumatic experience had the opposite effect on me, however, because of a valuable lesson my mother taught me as she was dying.

As Mother's lungs filled with fluid (in effect drowning her), she lost her voice, became bedridden, and had to be heavily sedated. Nevertheless, when visitors came over, she would manage to worry about them and ask if we were serving them food and drink. When we gave her pills, she would lift her weak arm and throw the pills back at us, just to make the guests laugh. I found this remarkable. How does someone at death's doorstep muster up the strength to be so concerned about other people? Her suffering did not make me think God did not exist; rather, it made me think God must exist, because I saw his grace before my very eyes.

In her dying, my mother taught me that there is something much worse than death, something we should fear a great deal more: meaninglessness. My mother had a mission in life—a purpose—and that purpose was to serve people in the name of Jesus Christ. This motivated her life and gave her days meaning. She practiced it literally as long as she breathed. The real tragedy for her would have been to live without this sense of purpose, which had driven her to accomplish much and be loved much in this lifetime.

After her death, I changed. Prior to her "graduation," I was a college drop-out, wasting any talent that I might have. After witnessing the grace with which she lived and died, I made major changes in my own life. I returned to college and eventually earned a master's degree. I tried to consciously live a more selfless life. I recommitted myself to a life in Christian ministry. And I traveled—a lot.

I have always loved traveling, particularly since I grew up on the mission field in Central America. But after my

Atheism in Cuba

mother's death, I began a ten-year period of trying to visit as many countries as I possibly could. I tried to look at the world the way Mother would have. Although I don't have her amazing spirit of charity, I do find that same strong sense of meaning through sharing my faith in Christ.

So it was that, nine months after my mother's death, Dad and I were on our way to Cuba, a nation that was officially atheistic. Mom's passing had inspired me and filled me with faith. Now I was traveling to a nation that taught its people that there is no God. For the Cuban government, the Spirit of God could not inspire people; only the government and its ideology could do that; only the state could meet the needs of people. However, those needs weren't being met, and we would soon see the consequences firsthand.

Atheism and the Rise of Secularism

I do not admire atheism as a belief system and would never want to claim it as my own personal philosophy, but I do find that atheists possess the greatest faith of all. Dismissing all religions as nonsense and declaring that all gods are nonexistent is quite a bold act of faith. While atheists may respect the world's religions and abide by their own codes of ethics, they simply do not believe that there is enough evidence to merit believing in God.

I think it defies logic to conclude there is not enough evidence to warrant belief in a spiritual world. Not only have all civilizations believed in a spiritual dimension of life, but they have based their national identities on those beliefs. The vast majority of people who have ever lived professed a faith of some kind; most people around the world still believe in a spiritual realm. It has always been considered so obvious that thinking otherwise seemed ludicrous. In fact, I would say that most people of the world acknowledge spiritual influence on a daily basis.

As I've traveled around the world, I've ridden in my fair share of taxis. In most countries, the taxi driver will have some religious symbol or statue hanging from the rear-view mirror or sitting on the dashboard. I would venture to say that most of those drivers have had a spiritual encounter of some kind which led to this practice. It is not just blind faith, but rather a belief borne out of personal experience or the experience of their communities.

The "enlightened" skepticism of the West has failed to take root in the rest of the world, where people view themselves primarily as spirits in a material world. Just because the academic institutions and mass media of the West do not take spirituality very seriously, we should not assume that most of the world's 6.5 billion people also do not. To be an atheist is to proclaim disbelief with enough certainty to dismiss the experience of almost every human being throughout history. The burden of proof rests with the atheist. Only in an ultra-secularized and materialistic society would the burden of proof fall on the religious person. Atheists are a minority in this world.

Atheism is a relatively new phenomenon and has been embraced by only a small fraction of the world's population. True, the early Christians were viewed as atheists by the Romans because they did not believe in the Roman gods, but rather in that strange new god named Jesus. A few groups of people in antiquity, such as the charvakas of Hinduism or the Epicureans, also could be labeled atheists. But it was really only after the Enlightenment, during the period that we call modernity (1789–1989)[1], that atheism established any real foothold in human society. The Enlightenment was a philosophical movement of the eighteenth century that emphasized the power of human reason. It had a profound impact on Europe, the United States, and ultimately much of the world. More than in any other period of history, many people began to think of progress and religion as natural enemies.

Within the Christian community, deism arose. Deists sought to reconcile this new "age of reason" with religion. They believed in a God who had set the world in order and then allowed human beings to manage it as they pleased. Deists found many of Christianity's supernatural claims untenable.

If often surprises American Christians to learn that the founding fathers of the United States would not be recognized as Bible-believing evangelical Christians. Thomas Jefferson, for instance, believed that the teachings of Jesus' divinity, the virgin birth, and miracles were nonsense. In fact, Jefferson produced his own version of the Scriptures using his scissors; the Jefferson Bible contains the story of the Gospels minus anything supernatural. Though often attacked for his beliefs, Jefferson held that many of the teachings of Christianity were myths. He respected Jesus as an ethical teacher but not as the Son of God.

While there certainly were committed Christians in America's early days as well as massive Christian revivals, we should not be surprised to learn that many of our country's first leaders were skeptical about Christianity

---

1. Theologian Thomas C. Oden uses these dates to identify the period of modernity—from the French Revolution of 1789, based on the ideas of the French Enlightenment, to the collapse of Marxist humanism with the fall of the Berlin Wall. The idea that human beings could achieve perfect modern societies started with the troubled French Republic and collapsed in Berlin at the end of the bloodiest century of human history.

and its supernatural claims. They were merely products of the Enlightenment. Jefferson thought it ridiculous that Harvard, Yale, and Andover would teach the Bible in any serious manner.[2] American institutions of higher learning were still committed to orthodox Christianity and to producing church leaders. Soon, however, secular leaders would become so influential that a huge chasm would develop between religion and the academy.

By the late 1800s, the writings of Charles Darwin, Friedrich Nietzche, Sigmund Freud, Karl Marx, and Friedrich Engels were having a powerful effect on the Western world. New inventions and theories of science were also challenging ancient religious assumptions. Sigmund Freud suggested that religion was merely a coping device for human beings seeking security by way of a projected father figure. He thought more developed human beings would discard such immature ideas. German philosopher Friedrich Nietzche placed his faith in humanity and believed that, free from religion, human beings could achieve almost anything through their own sheer will. Charles Darwin's theory of evolution was viewed as an alternative explanation for humanity's origin. Economists Marx and Engels questioned the fairness of the Industrial Revolution and sought to expose the way that elites in Europe exploited the masses for their gain. While these two men did not really focus on the role of religion to any great extent, Marx is well-known for saying that "religion is the opiate of the people." He was pointing out that religion kept common people focused on the next life, leaving them victims of bad economic systems in this life.

---

2. Joseph Ellis, *American Sphinx*, 310.

Atheism in Cuba

Religion seemed to be attacked on all fronts: psychological, philosophical, scientific, economic, and political. In light of these attacks, discarding religion seemed not only acceptable but progressive. The new ideas of secular humanism, which claims that moral order can be established without the influence of a supernatural authority through the inherent goodness of humanity, caught on quickly in the West. The secularization of Europe occurred rapidly and thoroughly. In the United States, secular humanism was propagated mainly through the university system. The great educational institutions such as Harvard, Yale, and Amherst that had been founded to train people for ministry became completely secularized at the start of the twentieth century. The acceptance of this "enlightened" skepticism became more widespread after the late 1960s. It is no accident that the Baby Boomer generation became the first to widely accept "enlightened" skepticism, as it was the first generation so deeply influence by the American university system.

But secular humanism and the beliefs it spawned ran into obstacles in the United States. Even if some of the founding fathers were deists, most of the early settlers believed in Jesus Christ. The nation had also experienced several great religious awakenings (1740 and 1790). And many Christian denominations and theological movements were born on American soil, including the nemesis of "enlightened" skeptics, Protestant fundamentalism. The more Darwin, Freud, and Marx were taken seriously, the more Christians in the United States mobilized to provide an alternate world view. The modern Christian fundamentalist movement is a direct result of the perceived threat by the atheistic ideas of secular humanism.

Passport of Faith

In the rest of the world, however, variations on secular humanism made inroads, particularly after the cold war divided the West from the East. The Soviets propagated Marxist thought throughout the world. Countries that had never considered atheism to be a viable option found themselves dealing with a new class of atheistic people, and in some cases atheistic governments.[3] Marxist thought swayed people throughout Africa, Latin America, and Asia.

One of the young men who followed the tide of secular humanism was a Cuban named Fidel Castro. Though educated in a Roman Catholic school, he became a professing atheist. In 1959, he led a revolution and established a socialist state on the island of Cuba in partnership with another revolutionary, Ernesto (Che) Guevara. Castro came to be viewed as a hero, not only for having led the socialists to victory, but for having created a socialist paradise a mere ninety miles from the United States. This state based on the philosophy of secular materialism was expected to show the rest of the world the folly of capitalism and religion. A great society would be created without the religious underpinnings of Judaism and Christianity, which were the basis of social order in the United States.

---

3. *Marxism* is a very general term. There are many different forms of Marxism, but it generally means ideas based on Karl Marx's *The Communist Manifesto*, which argues for the abolition of private property, a state-controlled economy, and a class struggle by the working people against the elite. *Socialism* is another broad term, but it broadly refers to collective ownership of all industries by the citizens. Marx believed that socialism was a stage of social reform on the way to communism, in which government would no longer be needed because all persons would be equal and social classes would cease to exist.

Atheism in Cuba

Smuggling for Jesus

After years of watching *Miami Vice* on television, I was thrilled to get my first smuggling assignment. I would not be smuggling narcotics, but Bibles and other Christian materials to the atheistic totalitarian state of Cuba. The trip was sponsored by an organization that focused on taking the gospel to nations where Christianity is outlawed or where Christian followers are severely persecuted. In 1991, Cuba was certainly that kind of place, and it was to that beautiful but impoverished Caribbean nation that I was headed to spend Thanksgiving week.

American citizens were forbidden to travel to Cuba, although Cubans themselves allowed *gringos* into the country because they needed the extra cash. If we were caught returning from Cuba, the United States government had the right to imprison us, fine us heavily, or take away our passports (a terrible fate for me). Because of these restrictions, our team of smugglers met in Toronto, Canada, for a day of orientation before catching a Cubana flight to Veradero, a resort city on the northern coast sixty miles from the capital city of Havana.

Our team was made up of two women and four men. I had just turned twenty-one and was attending a university in the Midwest, far from my home in Oregon, so Dad and I met on the Air Canada flight departing from Chicago for Toronto. It had been a while since we had seen each other, yet here we were together, getting ready to break the law. I was thrilled to see my father, but felt the whole smuggling thing was going to be less exotic with Dad coming along. Nevertheless, I have always seen my dad as a master missionary, so doing this assignment with him was a privilege.

Passport of Faith

When we arrived in Toronto, it was snowing heavily. The weather in Indiana had been bitterly cold. It was hard to believe that the next day we would be only ninety miles away from Florida, basking in the beautiful Cuban sunshine. For now, the temperature remained cold and the conversation was serious. Our leader, "Steve," was giving us our materials and final instructions.

I felt perfect for the job. For most of the 1980s, I had put gel in my hair and tried to capture that *Miami Vice* pastel look. Like Don Johnson and Philip Michael Thomas, stars of the hit TV show, I wore such outfits as a white jacket and pants, pink dress shirt, and chartreuse leather tie. I thought I looked incredibly cool. (I still think those clothes are cool, but I am forbidden by my wife to dress like that.)

Although Cubans welcomed Americans into their country for tourism, they definitely did not permit tourists to bring in Christian materials. Steve warned us that we needed to pack very carefully, burying our Christian literature beneath other books and clothes. I buried mine below my college textbooks. He also warned that we needed to be very low-key when we arrived at the Cuban airport. We were to separate and act as if we didn't know each other. Above all, we were to act like tourists. Once we passed customs, we were to pretend that we were just Canadians in Cuba to have a good time. If we became separated from one another, we should just continue alone to the hotel where we had reservations. If we were caught by the Cuban authorities, we were to make a bit of a scene and remind them loudly that "Cuba is a free country where people can believe anything they want." Of course this was not true, but the idea was to embarrass the officials into letting us get into the country with our Bibles.

Atheism in Cuba

It all sounded very exciting to me. I looked at the information book in our hotel room and familiarized myself with Toronto, in case someone asked where I was from. I decided to say I was from Toronto, particularly the neighborhood of Scarborough. I felt quite satisfied that I had the right stuff to be a smuggler.

The next day, we headed back to Lester B. Pearson Airport in Toronto to begin our journey. I was violating my own country's laws for the sake of the gospel; I was risking my life, health, and passport to take the good news of Jesus Christ to oppressed people. It felt good.

The adventure started once we were on the plane. At the time, Cubana operated a fleet of Soviet-made Tupelov commercial aircraft. The interior of our Tupelov 64 looked like it hadn't been cleaned since Castro was in diapers. Safety didn't seem to be a concern, either. The chairs folded up and it was possible to kick the seat of the person in front of you and send them flying into the cockpit. The only good thing about the food was that it helped prepare us for the meals we would have in a Cuban prison, should we be caught. The flight attendants were large Soviet women who looked like they could break me in half with their bare hands.

The cold war may have ended between the United States and Russia, but it definitely continued with Cuba. Our aircraft was not allowed to fly over U.S. airspace, so we had to fly along the St. Lawrence Seaway, head south a good distance off the shore of the East Coast, then bypass Florida altogether on our way to Havana. The Cuban government and the United States government remain very hostile toward each other. That's why we had to fly out of Canada; there were no regular direct flights between Cuba and the United States.

Passport of Faith

It hadn't always been this way. Prior to Castro's 1959 overthrow of the Batista regime, Cuba was a major destination for American tourists and business people—a tropical paradise for America's materialistic and hedonistic pursuits. The Batista regime was corrupt, propped up by the economic support of the United States government and the Italian mafia, but Cubans still had more personal freedom in those days. Like the revolutions of Mao Zedong, Vladimir Lenin, and other Marxist leaders, Castro's revolution had begun with promises that the little guy would finally get everything he deserved. As happened in the Soviet Union and China, the new leaders of Cuba turned out to be just as corrupt as the previous leaders, only basic human rights were systematically and overtly violated in order to keep the people under control. By 1991, Cuba was a grim place to visit.

Smuggler's Blues

Our plane touched down with all the grace of a Sumo wrestler playing the female lead in a Russian ballet. Once we disembarked, we faced the immigration officials. I had decided to play the part of a college student on vacation, which in fact I was. I brought a stack of CDs and textbooks, and kept my headphones around my ears at all times, as if I were some spaced-out college twit, which in fact I was. Although I can speak Spanish, I pretended that I could not understand a word, so as to look even more like the average tourist. I was also hoping to hide behind my Germanic name *Nachtigall*, which means "nightingale."

The airport looked no different that any of the airports in Central America—a perfunctory concrete building with lots of soldiers standing around. As usual, the first stop was

Atheism in Cuba

the immigration desk. Immigration officials the world over look bored out of their minds as they inspect your passport. Next was the luggage carousel, where I was glad to see that my luggage made it in one piece.

I picked up my suitcase, placed my headphones around my ears, and acted as though I was lost in the music. The customs officials had me place my luggage on a table. They opened it up and began to prod around in my stuff. One official saw my books and suddenly became very suspicious. He looked at me. I rocked my head back and forth, listening to the music and acting oblivious. The official looked at the books again, and I looked at the wall behind his head.

Unable to read English, he called over another agent, a dour, middle-aged woman. Apparently, she could read English and began sorting through the books. The Bibles were immediately beneath my university textbooks. I prayed silently that God would blind her and protect me from being caught. She picked up the first one: *History of Modern Japan*. She picked up the second one: *The MLA Handbook for Writing Research Papers*. She picked up the third book: *Introduction to Sociology*. With that, she said in Spanish, "These are all textbooks. He's just a student."

Feeling embolded, I spoke in Spanish with my worst American accent, "*Si, estudiante,*" and gave her my dumb, surfer-guy look. She let me past the checkpoint and into atheistic Cuba, carrying my cargo of Bibles.

In the old days, communist countries strictly regulated where tourists went, where they stayed, and what they saw. When I first visited China, we were escorted everywhere by official tour guides. Today, only communist North Korea is that stringent, following guests in the country everywhere they go. Back in the early 1990s, Cuba did give tourists some freedom, but they immediately ushered me into a waiting bus. I was one of the last people to board this particular bus; the rest of my team was held up in customs. I hoped this shuttle would take me to the right place.

On board were some rowdy Canadian tourists, eagerly awaiting the start of their hedonistic vacations. I sat in the last seat, next to two Mexican-Canadians. They asked if I spoke Spanish. I said that I could, so they proceeded to ask me questions in Spanish.

"Where are you from?"

"Toronto," I replied.

"Where in Toronto?"

"Scarborough," I said proudly.

"Are you here for a vacation?"

"Yes!"

"Would you like to party with us?" they asked.

"Well…," I stammered.

They then told me that their weeklong celebration would begin at a brothel. They offered to take me there and introduce me to some of their "friends." Needless to say, it became quite awkward. The Mexicans were so boisterous that the whole busload of tourists soon turned to face us as they described their plans for the week. My smuggler persona had already gotten me into trouble. How could I explain to my new Mexican friends that I couldn't go to the local brothel with them since I was actually in Cuba to smuggle in the gospel of Jesus Christ?

Everyone on the bus was in a festive mood. The trip to the hotel seemed to take forever. As everyone began pairing off, preparing to take full advantage of their holiday, it became clear that I needed to lose the Mexicans as soon as possible.

Atheism in Cuba

When we arrived at the hotel, I made a quick exit from the bus and headed to the receptionist's desk. I wanted to get my key before Don Quixote and Sancho Panza took me off to the brothel or something of the sort. They were soon in line behind me, looking happy to have found an accomplice. I got my key and ran.

The hotel was not fancy by Western standards. Cuba was just opening up to European and Canadian tourists and had not yet developed Western-style resorts. This place looked more like an army compound: concrete blocks with rooms that were always connected to at least one other. The showers were open, like those in high-school locker rooms. There were no television sets, and the phones were definitely bugged.

My father and the other two men still had not arrived from the airport. I had visions of them hanging upside-down by their ankles and being ordered to renounce Jesus Christ. Most likely, they were waiting in line to change their currency.

I spent my time dodging the Mexicans and getting a feel for the area, even though it was nighttime. Lizards ran around the little paths that connected the villas on the compound. It was very warm, and the air was filled with the sounds of the ocean and chirping insects. I wandered into a recreation room that also served as a bar. One of the passengers on our plane was there and recognized me as one of the "Mexicans" in the back of the bus. He looked exactly like the actor Dabney Coleman, who played the cruel boss in the movie *9 to 5*.

"So you're here for a vacation?" he asked.

"Yes."

"Where are you from?"

"I'm from Toronto," I said, keeping my useful cover.
"Really! So am I. What part of Toronto?"
"Scarborough."
"Really! So am I."
I immediately thought, *Oh, no! You've got to be kidding!*
"What part of Scarborough?" Dabney asked.
I quickly realized I needed to brush up on my smuggling skills. "Umm… I live over by the Tigard section." (Tigard was actually the name of my home suburb in Portland, Oregon. Since I knew no place in Scarborough, I just blurted it out.)
"Tigard? I never heard of it."
"Oh, yeah…. It's over by the…, you know, …the new mall."
"New mall? There's a new mall?" he asked.
"Oh, yeah….Well, they haven't built it yet, you know. I live over by where they are going to build it, on Eighty-Seventh Court. Anyway… Hey, look, I've got to get going!"
With that, I decided to abandon my Scarborough identity and just stick to my American one. Being a smuggler was just too complicated.

MEN OF REVOLUTION: THE SAINTS OF CUBA'S ATHEISM

My father and the other two guys—our leader Steve and a man named Greg—finally arrived at our hotel. They had been busted. All of their materials were confiscated at the airport, and they had been given a stern warning. They were fortunate not to have been arrested, immediately returned to America, put into prison, or—worse yet—forced to listen to one of Castro's speeches, which have been known to last ten hours or more.

Atheism in Cuba

Our guys were safe. Going to our room, we turned on the faucets and shower and spoke in whispers, just like in the movies. The main question Steve had was, Did I smuggle anything in? I had. The only Christian literature that had gotten past customs was what I brought in under my surfer-dude persona. (Sometimes, it pays to look stupid!) If the female customs officer checking my suitcase had looked just beyond my third textbook, she would have found a stash of Bibles and Christian pamphlets.

We spent the next day at the resort just blending in. I waded out into the surf and discovered that the water was unbelievably warm and shallow. The ocean was a radiant sky-blue and the sand a brilliant white. Behind the beach, the land was mountainous; dense tropical trees provided a lush green backdrop. There were many European tourists on the beach and clothes had become optional. This was not how the Communist government preferred it, but they were not about to offend the foreign guests whose money was keeping the nation from financial ruin. A strain of Puritanism runs through these communist regimes. They may be atheists, but they try to do away with drugs, prostitution, and other forms of crime as soon as they rise to power. They are usually successful for a time. It was a sign of Cuba's weakening that these vices were resurfacing in the early 1990's.

Before setting out across the countryside to look for Cuban Christians, we rented a car from a local dealer. Ladas were poorly made Russian cars; Volgas were slightly bigger sedans. Both were hideous to look at, ran terribly, and covered the streets of all Communist Bloc nations. In Cuba, however, people also drove American cars from the 1950s, including lots of old Plymouths and Fords. It was not unusual to pass a 1957 Chevy or an even older car in mint condition. The people of Cuba were so poor that they had to keep these old cars running; they couldn't afford new ones. We were lucky to find a silver Toyota for rent.

Driving across the countryside, Dad and I passed billboard after billboard with socialist slogans on them. The most common one was a picture of Che Guevara with the caption ¡*Victoria Hasta Siempre!* (Victory Forever!). Another common one read, "Socialism or Death!"—unfortunately, in Cuba the two went hand in hand.

Communist regimes the world over make it a priority to disband organized religion. Their leaders believe the addictive drug of religion must be removed as part of the clean sweep that totalitarian governments demand. In China, when the Communists took over in 1949, they quickly expelled all Christian missionaries and foreign-mission agencies. Like China, the Soviet Union, Vietnam, Burma, North Korea, and the Eastern Bloc nations, Cuba began to persecute Christians as well as the adherents of other faiths. The fear that religion would compete with their authority drove these governments to clamp down hard on people's belief systems.

Ironically, however, atheistic regimes tend to then create their own gods out of mere men to supplant the religions they've abolished. Faith is vital to being human; we instinctively look to something bigger than ourselves to provide direction in our lives. Even countries that negate the importance of faith ultimately use faith and transcendent symbols to survive. In China, Mao Zedong was viewed as godlike throughout the Cultural Revolution. While Bibles were prohibited, *Quotations from Chairman Mao*, a collection of Mao's thoughts, became a holy book of sorts; everyone in China was expected to obey it and memorize every word.

Atheism in Cuba

Karl Marx's pamphlet *The Communist Manifesto* also became a revered book, as did Che Guevara's *Guerilla Warfare,* which inspired people around the world to stage Marxist military revolutions. In North Korea, the government constructed a theology called *Juche* that cast their dictatorial leader, Kim Il Sung, as the head of a holy trinity, with his son, Kim Jong Il, playing the Jesus figure. And in Cuba, Che Guevara and Fidel Castro became those symbols.

Castro and Guevara both came from relatively wealthy families, yet both developed a burden for suffering and impoverished people. Hoping to make a difference, these two men latched onto the principles of secular humanism, particularly Marxism.

Fidel Castro attended a Roman Catholic school, studied law, and excelled at baseball. He might have played professionally in the United States had he not become the poster boy of banana-republic despots. Not only was Castro tall and handsome, but he could captivate an audience's attention with his oratorical skills. But in the wake of an unsuccessful coup against Batista, he landed in prison. Eventually, he fled to the United States and then Mexico.

Che Guevara was born in northern Argentina to a family with aristocratic roots. Originally trained as a doctor, he was moved by the plight of the poor during his travels in Latin America. He felt that the oppressed were ultimately victims of imperialism, primarily American imperialism. His life became a crusade against the United States in the name of underprivileged victims of capitalist exploitation.

Che developed a reputation as a fierce warrior. He was unrelenting in his hatred for the United States, and in armed struggle, he had no reservations about killing the enemy. He was a master of guerilla warfare, brave and even reckless in battle. He was angered by anyone who subjugated the poor. He even directed his anger toward the Soviets, whom he felt were far too weak in their confrontations with the United States and exploited people though their system of satellite nations. Che's concern for the poor inspired many people. His machismo, bravery, and ruthlessness also appealed to many and put fear in his enemies.

There is a classic portrait of Che Guevara that can be found on every street corner in Cuba, as well as on mugs, key chains, T-shirts, and posters hanging in college dorms from Argentina to Thailand. In the picture, Che is wearing a beret looking fierce and determined. It is an iconic image, powerful in establishing the myth of the guerilla Che Guevara. Most Americans do not realize how influential and inspiring the myth of Che has been around the world, particularly in Latin America. He is revered as a sort of secular saint and, in Cuba, has become a link to the spiritual for Castro and his propaganda machine. To many, he is a hero. He represents the classic socialist warrior fighting corrupt capitalism in the name of the poor and oppressed. In Cuba, Che became an example of all that people should strive to be.

Che and Fidel returned to Cuba by sea and launched their revolution from the east side of the island. By 1959, President Batista was on the run and Castro had become the leader of his nation. He then faced the question of all successful revolutionaries: What do we do now? Castro was not initially opposed to the United States, but the American government was at the height of its effort to root out communists, so it viewed Castro as a threat to freedom. Guevara was completely opposed to forming a partnership with the United States. In the end, Castro sought financial assistance

Atheism in Cuba

and support from the Soviet Union, support which lasted until the fall of the USSR roughly thirty years later.

Che soon grew bored with governing Cuba and attempted to continue the socialist revolution, hoping to spread it throughout the world and ultimately bring down the United States. In Africa and South America, he waged earnest campaigns to overthrow corrupt governments, but they all ended in disaster. He was eventually captured and executed.

Under Castro's rule, Cuba developed a high literacy rate, excellent medical laboratories, and a wonderful national baseball team. But it also became a nation of secret police, informants, nonstop propaganda, persecution, and prisons. Castro could be ruthless when confronting dissenters; executions were common. Hence the extreme paranoia that we witnessed throughout our visit. At least one Cuban prison cell was occupied by a relative of mine, Tom White, who was forced to make an emergency landing when his Bible-smuggling plane ran out of fuel. Tom spent a year and a half imprisoned under Castro. When released, Tom became even more committed to spreading the gospel around the world, continuing to work inside nations hostile to Christianity.[4]

MEETING THE REAL SAINTS OF CUBA

My father and I drove west toward Havana. The highway had no other cars, except for one that drove behind us for a long stretch of the road. We thought we were being followed. Eventually, the suspicious car seemed to lose us, or we lost it. We decided to stop in a seaside town for lunch.

---

4. White, *Missiles over Cuba.*

Passport of Faith

We pulled off the highway. The weather was perfect, but few people were out on the streets. It felt like a ghost town. We saw some children were playing with an old rubber tire and passed some older men, who stared menacingly at us. A large hotel on the shore looked like the only place in town that might have something to eat. We parked the car and walked past the driveway into the lobby. There were no tourists and the few hotel employees seemed surprised to see us.

"Can I help you?" asked one.

"Yes, we're looking for a place to have lunch. Do you have a restaurant?" Dad asked in Spanish.

"Yes, we do," the man responded, but he had a strained look on his face. He told us to wait and he would be right back. The hotel didn't look too bad; it was much better than the place where we were staying. After a few minutes, the hotel employee returned, looking embarrassed. "I'm sorry, sirs. The restaurant is open, but it has no food."

"No food at all?" my father asked.

"No. All we have is rice."

Nothing on our trip struck me as more pathetic than our conversation with this gracious hotel employee, who had to tell us that his restaurant had no food. There was no way to hide the fact that times were not good. I felt sorry for the Cuban man who had to turn us away. In other poor countries, nice hotels can offer a great deal to tourists, even if they are surrounded by shanty towns. Hotels that cater to tourists are the only places where an image of progress can be maintained. But in Cuba, there was no hiding the misery that socialism had brought.

Dad and I hit the road again, driving past mountains that were getting higher as we neared Havana. The miserable economic condition of the country contrasted sharply with the stunning scenery. Buildings were in terrible condition from neglect—pastel-colored structures, the color dulled by weather and the paint peeling.

We didn't have a definite plan for contacting local Christians. We were just supposed to drive until we found some. It sounded insane but, sure enough, it worked. Dad and I stopped in another desolate seaside town. The few people we saw had a glazed, distant look in their eyes. About to move on, we noticed a two-story building that looked residential. Above one of the upper windows was a little red cross painted on the outside of the building. We felt led to find the residents of that particular apartment and ask them about the cross.

The door was opened by a young lady of about nineteen. She had a warm smile and a sweet countenance, not at all like the other people we had encountered in Cuba thus far. Dad told her that we were tourists visiting Cuba and that we had seen the cross above her window. We wondered if they were Christians. She said her name was Angela, and yes, indeed, they were Christians. Dad then told her that we had brought some Christian supplies, including some Bibles that we wanted to leave with them. Her eyes lit up and she invited us in, telling us to wait while she went to tell her father of our arrival.

Both her father and mother came out shortly. They were extremely warm and friendly. They seemed to trust us immediately. My father explained again who we were, and they were both quick to believe us. The home was very dark, even on this perfectly sunny day, but their hearts were radiant as they made us feel at home immediately.

Passport of Faith

They told us about the difficulties of being Christians in Cuba. They described their inability to worship freely or to trust their neighbors, since so many worked as spies for the government. They were aware of how backward Cuba had become. Their small black-and-white TV didn't receive any channels very well, but Angela mentioned that they were able to listen to music from radio stations in Florida. They knew that there was another world outside, a world far different from the one Castro described in his speeches.

One of the most inspiring aspects of Christianity for me is the fact that you can travel to any country and, upon meeting another Christian, immediately experience a profound intimacy because of the shared experience of salvation through Jesus Christ. Even though two Christians may have grown up on opposite sides of the globe, there is a shared culture between them, and a shared hope and belief in God's providence. Two Christians meeting for the first time share a deep belief about the purpose of life. There is an unspoken understanding that we are part of God's family that will be united at the foot of his throne.

We felt that camaraderie with Angela and her family. It was a joy to spend time with them. I'll never forget the expression on her father's face when we told him that we had a Thompson Chain-Reference Bible. I felt ashamed that I had never known such reverence and awe for Holy Scripture. Angela and her family lived in an atheistic country where the futility of life without God was constantly demonstrated, yet the truth of Christ filled them.

The instant camaraderie that we felt is uniquely Christian. In their struggle against the exploitation of the masses, capitalism, religion, and other supposed social evils, the communists had long tried to establish this kind of camaraderie in which people genuinely view each other as brother and sister. But the communists failed because they suppressed the spirit and the spiritual, failing to recognize their vital importance.

Che Guevara was known as a man who had compassion for the oppressed of the world. Bothered by the plight of the poor, he was willing to take up arms against those that exploited them. Che's bible was *Guerrilla Warfare*, his book that inspired hundreds of thousands around the world to take up arms in order to bring equality to corrupt societies. After the successful Cuban revolution, Che found that the other revolutions he tried to start in the Congo and in Bolivia did not quite work out. Being united in poverty was not enough to foster an intimate unity of spirit. Che found that many so-called oppressed people were not interested in waging a violent revolution based on secular Western ideas.

When reading about Che's adventures in the third world, sometimes I can't help but laugh and cry at the picture of this angry guerilla trying to rally troops to revolution only to find that they would rather sleep or practice their religion than risk their lives for humanistic philosophy. In many ways, communism was and is very arrogant. It claims to liberate the masses but actually disregards many of the things the masses hold most dear. At the top of that list is religion, which is always forced out.[5]

Castro's Cuba had failed to create a nation filled with selfless people. Instead, it had become a country where people lived in fear and were ready and willing to turn each

---

5. Some people, even if only in small numbers, will always continue to practice their faith. In Cuba, despite the government's efforts, Christianity and Santeria, a syncretistic mix of African religions, were practiced covertly.

other in at the slightest provocation. In this atheist nation, Fidel had become god, Che had become a saint, and the people lived in fear.

Dad and I had to be very careful as we carried the Bibles and Christian books into Angela's home hidden in a suitcase and in brown paper bags. It had to be done as quickly and discreetly as possible to avoid prying neighbors and suspicious passers-by. We said our farewells and were on our way. Part of our mission had been accomplished.

LIBERATING HAVANA

The hotel that we stayed at in Havana was the country's most famous and best hotel at the time, and that's not saying much. It had originally been the elegant Havana Hilton, but the name had been changed by the Communists. It was now called *Havana Libre* (Free Havana) in commemoration of the liberation of Cuba in 1959 by Castro, Guevara, and the rest of the revolutionaries. A bland, gray, uninspiring structure, it was the tallest building in Havana. In 1991, this "luxury" hotel was shabby, and run-down. It had old carpets, poor service, and a pathetic disco lounge on the bottom floor, which continually played a concert of Paul McCartney and Wings on laser disc.

Dad and I still had more materials to give away. We had the phone number of a Christian man to whom we were supposed to deliver materials. While Dad made the call, I left the room to wander around the hotel. In the lobby, I purchased a copy of *USA Today* and sat down on one of the stools in the snack area. It was November 1991; the front-page story was about the death of Freddie Mercury, lead singer of the British rock group Queen.

Atheism in Cuba

Noticing that I was reading the English paper, the girl behind the counter asked me where I was from. "I am from the United States," I answered. We had to show our U.S. passports in the Cuban hotels, so there was no point in using the Canada story with hotel employees. They didn't care, as long as we paid.

"What's your name?" I asked.

"Jessica," she answered.

"Do you like working here?"

"Yes, I enjoy it very much because I get to meet people from all over the world. In Cuba, everyone has a job. Do you like Cuba?"

"Yes," I replied. "It's a beautiful country with beautiful people. Do you like the United States?"

"No," she said. "It's too dangerous. There's too much crime. You can get killed there."

"Wouldn't you like to at least visit?"

"No, I would not. I think it would be sad. In America, there are homeless people on every street. There are so many poor people and no one cares about them. It is the opposite of Cuba. In Cuba, everyone has a job, everyone gets an excellent education, and everyone has access to a doctor."

She was partially correct. In Cuba, the state attempted to provide jobs for everyone and ensured that people had access to education; the literacy rate was actually higher than that of the United States. Though the average Cuban may have been forced to regurgitate Communist propaganda in their schools, they were also a very well-read group of people. Jessica was also correct in saying that the Cubans had more affordable health care than in the United States. There were many doctors in Cuba, and many had been inspired by communist rhetoric to choose medicine as a profession. They were then sent to rural villages and paid a pittance. Many ended up driving taxis or working at other mundane jobs to make ends meet. But Cuba was also a cutting-edge leader in medicine and pharmaceuticals. In that sense, Jessica had reason to be proud of her communist country.

But Cuba was and is a police state. Religion hadn't become a tool for oppression in Cuba as Marx might have feared; instead, the lack of religion created a vacuum, allowing Castro and Guevara to become the local socialist deities and oppress the people with fear. One wrong word could land you in one of Castro's notorious prisons. Never have I been to any country where people were so obviously nervous and afraid. It was contagious.

I decided to walk toward the Malecon, the sea wall that is one of Havana's most famous landmarks. The streetlights were quite dark. When I'm traveling, I always notice streetlights: the richer the country, the brighter the lights. In poorer countries, the lights always have a dim yellow color. It's as if the economic vitality of a country comes shinning through in its lights. In Cuba, the situation was even worse. Those areas where the tourists stayed and visited were better lit than areas just a few blocks down the street where tourists didn't go.

Despite functioning lights, the Malecon, a tourist area, was still pretty dark. I walked the length of the wall. The waves made a nice sound as they lapped against the wall. I couldn't see anyone doing anything illicit, but it didn't feel as safe as Jessica implied that it was. The people, most of them young, didn't look particularly happy. They were smoking, talking loudly, and hanging out in gangs. Occasionally, I passed a couple holding hands and taking a romantic stroll.

Atheism in Cuba

I noticed a lot of interracial couples. Although racism exists everywhere, socialist Cuba had staunchly condemned it. In fact, when Castro visited New York City, he stayed in a hotel in Harlem just to make a point. Cubans are both olive-skinned and black. While racism exists wherever sin exists, Cuba had done better than most countries in eradicating racial prejudice.

In many countries, I can just blend in because I have olive skin, black hair, and brown eyes. I like to take advantage of that fact. From Egypt to the Philippines, people have mistaken me as a local. I've been spoken to in Arabic, Tagalog, French, Hebrew, and, of course, Spanish. This helps if you are going to be a spy for Jesus. Even in European countries, people assume I am a local: they assume I am a Turkish, Algerian, or Pakistani immigrant, depending on the country. In London, some tourists once asked me for directions on how to get to the Tower of London. I told them—in my best Birmingham accent.

As I walked along the Malecon, however, I didn't fit in. Most likely my clothes, as simple as they were, were too expensive. It was 1991 and I had just turned twenty-one, so I am quite sure I was probably wearing a pair of Air Jordans on my feet. I started to feel like I was being followed. A young man, taller than I, seemed to be walking behind me through the crowds of young people. I left the sea wall area and walked through a park. The young man was still there. I walked down the street, turned the corner, and began heading in the direction of my hotel. The young man was still following. Now I was considerably nervous and began taking shortcuts back toward the Havana Libre. I began speed-walking. The young man sped up as well. A block from the hotel, I began to sprint. I ran as fast as I could, not really sure what I was running from. The lobby was crowded and I felt safe as soon as I got in the elevator and made my way back up our room. The young man could simply have wanted to meet me, or sell me official Che Guevara souvenirs, but everyone's paranoia was starting to rub off on me.

The next day, outside the "Free Havana" Hotel, Dad and I met with our Christian contact and brought supplies to him in his car. As the sound of the torrential tropical downpour hitting the roof of his Russian-made car filled the air, we made plans to go to a Cuban church the next day where we would meet one of Cuba's great Christian leaders. As we had this conversation, however, this Christian brother insisted that we turn up the radio as loud as we could and that we whisper in hushed tones. I still remember the sound of the rain, the radio, and the hushed tones as we talked of Christianity.

The next day we met this well-known Christian leader and got to see a Cuban church. We also went into the suburbs of Havana to meet some Christians in their homes, which looked as if they were once beautiful, but now looked like they violated every building code imaginable. My greatest memory of that day is of the time I spent talking to James, a young Christian about my age.

While the adults talked business inside, James and I stayed outside and talked about our lives. I told him all about my life as a college student in America, my home in Portland, my jobs, church, and experiences. He did the same. I felt self-conscious; my life was so obviously blessed and full of privilege in comparison to his.

Toward the end of our conversation, James said that he had no future in Cuba. People had no food, no money, and, increasingly, no jobs. He mentioned that though very well-educated, he and his friends knew that they would never find jobs in Cuba. James's future was actually quite bleak. Nevertheless, he spoke of having a tremendous sense of peace and joy because of his faith. He then commented:

"I actually feel sorry for those Christians in the United States. They have so many things: so much money, so much television, so many distractions. In a place like the United States, it would be so easy to forget about God. Here in Cuba, our struggles bring us so close to God everyday."

I thought back to Angela's father cradling that Thomson Chain-Reference Bible as if it were gold, and I looked at James and his joyful, hopeful optimism springing from somewhere deep inside—and I felt ashamed. I felt ashamed that I had become so numb to the privilege that it truly is to know God, to serve God, and to have the freedom to worship the one true God who is our creator.

I suppose Marx and Castro would say that James is using religion as a drug to cure his pain. The pain he was experiencing, however, was not being inflicted by capitalist oppressors but by the failed socialist agenda in Cuba. Nevertheless, James had a kind of freedom that is difficult to find even in the United States. It was not political freedom that gave these Cuban Christians joy; it was freedom of the soul. "And you shall know the truth, and the truth shall make you free," said Jesus (John 8:32). James and the other Christians in Cuba knew the truth, and if there was any liberation occurring in Havana in 1991, it was occurring in the hearts of Christians who could see the folly of atheism and who were experiencing an internal revolution of the spirit propelled by the living Christ.

2

Losing Stock in the Sun Goddess:
Shinto in Japan

The Japanese have three hearts, a false one in their mouth for all to see, another within their breast for their friends, and the third in the depths of their hearts, reserved for themselves alone and never manifested to anyone.
—João Rodrigues, Portuguese translator for the Emperor of Japan in the sixteenth century

Nine thousand miles away from Cuba is the island of Japan, which has also embraced materialism; unlike Cuba, however, Japan managed to become the second richest nation in the world. Japan's spectacular rise was not simply the result of U.S. support in the aftermath of World War II, though. The Japanese were an efficient, hard-working, loyal people prior to the war. In fact, it was these very characteristics, used nefariously by Japan's leaders, that led the nation down the path of imperialism, war, and ultimately tragedy and defeat at Hiroshima and Nagasaki. In large part, Japan rose from the ashes of defeat because of the imprint on the culture made by the animistic religion of Shinto.

Animism and Shinto

Animism is the belief that every object, including inanimate objects are inhabited by spirits. The term is derived from the Latin word *anima* meaning "breath," "spirit," or "soul." Animism has been widely practiced in cultures around the world throughout history—from remote islands in the Pacific where volcanoes were believed to be gods, to the beliefs of Native American tribes who believed powerful men turned into animals, to the pygmies in the Congo who worship the forest.

In the West, animism is generally considered as religion at its most basic level. It is often thought of as the religion of primitive people—not nearly as sophisticated as Christianity, Judaism, Islam, or the Eastern faiths. British anthropologist Sir Edward Burnett Tylor coined the term in 1871, defining it "as a general belief in spiritual beings"; he considered it "a minimum definition of religion."[1] Today scholars argue about the proper definition of animism and what it entails. For our purposes, I define animism as the belief that spirits inhabit everything. Not only is this basic belief present among rural jungle tribes in South America and Asia, but it is clearly present in modern urban cultures as well.

In the United States and Europe, for instance, the New Age movement continues to grow, encouraging animistic beliefs about spirits in nature. Most Westerners, however, base their ultimate core beliefs on Judeo-Christian ideas and humanistic ideas rather than on polytheistic beliefs like those found in animism. Those in the West who do hold animistic beliefs often seem to be back-to-nature types—a little left out of the modern world, although they enjoy its benefits. That is why it is so fascinating that animism continues to thrive in a country as sleek, technological, and sophisticated as Japan; in fact, animism has helped to form the core iden-

---

1. Tylor, *Primitive Culture*.

Shinto in Japan

tity of what it means to be Japanese. Animist myths have been used to inspire Japan to excel in the modern world.

In Japan, animism is the basis for the indigenous religion of Shinto. *Shinto* means "the way of the *kami* (gods)." Like animism itself, the origin of Shinto is shrouded in mystery. The term *shinto* dates back to the sixth century AD and is derived from two Chinese characters: *shen* (divine being) and *tao* (way).[2] It has no founder, no scriptures, and no doctrine. The ancient Japanese believed that kami inhabited fields, streams, rocks, and woods, as well as animals such as snakes and foxes. Like China's Taoism, Shinto placed great emphasis on nature, which was to be respected and cared for at all times. The spirits that existed in nature were not all good. Rituals with charms, amulets, and Shinto priests were performed to expel evil spirits and bring about purification. But unlike Christianity and the other monotheistic faiths, the concepts of good and evil were never clearly defined.

The basic beliefs and rituals of ancient Japan are practiced today in modern Japan, though they have become more complicated and subtle. While the kami of Shinto primarily served as local protectors of small villages in ancient Japan, today, it is the ideas behind Shinto that help hold modern Japanese society together.

Land of the Rising Yen

No country that I have visited has impressed me as much as Japan. When I first went to Japan, I had not yet been to Europe or other countries in East Asia, and it was the first non–third world nation that I had visited other than Canada. After years of traveling in nations where electric-

---

2. Bowker, *Oxford Dictionary of World Religions*, 892.

ity is a luxury, time is irrelevant, traffic lights are optional, and transportation is life threatening, I was stunned by the order, cleanliness, and sophistication of Japan.

I had grown up in the 1980s when the American auto industry was being overtaken by better-built, economical Japanese cars. At the time, Japan had a reputation for being so progressive and advanced that it might one day completely overtake the United States economically and technologically. The Japanese were buying up prime pieces of American real estate, including the Rockefeller Center in Manhattan and Pebble Beach Golf Course in California. And Japanese buyers were snapping up American companies like Columbia Records and major film studios. Many Americans had a perception that the Japanese were taking over the United States by purchasing their most valuable land and companies. Movies like *Rising Sun* (based on Michael Crichton's best-selling novel) and *Black Rain* captured the dazzle and danger of Japan as it interacted with America. Japan was impressive to Americans, and threatening as well.

In Tokyo, one of the first books that I picked up was a very popular title by Shintaro Ishihara, *The Japan That Can Say No*. In this controversial book, Ishihara argued that Japan would emerge as a world leader as it continued to gain economic and technological strength. He hoped to prepare the Japanese and the Americans for Japan's new era of supremacy. The Americans, he believed, were annoyed by the fact that "an oriental country was about to supplant them in some major fields."[3]

Unfortunately, the release of Ishihara's book coincided with the end of Japan's economic boom. The Nikkei, Tokyo's

---

3. Ishihara, *Japan That Can Say No*, 30.

Shinto in Japan

stock exchange, peaked in 1989. Japan's major banks began to close, millions lost their savings or full access to their bank accounts, unemployment soared, and the nation teetered on the edge of bankruptcy with a credit rating at about the level of the African country of Mali.[4] Though Japan did not become a third-world nation, this economic bust was a staggering blow to a nation that prided itself on having built up an economic juggernaut from nothing. Homelessness had been a problem found in America, not in Japan, but not long after Ishihara's book came out, that changed.

Back in 1991, however, as I wandered around Tokyo's immaculately clean streets and experienced Japanese efficiency firsthand, Ishihara's argument seemed convincing. Japan appeared to have found a new way of doing things, and it had a lot to teach the rest of the world. With one foot in a glorious past and one foot firmly in the twenty-first century, Japan appeared to be a modern-day miracle. I knew that Japan's state religion, Shinto, remained an important part of the country's identity and was still practiced by her emperor. I wondered whether it was part of her success.

The efficiency of modern Japan was fully on display the second I arrived at the New Tokyo International Airport in Narita. I was to stay at the Grand Palace Hotel in Tokyo and had arranged with a tour agency to be escorted from the airport onto a bus that would take me downtown only blocks away from the emperor's residence. In Japan, transportation is tricky because the transportation systems are so complex.

---

4. This does not mean Japan and Mali were at the same economic level; rather it meant that Japan was no longer a safe place to invest. The Japanese have been able to resuscitate their economy slightly, but the days of evenly distributed wealth throughout the land are most likely gone for good. Socioeconomic class will be a bigger issue in the future.

Passport of Faith

The subway system in Tokyo, for instance, is a multilayered maze with twelve lines and three hundred stations. Not only do you have to find the right type of train and the right line, but also the right level.

As I made my way out of the airport, two young Japanese airport employees, a girl and a guy my age, came running toward me. The young man said to me in the thickest Missouri accent I had ever heard, "Where have ya been? I reckon' yer flight must have been delayed on account of the weather 'n' such?" I stood there flabbergasted.

"Where did you learn to speak English so well?" I had to ask.

"Missouri. Lived in the Ozarks. Used to go fishing!"

Wow, I thought. *Not only do they send you a guide who speaks perfect English in Japan, but they even speak with a regional dialect from your native country! Fantastic!* I told the young Japanese that our flight had arrived late because the pilot had put one of the engines in reverse during take-off.

I walked away extremely impressed. I was used to getting off planes in dusty capitals only to be assaulted by poverty-stricken children wanting money, candy, or AK-47 rifles. It was strange to be greeted at the airport by someone I was pleasantly surprised to see. It turned out that the young man had spent a year as an exchange student in a high school in the Ozarks. He had returned to Japan speaking perfectly fluent Ozark English. He put me on a brand-new bus that went directly from Tokyo's Narita airport to the Grand Palace Hotel.

As the bus traveled south toward Tokyo, I was able to see the famous neon signs lighting up the night in the Ginza district, houses with shiny blue roofs (for luck), skyscrapers in the business district, and baseball teams playing on lighted fields. Everything about Tokyo seemed new, shining, and utterly sophisticated. Many visitors view Tokyo as a modern urban nightmare, and in some ways it is. There are very few street names, for instance, in this mega-city. You just have to know where you're going and how to get there because street names are few and far between. For me, however, the buildings, neon lights, and superhighways contrasted so greatly with the other countries of my experience that I was completely enthralled. Clearly, modern Japan was a wealthy nation with a tremendous infrastructure.

When I arrived at the Grand Palace Hotel, I was thrilled to be staying in a real luxury hotel. It really did look like a grand palace to me. Through my window, I had a view of the Tokyo Dome (also known as the "Big Egg" because of its inflated white roof). Just down the street a few blocks was the Budokan Arena, a pagoda-shaped coliseum where many of my favorite performing artists from the 1970s and 1980s had given concerts. A short walk away was the emperor's palace and grounds. Inside my hotel, the rooms were outfitted with gear that was so high-tech that figuring out how to turn on the television and lights, or even opening the door, seemed to require a computer science degree. In case of an earthquake (a common occurrence in Japan), the television would automatically turn itself on and broadcast the necessary information to those in the room.

On Tokyo's streets, nature was losing its battle to progress. The Tokyo–Yokohama area had developed rapidly and consisted of twenty million people covering the Kanto plain on the main island of Honshu. There was not much room left for wildlife. About five-eighths of Japan is so mountainous that it cannot be built upon. So wherever there is space, the Japanese have moved the animals out and built sprawling cities. As with many East Asian cities, city parks are a rarity. It is paradoxical that a nation with a history of idealizing nature has destroyed so much of its green space in the name of progress. Even odder was the fact that there was less rubbish in downtown Tokyo than on Mount Fuji, Shinto's holiest site, where the trails were littered with garbage.

SPIRITUAL BUT NOT RELIGIOUS

The past and the present coexist in interesting ways in Japan. Consequently it can often appear to be a land of contradictions. Japan's religious roots are visible in every facet of Japanese life if you look closely enough, yet the Japanese themselves are not particularly religious. This is not to say that they are not spiritual; in fact, the Japanese can be very superstitious, worrying about the effects of spiritual influences on family, marriage, and even business. It is not uncommon to see new buildings receive a Shinto blessing from a priest before they are erected. But Japan is not a particularly religious nation in the Western sense of the word. Organized religion seems foreign and unnecessary to the Japanese mind.

In the West, when we think of belonging to a particular faith or of practicing religion, we usually assume this means that you are familiar with that religion's history, doctrines, and core beliefs. You probably have committed to attending a synagogue, church, mosque, or temple. A new convert might go to the local bookstore and stock up on books explaining the faith in detail. In the West, to say, "I am a Christian," carries a lot of weight. A listener might assume that you know the story of Jesus Christ, that you believe in God, that you are comfortable with at least some of the Bible's supernatural claims, and that you will make an effort to adhere to biblical codes of conduct. When Westerners tell someone that they are Christian or Buddhist, it is not a statement to be taken lightly.

In contrast, East Asians may call themselves Buddhists, practice Shinto, and do Taoist spiritual exercises yet remain completely oblivious to the main theological or philosophical points of those faiths. In much of East Asia, to be religious simply means to do rituals. I do not mean this in a pejorative sense. East Asians, for the most part, do not view religion as a particularly special part of life in the way Westerners do. In China, a Taoist woman might go to the local shrine to burn incense for luck, nothing more. She might be completely unaware of any of Taoism's core beliefs. If you ask her, she would say that she's not religious at all and wonder why you are asking her that as she waves incense in her hands. That is how detached the practice of religion can be in the Far East.

In the West, Christians, in particular, would view such activity as nothing more than empty ritual. We expect people to rationally and systematically know what they are doing and why they believe as they do. Westerners, because of the influence of Judaism and Christianity, also expect religion to be a very personal and private matter. We go on religious quests to discover which religion speaks to us as individuals. Young men grow a ponytail, put on jeans and a wool sweater, and go to Colorado to find themselves and achieve Zen. We seek a faith that touches our core and offers guidance for our lives. We then become supporters of that religion and explain to others why we believe in it. It is all very personal in the West: religion is about us. This contrasts greatly with most East Asians, who often grow up believing an Eastern faith and never learn much about it because they live in societies that don't view systematic ideas about religion to be very important. Things just are. You don't ask why; you just accept.

You can thus imagine the frustration of a Christian missionary who goes to Tokyo with a tract explaining the important Christian doctrines in Japanese and asks people to "accept Jesus Christ into their heart as their Lord and Savior." Many Japanese will not be at all interested in the pamphlet and will wonder why this Westerner is so obsessed with the topic of religion. Others may take the pamphlet and gladly accept Jesus Christ because they have no problems accepting every religion. As far as they are concerned, they have just purchased extra insurance in case there happens to be an afterlife. Yet other Japanese might "accept Jesus" just to be polite and to get rid of this impolite and presumptuous *gaijin* (foreigner). The reaction of the average Japanese will probably not be one of acceptance, however, and few would view this new faith as something that will fundamentally alter their lifestyle, behavior, and worldview on a personal level. These responses, of course, are not what the Western Christian missionary wanted, but the missionary was expecting the Japanese to base their decision for Christ on Western ideas of religion and individuality.

For the average Japanese, core beliefs about personal identity and reality were culturally ingrained centuries before birth and thus are not easily subject to change. The individualistic religions of the West generally have little effect on how they view ultimate reality. This is why it so difficult for Christianity to penetrate Japan. Ironically, the cultural attitude that finds all religions acceptable yet unimportant is the result of the Shinto religion.

Shinto in Japan

Follow the Crowd Instead of the God

Animism laid the foundation for Shinto. Shinto, as the official state religion of Japan, was then used to shape the essence of what it means to be Japanese. Japanologist Shichihei Yamamoto coined a phrase for this phenomenon: *nihon-kyo*. Dr. Neil S. Fujita translates it as "japanism."[5] To be Japanese is to be linked to the national identity of Japan in a very deep, ultimately spiritual way.

Although Japan is a modern nation engaged in cultural and economic exchanges with the entire world, there is still a tremendous amount of internal societal pressure to remain pure and unaffected by that external world. This is an example of Japanese comfort with what we in the West consider contradiction. On one hand, to be Japanese means to conform to the group and behave in the fashion that nihon-kyo dictates. Uniformity is what nihon-kyo demands. Differing ways of existing are not acceptable. On the other hand, the Japanese are fascinated by foreign things and willing to adopt them. They have become known for their ability to borrow ideas from other cultures and make them uniquely their own, whether it's automobiles, televisions, pop music, or Buddhism. The old and the new exist side by side in harmony as long as "japanism" is not threatened.

An excellent example of Japan's love of the foreign *and* the need for conformity is the Japanese propensity for outlandish crazes and fads. In the 1990s, for instance, it suddenly became hip for young people to get tan. This seeming act of nonconformity was followed by just about everyone. Millions of young people flocked to the beaches and put on tanning lotion in an effort to become as dark as Brazilians or

---

5. Lundell, "Behind Japan's Resistant Web."

other Latin Americans, making them look very un-Japanese. The fad lasted an incredibly short time before a new fad took its place: get as white as humanly possible. Fads work in Japan because they don't truly upset the system. Young people vent off some steam through an individualistic act (committed in mass), dabble in something foreign, but stay essentially Japanese. A commitment to Christianity, however, would alter too many of the essentials of Japanese identity. Christianity (from the Japanese point of view) would demand that the Japanese individual be more confrontational and take direction from God instead of from society.

Surveys reveal that most Japanese spend little time thinking about religion. They respect all religions but don't identify with any one faith. Their personal beliefs don't tend to be either systematic or exclusive, thus systematic and absolutist faiths like Christianity and Islam are largely rejected. Such faiths are a threat to japanism. Shinto's animism leads them to be polytheistic: gods are everywhere, in every rock and stream. So to the Japanese, the notion that there is just one God and that he is Yahweh or Allah is unrealistic and, in fact, quite arrogant. For five hundred years, Western Christian missionaries have struggled to win converts in Japan with very little success. Today, Christians still constitute less than 1 percent of the Japanese population.

But a more covert form of religion does survive in Japan. That is what nihon-kyo is ultimately about. Yamamoto even created the phrase to mean "Japanese religion." In coining this phrase, he was trying to describe the Japanese view toward religion.

Shinto in Japan

The Shrine of Asakusa

A good place to see Shinto and nihon-kyo up close is at the Shrine of Asakusa in central Tokyo. It is probably the most visited religious site in this city filled with temples and shrines.[6] Since Tokyo is difficult to navigate if you don't speak Japanese, I made it to the temple by joining a day tour.

The shrine is surrounded by high-rise apartments, art deco buildings, skyscrapers, and fast-food restaurants. In that sense, Tokyo looks like any other world city. But in other world cities, it is not common to stumble across a shrine squashed between office buildings, garages, gambling parlors, and comic book stores. After the massive destruction of World War II, Tokyo was reconstructed quickly and without much urban planning. Thus, it is not unusual to walk past a 7-Eleven convenience store and a McDonald's restaurant only to find yourself on sacred ground. Space is at a premium: even the gods have to get used to living in cramped quarters.

Shinto shrines usually have a gateway called a *torii* that leads to ceremonial halls or beautiful nature sites with rocks, streams, and bridges. They look like the facade of a Chinese pagoda with a curved roof suspended by two posts. Usually, the gates are made of timber painted black and red. The torii separates the secular from the sacred. As worshipers enter the sacred ground, they bow to the gods. At the Asakusa Shrine, I entered through the vermilion-laquered Kaminarimon gate, which had a giant red lantern suspended from it with a Chinese character written on it and two ominous

---

6. Shinto traditionally has shrines while Buddhism has temples. It gets confusing as both can be found in the same complex. Originally, Shinto shrines were simple structures that housed *kami*.

wooden statues peering down at me. The two statues were the God of Wind and the God of Thunder.

Surprisingly, the first thing I encountered inside the gate on holy ground was a market. In front of the main Asakusa building was *nakamise*—a long promenade with stores and stalls filled with vendors selling a wide array of things: T-shirts, wedding dresses, postcards, maps of Tokyo, Japanese-style kimonos made in China, plastic ninja swords, badminton paddles, pictures of Harrison Ford, and, of course, women's underwear. If Jesus had been a pious follower of Shinto instead of Judaism, he would not have been so angry with the temple hawkers.

Next to a tree on the grounds were small wooden plates on which you could write a wish. Others tied pieces of paper around the branches of trees to receive a blessing. You could also get your fortune told for a small fee or buy amulets, lanterns, and purification wands from hawkers. A section of the compound contained other temples. The artificial streams, trees, and bridges could easily make you forget that the whole complex is in the middle of one of Tokyo's busiest districts.

I purchased a kimono with Chinese writing on it and proceeded toward the main building. A group of old ladies was walking up to a large bowl burning incense. They each took turns leaning in toward the bowl and covering their faces with the smoke. They did this to purify themselves, which is expected of all those who come to worship. The purification ritual usually involves washing your hands and mouth with clean water at a pavilion outside the building, rubbing the smoke on yourself, throwing a coin into a box at the front of the sanctuary, bowing twice deeply, clapping your hands, bowing again, and praying for a few seconds.

Shinto in Japan

For the sake of purity, those with open wounds or those who are sick are expected to refrain from visiting.

I followed the old ladies up the stairs toward the shrine. They might have been there to receive good luck, to seek protection from someone threatening them, to receive a blessing before an important occasion, or possibly to court financial favor from the gods. It is for these kind of everyday occurrences that the Japanese petition their gods. They are not looking for a direct message about their lives, but rather they are seeking general help in dealing with everyday issues. Entering, the old women clapped their hands and bowed in prayer. It was extremely crowded and people were crushing each other as they made their way to the altar to throw their coins into the offering box.

This main building of the Asakusa Shrine was constructed by the third shogun, Iemitsu Tokugawa, in 1649. Inside the shrine, as in most Shinto shrines, there is an inner chamber, a priest's house and office, and other buildings. Somewhere within the shrine, statues or artifacts symbolizing Shinto deities are kept, but these are off limits to the public.

Though it is a Shinto shrine, Asakusa is actually a Buddhist female deity of compassion. The shrine is dedicated to the Hinokuma brothers, Hamanari and Takenari, and their lord, Matsuchi Haji, who according to legend found a statue of Asakusa Kannon in the Sumida River in AD 628. The men threw the statue back into the river numerous times only to have it come back to them each time. A host of other minor Buddhist deities also appears on the grounds and mingles freely with the Shinto deities. On the way out of the shrine, you might pass the Bensai-ten, the goddess of creative arts (who also serves as the goddess of money-making); Jizo, the spirit of ambition in children; and Awashima-do, who commemorates the faithful service of needles and pins.

So even the holiest of Shinto shrines is not off limits to the deities of other faiths. And no one sees this mixing of religions as problematic. After all, if gods are everywhere, as Shinto proclaims, why not embrace all deities. In fact, the most popular festival at the temple is a Brazilian conga festival in which scantily clad Brazilians join Japanese people in dancing down the street. It has nothing to do with religion; it is simply about having a good time.

The Asakusa temple experience was a wonderful introduction to East Asian religions and to polytheism. In the Far East, all religious ideas are welcome. It is a pragmatic approach to spirituality in which people only seek when they need something, leaving them free to ignore the deeper, existential issues pursued by Westerners. Shinto is a prime example of this. It is viewed with respect and followed to some extent by most Japanese (even if only by attending annual festivals with their family), yet the Japanese are not protective of Shinto in a theological sense when it is confronted by other religions and philosophies.

But Shinto is more than just religion. It is part of what defines being Japanese. It is part of nihon-kyo. The religious aspects are almost secondary. This is similar to the Jew living in Brooklyn who is not religious at all but feels a strong affinity for the nation of Israel and the Jewish race. Such a Jew is not a practicing Jew but is still culturally Jewish. Culture is the key.

Though not protective of Shinto, the Japanese are very protective of their identity. As a result, they tend to be xenophobic. Distrusting foreigners and feeling that they are not equals is logical given the cultural mindset, not racist

Shinto in Japan

as Westerners would claim. It is the result of the Japanese national myth created through Shinto. For those who have grown up in pluralistic societies with Judeo-Christian ideas about the value of all people regardless of race, creed, or gender, Japan's prejudice can be off-putting. But for the Japanese, it is part of life as a Japanese person, a life defined by Shinto. As we will see, Shinto is the key to understanding the strength of the Japanese identity in the midst of a pluralistic world.

Inventing a New Religion: Japanism

Shinto in Japan has not changed people's individual lives much in a theological sense; rather, Shinto was used by Japanese officials to create a new culture—the culture of japanism. Ironically, the early success of Christianity in Japan helped to form the impenetrable shell of Japanese indifference to religion that has plagued missionary efforts ever since.

Five hundred years ago, the Japanese islands were still divided among many clans, each of which worshiped its own patron god.[7] Introduced in 1549 by Jesuit missionary Francis Xavier, Christianity enjoyed a peaceful coexistence with other religions in Japan. In this relatively open religious atmosphere, Christianity experienced tremendous growth. By the end of the sixteenth century, nearly a million people called themselves Christians.[8]

By the late 1500s, a general named Hideyoshi Toyotomi had subdued the various clans and even some militant Buddhists, bringing stability to all of Japan. Initially Toyotomi was viewed mostly as a friend to Christians, but the San

---

7. Hane, *Modern Japan*, 11.
8. Fujita, "'Conic' Christianity and 'Donut' Japan."

Passport of Faith

Felipe incident of 1597 marked a tragic turning point for Christianity in Japan and was the last in a series of incidents that helped to usher in the new Japanese religion of nihon-kyo.

Sailing from the Jesuit stronghold of the Philippines to Mexico, the San Felipe strayed off course and landed on the southern Japanese island of Shikoku, where it was boarded by Japanese officials. An overzealous Spanish officer showed the Japanese officials a map of the vast Spanish Empire, which the Japanese understood to be expanding through force and with the help of colonizing missionaries. The ship itself was filled with Franciscan priests and ammunition. Incensed, Toyotomi ordered the arrest of numerous Christians and marched them on a monthlong journey of humiliation to the port of Nagasaki, where they were crucified. Toyotomi, somewhat accurately, perceived the Catholic missionaries as a threat to the Japanese empire, even though most priests were genuinely only interested in spreading the gospel. Many Christians were banished or crucified under his regime. Toyotomi died the very next year.[9]

Three years later, in 1600, Tokugawa Ieyasu was designated *shogun* by the Japanese emperor.[10] Traditionally, Japan has avoided concentrating power in one central ruler. The emperor did not serve as the leader of the military aristocracy; that job fell to the shogun. As shogun, Tokugawa Ieyasu moved to ensure the complete and continued dominance of the Tokugawa clan in governing Japan.

The leaders of Japan began to use religion and established codes of conduct to mold the Japanese people. Through traditional religious movements, such as Kokutai, Hotoku, and

---

9. Ross, *Vision Betrayed*, 76.
10. Hane, *Modern Japan*, 84.

Shinto in Japan

Shingaku, core values were strengthened among all classes of people, values which included selflessness, loyalty (particularly to one's lord), and a concern for the welfare of the nation. These values provided the motivation and the ethic that ultimately allowed the Japanese people to make the tremendous personal sacrifices required to advance the state. It was this subtle relationship between religion, politics, and culture that enabled the Japanese to quickly come together after World War II to rebuild Japan into the world's second largest economy.

The religious emphasis on the values of selflessness, loyalty, and concern for the welfare of the nation merged with the samurai ethic of *bushido*, a strict code of honor demanding complete loyalty and obedience to the superior as the ultimate virtue. Any samurai failing to adhere to the code was expected to commit suicide in a highly ritualized disembowelment procedure (*hara-kiri*) that avoided major internal organs, but that ultimately assured death and restored dignity.[11]

In modern Japan, the company man, or *sarariman,* is often called a modern samurai because of his loyalty and obedience to the company. But beyond that, working hard for the company means working hard for all of Japan. Even Japanese baseball players are expected to wake up early and exercise with their fellow players in a sign of solidarity and commitment to the team they represent. A sports team really *is* a team. Bushido clearly continues to this day to be an important part of the Japanese psyche.

---

11. Ross, *Vision Betrayed*, 7.

Passport of Faith

The Emperor God

Another important component of the subtle interplay between religion, politics, and culture is the emperor system. Beginning during the Tokugawa period, the imperial family was explicitly connected to the Shinto kami. The Japanese myth that was formed helped to preserve Japanese unity and spirit in the face of constant contact with foreign powers that were forcing their way into Japan. The Tokugawa regime fell shortly after U.S. Admiral Perry forced Japan to open to U.S. trade in 1837, supplanted by a small group of court aristocrats that hovered near the young emperor Meiji.[12]

In the years that followed, the Japanese were taught that their country was not only divinely protected by Shinto deities but that their emperors were descendants of Amaterasu Omikami, the divine sun goddess, through the male line from the age of the gods to present.[13] Amaterasu is the key figure in Japanese understanding of their origin as a nation. She is the Heaven-Shining Deity who was a radiant child. Her brother was an unhappy storm god named Susa-no-no. Together, they gave birth to the deities that ultimately produced the emperor's ancestors.[14]

Temples like the Asakusa temple were declared national shrines during Emperor Meiji's reign. In the great promulgation campaign (1870–1884), the three great teachings (*sanjo nyo kyosoku*) were taught to the public. They were (1) respect for the gods and love of country, (2) understanding the principle of heaven and the way of man, and (3) reverence for the emperor and obedience to the court.[15]

---

12. Hane, *Modern Japan*, 84.
13. Bix, *Making of Modern Japan*, 21.
14. Smith, *Japan*, 140.
15. Robert Lee, "Japanese Emperor System," 119.

Shinto in Japan

The Shinto shrines were no longer just places to worship nature but places to worship Japan. By 1900, the Bureau of Shrines and Religion within the Home Ministry had forced every Japanese to become associated with a local shrine and connected to a tutelary deity. The gods at the local shrines were then connected to the goddess Amaterasu Omikami, thus connecting them to the emperor.[16] Shinto, an informal animist religion, was systematized and used to create an ultimate god that all were supposed to obey without question.

Japanese leaders used Shinto beliefs not only to create a powerful Japanese myth and form their identity as a people but also to maintain their subjects' loyalty, reverence, and obedience toward the emperor (and ultimately those who govern for him). Most Japanese became deeply attached to the emperor as the ultimate leader of Japan, viewing him as divine and as the reason for their very existence. In actuality, those surrounding the emperor made sure to keep him relatively weak. The constitution of modern Japan still claims these divine origins for the nation and the emperor, who, as the high priest of Shinto, is expected to perform a variety of rituals at key times each year on behalf of the Japanese nation.[17]

The people of Japan became loyal subjects, viewing themselves as part of an extended family that included the whole nation as children under the care of the great parent, the emperor. People were expected to honor the stories that told of the divine origins of the state and to practice state Shinto. All of this was an effort to put the state ahead of private interests and needs.[18]

---

16. Bix, *Making of Modern Japan*, 31
17. Ibid., 2
18. Ibid., 27

The Japanese theocracy fueled by an invented myth came to a crashing end when General MacArthur occupied Japan at the end of World War II. MacArthur realized that the emperor system was too important to the Japanese people to be discarded, but he made sure that Emperor Hirohito renounced his divinity on New Year's Day 1946 in what became known as the Emperor's declaration of humanity speech. Hirohito himself seemed hesitant to give up the myth; his speech was vague and unclear. Long after the position of emperor had been reduced to symbolic status, Hirohito alluded to the fact that he hadn't really meant to renounce his divinity.[19]

The Soul of Japan

I made a visit to Japan's Imperial Palace, located in the center of Tokyo. The palace dates back to the 1400s and became an enormous complex under the guidance of Tokugawa Ieyasu, the man who made sweeping changes that helped to form the religion of japanism to which the emperor was later linked. The palace is a sacred place, and most of it is off limits to visitors. But I looked at the stone wall and walked along the moats.

Eventually, I made my way to the Ginza district, which I love. This is a place for people far wealthier than I to shop. It's unfortunate that such a beautiful country is so expensive. In Japan, even McDonald's is expensive. A cup of regular coffee in Japan costs at least $4, a trip by train to a nearby city costs as much as airfare to another Asian country, and some kinds of melons have been known to sell for $1,000. The fare from the airport to the hotel would be enough for a day

---

19. Chiyozaki, "Japanese Emperor System," 106–107.

Shinto in Japan

of sightseeing in most Western cities or enough to support a family for a month in most developing countries. Nowhere are the extreme prices more visible than in Ginza, an area of expensive designer stores whose neon signs light up the skies for blocks. In 1991, jumbo-tron screens were extremely rare, so Ginza provided quite a light show. I walked the streets during the day to see them and then waited for sundown to catch them lit up at night.

It is mainly the older generation of Japanese, the grandparents of today's teenagers, who still believe in the divine powers of the emperor and in Shinto and its many gods. For most Japanese, the Shinto rituals are performed for pragmatic purposes or for cultural reasons. My Japanese friend Mihoko, who is in her late twenties, enjoys going to the temple on New Year's Day with her friends. They stay out late, drink Asahi beer, and have a good time. "It is a social function, not a religious experience," she says. She is not a believer in religion and hates being dragged out of bed by her parents every year for one of the Shinto festivals that take place in the middle of the night. But it's a ritual she respects. It's what Japanese families do, so she goes.

After the Nikkei hit its peak in 1991, Japan's juggernaut economy took a nosedive. Having seen their nation outperform the economy of every nation in the world, the Japanese were shocked to find themselves in dire financial straits. The American automobile industry roared back in the 1990s, the value of the overpriced real estate that they purchased in America plunged, and the Japanese government developed a massive $666 trillion debt. The bubble of the Japanese economy collapsed under bad loans, corrupt bookkeeping, and extreme overspending by government officials that depleted the nation's banks. Payroll costs were too high, most companies had an excess of employees, and factories were going overseas to places where the labor was cheap in comparison to Japan. Japan's high tariffs and the lack of foreign competition were also hurting the economy. Japanese companies began to abandon the traditional guarantees of lifetime employment and financial success. Although salaries remained among the world's highest, the Japanese began to feel the burden of having less disposable income than Americans because of the high cost of living.[20]

Japan had become a country where sararimen worked from 5:30 in the morning to midnight six days a week, living lives completely disconnected from their wives and children. A number of Japanese men literally died from overwork. Divorce rates were climbing rapidly. The rigorous Confucian-style education system was producing children who were good at rote memorization but who were unable to think critically. Many young people collapsed under the pressure of examinations which determine who gets into the good schools. At the same time, student bullying and physical abuse from teachers became a serious problem. Hazing and punishing students who did not fit in was and is a common practice in a nation where there is no sin except not fitting in.

The Japanese people began to find the pressure to conform and succeed to be too much. The country entered into a period of soul searching. Japanese movies, books, and comic books gently explored issues regarding the perceived

---

20. The Japanese economy has rebounded to an extent, but I would argue that Japan's long-term prospects are uncertain due to many unresolved fundamental problems. Among those problems are an aging population, a failure to reform government spending, an unwillingness to make use of immigrant labor, and the continued marginalization of women in the workforce.

soullessness of a nation that valued conformity for the sake of money. Japanese art began to reflect the existential nature of the crisis as things worsened. A disproportionately large number of Japanese films began to include scenes of rape and violence.

Pornography in Japan flourished, and even mainstream movies focused on acts of sadism. Young school girls obsessed with materialism and status rented themselves out sexually to older men in exchange for money and gifts. Subways were routinely delayed because of suicides.[21] A series of grisly murders throughout the 1990s rocked Japanese society, which was very proud of its low level of crime and violence. And all of Japan and the world were shocked when the Aun Shinrikyo cult launched a sarin gas attack on Tokyo's subways in 1995.

The rise in crime in Japan was sudden and very different nature from traditional crime. Quite often those perpetuating the crime had a message for Japanese society. Shimizu Tateo, a journalist covering crime for the *Asahi Shimbun* newspaper, wrote an article for *Japan Quarterly* discussing the strange character of these crimes. In March 1997, for instance, a fourteen-year-old boy beheaded a classmate and wrote a letter to the newspaper in which he said, "I want you to acknowledge my real existence, if only in your minds." He went on to explain that murder was his revenge against "the compulsory education system that produced me and the society that produced the system."[22]

Tsuyako is from Kobe, and she has dyed her hair orange. She is twenty-six and unmarried; she enjoys life traveling the world as a single woman. The generation to which she

---

21. Tateo, "Gathering Thunder Clouds," 45.
22. Ibid., 56

belongs, sometimes referred to as Japan's Generation X, has grown up without much parental supervision and has seen Japan's economic miracle collapse just as it entered the workforce. Since the mid-1990s, Japanese magazines have repeatedly published cover stories on the soul of Japan and on Japan's "new youth," all pointing to a breakdown of tradition in Japan.

Young Japanese adults like Tsuyako are forging their own way out of the pressure cooker of Japanese society. Tsuyako plans to live outside of Japan. Utada, another friend, told me, "Outside of Japan, we can be ourselves." Even Mihoko has decided to leave Japan and raise her child elsewhere, preferring a less intense environment. Japan's Generation X desires less and less to be traditional Japanese; they have found that being Japanese in Japan is exhausting.

Animism gave Japan Shinto. Shinto helped to form a strong national identity and lay the foundation for economic success. But in the 1990s, as Japan's economic bubble burst for all to see, the Japanese were forced to reexamine the state of their nation, and possibly the state of their souls. There have been many others like Tsuyako throughout Japanese history. Whether through an invented religion imposed on the nation or through the rebellion of hair dyed orange, the Japanese seem to constantly be in search of identity. Shinto and japanism are not enough to satisfy the human spirit.

A Yen for God

Fourteen years after my first visit, I stayed in the Hotel Grand Palace once again and retraced my steps through the Chiyoda-Ku section of Tokyo. The Grand Palace didn't look so grand anymore. The building looked beaten and weathered. The high-tech gadgets were no longer so high-tech.

Shinto in Japan

The only thing that hadn't changed at the Grand Palace was the excellent service.

I walked the hilly streets around Lidabashi and Kudanshita with my two-year-old son Marco. These Tokyo neighborhoods still fascinate me. Japanese cities tend not to have very many high-rise buildings due to the frequency of strong earthquakes, so even the main streets do not seem large. The side streets can be extremely small and crowded. Various little apartments and commercial buildings all share an intimate space. It's fascinating to see, wedged between a 7-Eleven convenience store and a four-story commercial building, a miniature apartment building that hardly looks any different from the metal shed where my grandfather kept his large lawn mowers. Nevertheless, these tiny apartment buildings still look clean and cozy despite their ridiculously small size.

Marco and I walked to the Yasukuni Shrine, a Shinto shrine not far from the Imperial Palace. Every year, a tremendous controversy erupts when Japan's prime minister goes to honor the war dead from World War II. When built, the shrine was dedicated to war and deified all Japanese soldiers who had served their country. They are believed to be gods. So there is great anger in China, Korea, and other parts of East Asia each time the Japanese prime minister makes his visit.

Tokyo really is beautiful if you look closely enough. Scattered throughout the city are museums and auditoriums that represent the best of modern architecture. As Marco and I walked along the paradoxically miniature streets of this global mega-city, we passed by many noodle shops and sushi joints with their menus printed only in Japanese. Despite Japan's economic prowess and Tokyo's role as a hub for global commerce, it is surprising how few foreigners live in Tokyo and how many Japanese still do not speak much English. As Marco and I checked out one restaurant, I read the sign on the window: "We don't have an English menu and we don't speak English. How about trying Japanese?" I couldn't help but laugh as I pushed my son in his stroller, taking him back to the Grand Palace.

It is ironic that Japan managed to create the kind of society that Castro and Che would have loved for Cuba to have become. Now, both are experiencing financial bankruptcy as well as a spiritual bankruptcy of sorts. Both of these countries have produced an oppressive spirit in their people, one that I think is inevitable because the true God is not an option in either society. In Cuba, there is no god but an elderly despot with a beard. In Japan, there were certainly gods, but they kept mutating—from Amaterasu, to the emperor, to the almighty yen. People need more than the material in their lives. They need a God who will see them as individuals and give their lives a purpose that is much more profound than any manmade system could ever give.

It is difficult to live up to the standards set by nihonkyo. To be Japanese is to carry a heavy burden for society and country. It is something Westerners simply do not feel. The Japanese learn to suppress many of their inner thoughts and desires for the sake of the group. The Japanese truly value the group more than the individual.

As a Christian, however, I think it is fair to say that God calls all people in all cultures to derive their identity from him, instead of from a group or country. In the final analysis, we are God's children. Our ultimate meaning is to be found through Christ. Westerners can learn a lot from the Japanese attitude of selflessness and respect, but I believe there is a personal validation missing in the lives of most Japanese: a profound validation that can only come by being reconnected to the heavenly Father. There is nothing wrong with loving your country, but a country cannot offer personal salvation and ultimate meaning.

As sociologist Robert Bellah has pointed out, religion is always an important ingredient in economic growth and social unity. He suggests that religion serves to "supply a context of meaning for the central values of a society and to meet the threats to these values posed by the ultimate frustrations of the human situation."[23] According to Bellah, every central value system seems to imply certain religious beliefs and actions, which make the value system meaningful in the largest context and consequently motivate people to adhere to it.[24] That certainly seems to be the case in Japan.

Yet Japan, the Land of the Rising Sun, can never hope to be divine. That space is reserved for Jesus Christ. Many of the characteristics that have made Japan great will never be lost; they are too deeply entrenched in the culture to ever be shaken. But my hope and prayer is that the people of Japan will find a deeper inner peace and spiritual direction in their lives, one that will validate them as individuals yet preserve their selfless spirit. If the Japanese were to embrace Christianity in large numbers and Japan became "the Land of the Rising *Son*," I have no doubt that their spiritual influence on the world would make their economic influence look paltry by comparison.

---

23. Bellah, *Tokugawa Religion*, 179.
24. Ibid.

3

TAMING THE TIGERS:
HINDUISM IN SRI LANKA AND SINGAPORE

"Hinduism is all things to all men"
—Jawaharlar Nehru

Religion has certainly been at the heart of many bloody battles throughout history, but for the overwhelming majority of believers in the world, religion inspires peace and tolerance. If you were to speak to the average Buddhist, Taoist, Muslim, Christian, or Hindu, you would most likely find that their faith teaches acceptance of those of different faiths. All of the major religions have strong traditions of peace and tolerance running through significant portions of their teachings. In the case of Hinduism, for instance, it is impossible to imagine that a land as diverse as India could have held together for so long if not for Hinduism's tolerance of other belief systems. In cases where religion is used to wage war, it is often inspired by leaders deviating from orthodox religious beliefs and fueled by an extremist approach to economic or social problems.

Since 1983, Sri Lanka has been engaged in a violent civil war that has killed about sixty thousand people and displaced over one million.[1] The conflict has pitted terrorists from a Hindu minority group known as the Tamils against the predominantly Buddhist Sri Lankan majority. The Tamil Tigers (LTTE[2]), lead by the enigmatic Vellupillai Prabhakharan, have waged a campaign of terrorism against this island's citizens that has included assassinations, poison gassings, suicide bombings, and military operations using women and children. The Tigers were behind the assassination of Sri Lanka's former president, Ranasinghe Premadasa, as well as the unsuccessful attempt on the current president, Chandrika Bandaranaike Kumaratung, who had one of her eyes blown out in a 1999 attack.

Despite the fact that Hindu terrorists have set themselves against the Buddhist majority, this is not a religious conflict. Rather, the Tigers are an example of how terrorist organizations play upon religious sentiment to stir up rebellion for nationalistic ends. The Tamil Tigers believe that they have been marginalized from Sri Lankan society because of their ethnicity and religion. But they do not appeal to Hindu theology at all to support their attacks; rather, their reasons for war are ideological and political. Their attacks are carried out for the cause of nationalism.

Nationalism is devotion to a certain ethnic, cultural, or economic group. An extreme case was Germany's Third Reich under Hitler. The strong loyalty and sense of duty that the Japanese have for their nation (discussed in chapter 2) is also a type of nationalism, the most extreme form of which was visible during World War II. Taken to an extreme, nationalism becomes an ideology and a form of behavior; it can be dangerous.

---

1. Human Rights Watch, "Asia: Sri Lanka."
2. Liberation Tigers of Tamil Ealam.

Hinduism in Sri Lanka and Singapore

The Tamil Tigers are a nationalist organization originating in the Hindu community of Sri Lanka, though they are not representative of the entire community. They are from the Tamil ethnic group, which originally migrated to Sri Lanka from southern India. The Tamil Tigers are fighting against the Sinhalese, who are the dominant ethnic group of Sri Lanka and who speak a language known as Sinhala.

Seeds for the current conflict were sown as early as 1956, when the government of Sri Lanka (which was known as Ceylon at the time) designated Sinhala as the only official language. This had profound effects on ethnic relations: Tamil-speaking civil servants who did not also speak Sinhala were forced into unemployment. Both the military and the education system were also run in Sinhala. Most devastating of all, land that had been cultivated by Tamils for centuries was taken from them and given to Sinhalese. It was in this kind of environment of change and denigration that Vellupillai Prabhakharan was born in 1954. Hindu Tamils saw their influence in Sri Lanka shrink to virtually nothing. By the time Prabhakharan was eighteen, he had founded the Tamil resistance organization that would one day be known as the LTTE.[3]

Tensions were further aggravated in 1972 when the government gave special recognition to Buddhism (the religion of the dominant Sinhalese) but not Hinduism.[4] These official acts caused a sense of ethnic separation that led militant Tamils to wage war against the Sri Lankan government. The Tigers believe that the only solution would be for them to have their own Tamil nation-state.

---

3. Gopal, *Nationalism in Sri Lanka*, 154.
4. Seneviratne, "Religion and Conflict," 76.

Passport of Faith

Despite the current ideological and religious tension, it is religion that has enabled numerous faiths to coexist peacefully in Sri Lanka for most of its history. For centuries, Sri Lanka has been a primarily Buddhist nation. Long ago, Hinduism came to the island from India, where it is the dominant faith.[5] Throughout the island's long history, Buddhists and Hindus have typically worshiped in much the same way. The worship that takes place at Buddhist shrines is patterned on the Hindu ritual puja, the giving of offerings, devotion, and quite often flowers. And many Hindus participate in Buddhist festivals.[6] Sadly, the peaceful society that religion wrought has been torn apart by militants misusing religion, becoming synonymous, instead, with religious violence.

I chose Sri Lanka for my study of Hinduism because the civil conflict between Hindus and Buddhists is an example of the kind of civil wars that have been common since the end of the cold war. Yugoslavia, Chechnya, the Philippines, India, Sudan, and even Thailand, to name just a few, have seen a dramatic escalation in "religious" violence in recent years. It is important that we pay attention to these regions where religion is being used as an excuse to wage violent war.

We have also entered into a new era of terrorism. Globalization is benefiting global terrorists, allowing them to more easily raise funds, purchase weapons, and cross borders to safety. The kind of network that Al-Qaeda utilized for the

---

5. Hinduism is the dominant faith in India, Bali, and Nepal (the only Hindu kingdom). It is also practiced by a significant number of people in Afghanistan, Bangladesh, Pakistan, Indonesia, South Africa, Malaysia, and Fiji.

6. Seneviratne, "Religion and Conflict," 85.

Hinduism in Sri Lanka and Singapore

September 11 attacks was already in place in Sri Lanka years before. The Tigers were perhaps the first terrorist group to establish a transnational terrorist network, basing themselves all around the world. Their methods are both high-tech (as they raised and transferred funds with ease across borders) and low-tech (using very limited technology to challenge a larger, national military).

A Ruin with a View

Sri Lanka, a tropical island shaped like a teardrop, is located off the southern coast of India. It is a multiethnic society: in addition to the Sinhalese Buddhists and Tamil Hindus, there are the Veddas (the indigenous people of the island), Muslims (Moors and Malays who generally practice Sunni Islam), and Burghers (descendents of European settlers). The Sinhalese Buddhist majority make up about 75 percent of the population of this nation that is roughly the size of West Virginia. The Tamils make up roughly 12.6 percent of the population.[7]

This island has often been called "the jewel of the Indian Ocean" because of its beautiful beaches, lush jungles, abundant gems, and scenic mountains. It is an ancient land that has been the home of Theravada Buddhism for centuries and home to Sinhala, one of the world's oldest written languages. In the modern era, it has been known for producing excellent tea and providing the world with spices such as cinnamon.

When I arrived at the airport in Colombo, the capital city, in 2005, I asked the taxi driver what he thought of Villupillai Prabhakharran, the mastermind behind the Tamil Tigers.

---

7. Royston Ellis, *Sri Lanka*, 11.

"Prabhakharran is dead," he told me. "He was killed in the tsunami."

That was news to me. I was surprised that there hadn't been more publicity. If true, the Sri Lankan government had just lost a terrible thorn in its side. Prabhakharran was a brilliant strategist who had outwitted the government many times and who served as the hero of the Tamil resistance.

"We don't have confirmation," the Sinhalese driver told me, "but those are the rumors."

A few days later, I hired a car to take me to the ancient rock fortress of Sigiriya, located deep in the jungle. I had been told that renting drivers in Sri Lanka was a good idea since they were often inexpensive and could show you things you might not see otherwise. My driver was Ajidh, an elegant, shy man in his early forties with a gentle tone in his voice. I learned that he was a Methodist who had married a Buddhist. As we set out for the interior of the country, I asked him about Prabhakharran's supposed death.

"This is what I hear as well. He may have been killed in the tsunami."

Ajidh pulled the car over and pulled out a map of Sri Lanka. He pointed to the northeastern corner of the map, to a city by a harbor. It is the northern part of the country which the Tamil Tigers have often controlled and which they want to partition off in order to create their own Tamil state.

"Right here is the town of Trincomalee," he said. "This is located on a very valuable natural harbor. It is around this area that Prabhakharran has been living and hiding. But you see this area was hit very hard by the tsunami, and Prabhakharran and the Tigers hide in tunnels under the ground."

Hinduism in Sri Lanka and Singapore

"So you think the tunnels where he lives flooded and he died?" I asked.

"That is what I think," he responded.

If that is the way Prabhakharran went out, then he died with as much surprise as his many victims.[8] It's almost enough to make a nonbeliever believe in the Hindu concept of karma, which claims that your actions, negative or positive, can affect you in this life and in the next.

I asked Ajidh how he felt about Hindu Tamils and whether he had friends that were Tamil. "Yes, we all get along," he assured me as we passed road barrier after road barrier, each one designed to keep Tamil Tigers from crossing undetected into the middle of the country from their northern strongholds. I wondered if Ajidh's assurances were more about reassuring a tourist than dealing honestly with the erosion of trust that occurs during civil conflicts.

"We all get along well. Nobody wants this war. Even the Hindu Tamils in Colombo don't like the Tigers."

"Why?" I asked.

"It is because they take advantage of people in the city. If you have a business, perhaps you have to pay money to them so that they will leave you alone."

"Oh, like the mafia?" I said.

"Exactly." he replied.

Unfortunately, Sri Lanka has another problem lurking in its future. As the conflict between the Tigers and the Sinhalese has begun to dissipate, conflicts have sprung up between the Sinhalese and the Muslims living in the southeastern part of the island. The Sinhalese gave the Muslims

---

8. As this book was going to print, there were signs that Prabhakharan's was still very much alive and that the civil war was about to enter a new violent phase.

Passport of Faith

weapons to protect themselves against the Tigers, and now, inspired by Al-Qaeda, the Muslims have started to embrace militancy. Could it be that Sri Lanka is going to go from one religious ethnic conflict to another?

The countryside was beautiful—lush with coconut trees, palm trees, and tea plantations. It was about ninety degrees, humid, and perfectly sunny as we made our way toward the middle of the island. We drove past water buffalo, cows (which are sacred to Hindus), monkeys, and the occasional elephant. In one of those jarring intrusions of globalization that have become so common for travelers today, Alan Jackson and Jimmy Buffet were singing "It's Five O'Clock Somewhere" on the car radio.

I was surprised to see that Sri Lanka had not modernized very much. Aside from the occasional billboard featuring pop singer Britney Spears, everything in the country looked old. There were virtually no new buildings in the entire country. I had heard that Sri Lanka was trying to cash in on the technology economy of the 1990s, as India has in Bangalore and Delhi, but I saw no evidence of this. Instead, I was surprised by how weak the infrastructure was and the lack of any new development. Apparently, the twenty-year civil war had scared off potential international investors.

Corruption might be a factor as well. At one point, Ajidh veered across the center line and was flagged to a stop by a police officer. He jumped out of the car and smiled. "I'll need money." A few minutes later, he returned. I asked if he had bribed the police officer. "Of course!" he smiled. "It was either that or I would have had to come all the way back here later in the week to pay a fine."

As Ajidh drove into the mountains, I nodded off. The driving in Sri Lanka is chaotic, to say the least. I would wake up to find us traveling in the wrong lane, headed straight for a truck. At other times, I would wake up to see a vehicle in our lane, moving straight toward us. I never worried about it since I had confidence in Ajidh's driving. He later confided in me, however, that he was exhausted. "It's not like America, where you can drive for hours and not get tired because the roads are so nice."

Sigiriya is built on a giant piece of granite that rises six hundred feet from the jungle floor and is nearly three acres large at the top. It is an ancient fortress dating back to AD 477. Over a thousand years ago, a palace adorned the top of the rock; it must have been one of the world's most stunning feats of architecture. A model of civil engineering for its time, it is still very impressive. As I walked over the moat, which at one time was filled with crocodiles, I was amazed by the remnants of a beautiful, symmetrically laid-out garden with numerous pools. The complex had one of the world's earliest and most sophisticated hydraulics systems, with drains and pipes that collected rain water and distributed it throughout the complex. On rainy days, water still runs through the ancient pipes and down the drain, surfacing at the base six hundred feet below. In its time, the complex was filled with water fountains, swimming pools, and water for agriculture and horticultural use.

Climbing the stairs, I passed a room carved out of stone which served as the king's auditorium. King Kasyapa (AD 477–495) was a Sinhalese king who built this amazing complex after he killed his father, King Dhatusena. Kasyapa's brother, Mogallana, eventually brought an army to Sigiriya to avenge their father's death. During the battle, Kasyapa's elephant turned to avoid a puddle of mud. His soldiers thought he was retreating and deserted him. Without the protection of an army, the great stone fortress was breached. King Kasyapa killed himself before he could be taken alive; myth would have it, that, with great gusto, he slashed his neck and raised the bloody knife for all to see before dropping dead.[9]

Climbing on up, I passed another room carved out of stone where the king once presided over legal issues. Along the path, some of the giant stones had the shape of elephants; one giant boulder looked exactly like a cobra; other large boulders were meant to be hurled down on attacking foes. In the grotto half-way up the rock are paintings of the king's concubines half-nude, reminding me that even though Hindu and Buddhist parts of the world tend to be sexually conservative, their art is often very comfortable with the erotic.

Sigiriya means "Lion Rock." In order to reach the palace, you had to enter through the mouth of a giant lion carved out of the rock. The facade of the lion's head and throat which served as the passageway for the final ascent has eroded; all that remains are the giant stone paws of the lion. It is hard to imagine how tremendous this fortress must have been in its day. As I made my way toward the paws of the lion, I passed a cage with a sign designating it is as a refuge from attacking hornets. Looking up, I saw many hornets swarming around the plateau where the lion's paws are located. "The bees attack pretty frequently," one of the locals told me.

After taking some time to rest, I made it to the top where the palace once stood. It had taken me an hour and twenty minutes to do so; apparently that was pretty good time. The

---

9. Of course, there are other stories of how the king died.

view was amazing—green jungle as far as the eye could see, a muddy river intersecting the plains, and little villages barely visible below. Even atop this giant rock, there were pools where the king and his concubines must have surely enjoyed the best view in all of Sri Lanka. Twenty minutes later, I was back down on the plains, exhausted and stumbling my way to Ajidh, who was waiting by the car. "A lot of people get scared and don't go all the way up," Ajidh said.

Ajidh then took me to the Temple of the Tooth Relic in Kandy, a city high in the mountains of central Sri Lanka. It is the holiest Buddhist temple in all of Sri Lanka as it allegedly possesses a tooth of the Buddha. It was here, in 1998, that the Hindu Tamil Tigers detonated a bomb that killed twelve people, including a two-year-old. The relic survived unharmed, and today the temple still stands, although it is now heavily guarded. The Tigers' audacity in bombing such a holy site garnered them little international support; ultimately, it caused the Buddhist clergy to move away from peaceful negotiations.[10] As is so often the case when militants seek to win concessions through terrorism, their acts mobilize the victims to oppose the terrorists and their movements even more vigorously.

The story of Sigiriya—two brothers at war—seemed sadly appropriate as I contemplated Sri Lanka's long and tragic civil war. I wondered how Sri Lankans felt about each other and what they thought of the future. Was there really great hatred between the Hindu Tamils and the Buddhist Sinhalese? Everywhere that I went, though, I was assured that there really are no hard feelings between them. Walking through the towns of Sri Lanka, I marveled at how often

---

10. Gopal, *Nationalism in Sri Lanka*, 181.

a mosque would be just a block away from a Buddhist or Hindu temple, remnants of a society in which religions had once coexisted peacefully. But places like the Temple of the Tooth Relic were now scars on the land, and I wondered whether the wounds had healed completely.

The Basics of Hinduism

For many Westerners, Christians in particular, Hinduism does not seem like a religion at all. It has no founder, no central creed, no strong tradition of communal worship, no single truth to discover, no single authoritative text, and no single way to practice and believe in Hinduism. It is the product of a civilization more than it is of a religious group or leader. In fact, Hinduism is not one single religion, but rather a collection of Indian religions. The term *Hindu* was the Persian term for those people living along the Indus River; it did not come into common use until the eighteenth century.[11]

In Hinduism, God is everything and everyone, yet Hinduism also has over 300 million lesser gods that are worshipped by different groups. The various sacred Hindu texts clearly contradict each other on many points, making it impossible to come up with a clear, systematic theology. Western scholars have tried to examine the texts and defend the religion as coherent, but it is not. But to Hindus, the complexity and contradictions are not problematic: for them, it is a way of life, not a faith to be studied and analyzed, and they believe that there is no one path to truth. Not only is there an absence of absolute truth, but there is neither good nor evil. Everything in the world is simply

---

11. Flood, *Introduction to Hinduism*, 6.

Hinduism in Sri Lanka and Singapore

an illusion, all of which flows from the supreme spirit. It is confusing to the Westerner. For the Hindu, however, these issues are not important. Most Hindu believers do not seek to convert others; it is not a faith that has been transplanted outside of India in significant numbers—other than in immigrant communities.

Hinduism is a complete way of life that determines the cultural identity of its more than 800 million adherents, most of whom live in India. Their social class, politics, diet, and religion are determined at birth. Despite the many different sects, gods, and beliefs present in Hinduism, there is a clearly recognizable cultural core. Prominent in that core is the caste system, which separates people into four main classes (subcastes further divide these four): Brahmans (priests), Kshatriyas (warriors), Vaishyas (farmers and producers), and Shudras (laborers). Outside of the caste system are the untouchables, the outcasts. Traditionally, Hindu life has meant the acceptance of one's class and lot in this life, with no possibility of upward mobility.[12] One's place in the current life is defined by caste, current position in the lifecycle (age), and gender, all of which is decided at birth as the result of karma.[13]

Karma is neither a punishment nor a reward; rather, Hindus believe that each person's actions have consequences that will affect him or her in this life and possibly in the

---

12. The caste system has hindered India's economic development because it limits upward mobility and discourages change. In the past, as an agricultural society, this provided stability and order for small communities throughout Hindu areas. However, as the nation moves toward market economics and practices democracy, the caste system does not seem to be sustainable in its classic form. Historically, different manifestations of caste systems have been present in societies in East Asia and Europe as well.

13. Brekke, *Makers of Modern Indian Religion*, 2.

next. Hinduism incorporates the concept of reincarnation (*samsara*). An individual's karma is the deciding factor in determining how they will return in the next life. For instance, if you accumulate a lot of good karma, you might come back to earth looking like Brad Pitt, playing basketball like Michael Jordan, or making money like Bill Gates. If you accumulate bad karma, you might return as a mosquito, a warthog, or a bat.

The entire universe is part of the divine. The supreme spirit is Brahman. Out of this supreme deity come other well-known deities; among them are Vishnu, Shiva, Brahma, and Krishna.[14] Hinduism is polytheistic, yet it also claims to believe in just one supreme god. Unlike the God of Judaism, Christianity, and Islam, Brahman remains completely unknown and indescribable. Hindus believe that glimpses of Brahman can be seen through the millions of other gods at shrines throughout the world. For instance, Brahma, Vishnu, and Shiva are different aspects of Brahman: Brahma created the universe, Vishnu keeps the universe in existence, and Shiva destroys it. The importance of these deities, though, varies from sect to sect.

While Hinduism does not have one authoritative source and remains unsystematic, there are a number of holy books in Hinduism, including the *Veda* (1200–900 BC), *Brahmanas* (1000–650 BC), the *Upanishads* (400–200 BC), and the most famous, the *Bhagavad Gita* (200 BC). Written in story form, the *Bhagavad Gita* gives instructions on how to live

---

14. Brahman (or Brahma) is the one supreme spirit beyond attributes, not to be confused with Brahaman, the personal creator God who is one of the four highest deities. Neither should it be confused with *Brāhamana* texts that are part of Hindu's holy texts, or Brahman, the highest level of the caste system made up of priests and religious teachers.

life as a Hindu. It admonishes the believer to accept their caste, devote oneself to Krishna (a helpful and much revered deity), be honest in one's actions, not seek to influence one's lot in the next life, and pursue knowledge and devotion.

Families are of the utmost important, and parents are greatly respected. Parents are heavily involved in the choosing of mates. The sexual mores of Hindu communities tend to be very conservative. Meals are an important part of community life, and dietary habits are highly regulated; because of their belief in reincarnation, many Hindus avoid meat, fish, chicken, and eggs since these foods require killing living things. Dairy products are acceptable and the Hindu's reverence for cows is well-known.

Throughout India and Sri Lanka, rituals are practiced in the home, in temples, at smaller shrines, at places of pilgrimages (such as the sacred river Ganges in India), and in special pavilions.[15] The most important parts of life are the *samskara*, rites of passage such as birth, the initiation ceremony for those in high castes, marriage, and death.[16] Most Hindus are cremated—on the day of death, if possible—in order to control the pollution of death and to allow the spirit of the deceased to continue in its travels.[17]

WARTIME WOUNDS

After about three days, I realized I was the only adult on the island wearing shorts. Any wise traveler who likes to visit religious sites should always bring a pair of slacks to cover one's legs before entering temples and shrines. I know this, but on this trip I always managed to forget to take a pair

---
15. Flood, *Introduction to Hinduism*, 198.
16. Ibid., 203.
17. Ibid., 207.

of pants when sightseeing. At one Hindu temple, I stood outside looking in. It was here, though, that I encountered my first snake charmer. The experience was straight out of the movies. A man bent down next to me with some sort of flute in one hand and a small basket in the other. He pulled off the top of the basket and began to play his instrument. A cobra slowly rose out of the basket and made several strikes at the man as he played. The snake charmer asked me if I wanted to touch the snake or have him put it around my neck. I graciously declined both offers.

The temple itself was adorned with statues of Hindu gods. It looked very much like the first Hindu temple that I had ever visited, the Sri Veeramakaliamman Temple in Singapore. Twenty years old at the time, I had been taken aback by the frightening statues that covered every wall of the temple. The gods of Hinduism are often portrayed in harsh, violent poses or with mouths wide open, fangs showing. The temples and the gods within them are often very colorful—jarringly so. Red, sky blue, black, green, and yellow will appear on a single statue; within the same temple, there might be hundreds of statues back to back, all following a similar color scheme. To my untrained eye, they often look like evil monsters, the stuff of nightmares.

In Sri Lanka, for instance, Shiva is prominent, often accompanied by his son Ganesh, who is portrayed as a six-limbed, pot-bellied human body with an elephant head who sits upon a sky blue Shiva surrounded by snakes. Ganesh appears throughout Sri Lanka, even in Buddhist temples. He is a much loved god, who is said to bring wisdom and good fortune and who removes obstacles from the path of his followers. Despite his rather frightening appearance, he is, in fact, a lively, humorous god.

Hinduism in Sri Lanka and Singapore

Leaving Ganesh behind, I headed to the University of Colombo, Sri Lanka's best and most well-known educational institution. As I walked onto the campus, I was surprised by the modest facilities. The first thing I noticed was a very small, concrete building with a sign on the wall that read "Department of Nuclear Science." Walking around the campus, I found that important departments and classrooms were small, lacked air conditioning, and were badly lit and poorly equipped. I felt badly for the students and wondered how much wealthier the university might have been if not for the civil war.

I asked a group of college kids sitting together in the shade of a tree about their life in Sri Lanka.

"How's the economy?"

"It's terrible," replied one girl, a sophomore.

"Is it because of the tsunami?"

"No, it was bad before the tsunami, and it is bad after the tsunami. It's just always bad."

Another girl chimed in, "And we can't get part-time jobs at night because we can't go out at night."

"Why can't you go out at night? Is it because it's dangerous?" I inquired.

"No, it's cultural. Young women should not be seen out in the streets at night."

Another girl spoke up. "Sometimes we wonder if it is worth going to university because it means we don't make any money for four years."

I asked them what they planned to do after college. None of them were sure, but most of them were considering leaving the country. "We don't want to," they said, "but there are no jobs." I was curious whether Hindu Tamil students and Buddhist Sinhalese students got along at the university. "We get along," one student told me, "but we don't really spend time with each other. They speak Tamil and we speak Sinhala." As for the university courses, they told me that they were all in English.

After spending a few hours in the library, I made my way out into the courtyard again. A Tamil professor approached me and asked about the purpose of my visit to the university. I explained that I was trying to find out more about Sri Lanka's history and the relations between the Hindu Tamils and the Buddhist Sinhalese.

"I'll tell you," the professor said matter-of-factly. "I'm a Hindu and I deal with prejudice everyday."

I was thrilled to have a Sri Lankan speak so candidly to me.

The professor continued, "People will tell you that there's no problem. They even say this to me. They say, 'Look, you work at a university as a professor. What are you complaining about?' But there is subtle pressure every day. I can feel it."

"Sometimes people will joke," the professor related. "They will say, 'You are a Tiger!' They may laugh after they say such a thing, but there's something about that kind of comment. There is a division and a lack of fairness in this society."

"In 1983, when this whole conflict began, my house burnt down in the riots." As the professor spoke, I recalled what I had just read in the library about the July 1983 riots: Thirteen government soldiers had been killed by the Tamil Tigers. The government retaliated by gunning down thirty Tamils and killing another fifty-seven who were in jail. The result was widespread riots, arson, looting, and vandalism. Four hundred Tamils were killed, 152 industries destroyed,

1,100 shops damaged, and 50,000 jobs lost. When the Sinhalese president went on television that August, he never expressed a single word of sympathy for the Tamil victims.[18]

"I lost everything," the Tamil professor continued. "And these Buddhists, they call themselves Buddhists preaching peace, but they go against everything their religion teaches."

I asked the professor if he felt support for Villupillai Prabhakharran and the Tamil Tigers. "We don't need the violence; but yes, the ideas behind it make sense. Things are not fair. It's easy to understand why it happened, and we sympathize with the idea behind the Tamil Tigers."

"Are you looking for equality?" I asked.

"Not equality. I don't think you can even get that in the United States of America. No, we're just looking for fairness, but we don't want to fight in a violent way."

The professor stood lost in thought for a moment and then added, "I lost everything and I had to start over completely. It's not easy and it's never the same. It's never the same. Recently, we were hit by the tsunami. My car is still damaged from the water. But you know, we Hindus believe in karma."

Child Soldiers and Suicide Bombers

The Tamil Tigers, like Al-Qaeda, have taken advantage of the new openness and technology offered in this era of globalization. The LTTE has used the Internet to create a worldwide propaganda campaign and has solicited funds from Tamil immigrant communities throughout the world

---

18. Gopal, *Nationalism in Sri Lanka*, 155–156.

using front organizations coordinated out of an office in London. With access to assault rifles, surface-to-air missiles, and anti-tank weapons from weapons bazaars around the world, they have proven to be a formidable enemy for the Sri Lankan military. The Tigers are quick to use both modern technology (they were the first to use night-vision goggles) and low-tech tactics (suicide bombers).[19]

The Tigers have relied heavily on children, going so far as to use them as suicide bombers and even "recruiting" orphaned children in the aftermath of the December 2004 tsunami. UNICEF estimates that three hundred thousand children are exploited as fighters in conflicts throughout the world.[20] It is believed that up to 10 percent of the Tiger army consists of children.[21] Of these, it is estimated that only 5 percent join voluntarily; the rest are given no choice but to join the fighting—many are abducted into this form of slavery.[22]

The conflict in Sri Lanka has been incredibly violent; the Tigers have used their limited resources to full effect. In the 1980s, more people were killed per capita in Sri Lanka than anywhere else in the world other than El Salvador.[23] The Tamil Tigers have displayed an impressive tenacity. In the late 1980s, India sent one hundred thousand troops to Sri Lanka to help quell the Tiger rebellion. Prabhakharran and his followers were outnumbered ten to one, but they still managed to rout the Indian troops, causing India to

---

19. Homer-Dixon, *Ingenuity Gap*, 357.
20. UNICEF, "Child Soldiers."
21. Gopal, *Nationalism in Sri Lanka*, 154.
22. Human Rights Watch, "Children's Rights."
23. Bose, *States, Nations, Sovereignty*, 86.

withdraw them. A few years later, the Tigers assassinated the Indian prime minister, Rajiv Gandhi.

Sri Lanka also became the land of the suicide bomber. From 1980 through 2003, the world's leading instigator of suicide attacks were the Tamil Tigers of Sri Lanka—not Hamas or Islamic Jihad. These attacks were not carried out in the name of Hinduism, but for the cause of nationalism. Political scientist Robert A. Pape conducted a study of all suicide bombings that occurred from 1980 through 2003. In a 2005 *New York Times* article, he reported that "religion is often used as a tool by terrorist organizations in recruiting and in seeking aid from abroad, but it is rarely the root cause." His findings serve as yet another reminder that it is not religion per se that breeds and encourages conflict, rather it is other socioeconomic issues. Pape's study showed that all of the suicide attacks during this two-decade period had taken place as part of military and political campaigns, had occurred within democracies, and were all trying to establish or maintain political self-determination.[24]

Taking the advice of the Tamil professor that I had met, I looked up the International Center for Ethnic Studies in Colombo. The ICES is a nonprofit organization where academics from around the world come to do research to advance human rights, promote international peace, and work for cohesion within Sri Lanka itself. The very next day, I listened as Dr. Riaz Hassan, a professor of sociology from Flinders University in Australia, spoke about suicide attacks. Hassan's findings agreed with Pape's: suicide terrorism arises out of a desire to regain control of a territory. From Chech-

---

24. Pape, "Blowing Up an Assumption."

nya to Rwanda, Saudi Arabia to Sri Lanka and the West Bank, suicide bombers want land.

Numerous studies since the September 11, 2001, terrorist attacks have reported that suicide bombers are not necessarily from the poorer classes; rather, they tend to be well-educated, come from wealthy or middle-class homes, are usually in their twenties, and often have families of their own.[25] The bombers usually possess a significant amount of rage as well as a strong desire to find honor in a humiliating situation. Those that argue that it is the desperation of the oppressed poor that leads to such extreme actions are wrong.

As movements gain support over time, however, they often claim to champion the poor; as a result, the poor frequently become unwitting participants in the fight. Pol Pot's Cambodia, Mao's China, and Stalin's Soviet Union were all places where many of the poor did not understand and could not articulate the revolutionary ideas of their movements, but they got caught up in them nonetheless. This is a danger that we will face in the next thirty years or so as violent movements increasingly claim to represent religion and the poor in pursuit of political and socioeconomic agendas.

Neither should we make the mistake of thinking that fundamentalist religious groups inevitably promote militancy and terrorism. Few Christian fundamentalists advocate terrorism; neither do most Islamic fundamentalists. What fundamentalists do have in common with terrorists who use religion is that both groups are usually trying to counter the forces of global change. But fundamentalists usually

---

25. From a study done by Reuven Paz, the results of which were reported in Glasser, "Martyrs in Iraq Mostly Saudis."

Hinduism in Sri Lanka and Singapore

challenge governments through legal means. Terrorists and militant organizations are different; they are willing to wage war to counteract the forces of global change. We must be careful not to use labels indiscriminately; we must look closely at how religion is being used and by whom.

It is amazing to me that terrorist movements last when very little is achieved; historically, such movements have achieved very little success. But, as one senior Tamil Tiger commander said, "When the friends you live with, eat with, sleep with, die every day in front of your eyes, you don't give up the cause."[26]

TAKEN FOR A RIDE

Trishaws (also called *tuk tuks* in some parts of Asia) are tiny, three-wheeled, motorized vehicles that can get you about quite cheaply. I used them often in Sri Lanka because they are able to navigate the heavy traffic much better than taxis. But I saw a number of Hindu and Buddhist temples that I had not planned on visiting due to overzealous trishaw drivers eager to make more money off of me. Knowing that the country had just been hit by a tsunami, as well as the fact that I enjoy talking to people, I often found myself going along for the ride, even if it meant being overcharged and losing a few extra dollars each time.

One evening, I decided to walk along the oceanfront in Colombo. Determined not to be ripped off again, I set out, hoping to avoid the scammers. I can usually spot a scam a mile away, but that night in Sri Lanka I was had.

His name was Mohammed, and he was standing along the waterfront, dressed in a nice suit.

---

26. Bose, *States, Nations, Sovereignty*, 121.

"Hello, sir. Where are you from?" he called out.

"The United States," I replied.

"I am from the Maldives," he told me. The Maldives is a tiny nation consisting of a number of atolls in the Indian Ocean not far from Sri Lanka. I asked him how the Maldives had weathered the tsunami. He told me that they were doing fine and that the damage had not been significant.

As we walked along the oceanfront, he talked about his Muslim heritage and his deep belief in Islam. "I have been to the Hajj seven times," he said with pride. The Hajj is a pilgrimage to Mecca that every physically and financially able Muslim is expected to make in their lifetime.

Mohammed then told me that there was a Hindu temple and a festival occurring just up the block. He asked me if I would be interested in going. I said, "Sure!" He warned me that the beachfront promenade up ahead could be dangerous at night and recommended that I take a trishaw to avoid trouble. The entire time I had been in Sri Lanka, I had never felt as though I were in danger, even when I was being ripped off. Looking ahead, I saw many men loitering on the beachfront, so I figured that perhaps Mohammed was right.

"Come with me and I will get you a trishaw and tell them to drop you off at the Hindu festival." Trusting Mohammed, I jumped into a trishaw with him. Before long, I noticed that we had passed the area where I thought we were going. Suddenly, Mohammed starting talking about gems and jewelry and wanted to know if I had gotten gifts for my wife and friends. An alarm went off in my mind; I wondered if Mohammed was going to try to scam me. Sure enough, before long we pulled up to a jewelry store that had no customers except for me. The door opened just as our trishaw arrived. Mohammed told me to "just look," that he was just trying to "help me out" with my shopping.

Experienced travelers in the third world know the setup. As soon as you enter the store, the pressure is on. The proprietors are all smiles and want to know everything about you; it's a massive charm offensive. Then, they offer you a drink or a snack to induce guilt. They force you to listen to their spiel as they demonstrate every product in stock, hoping to wear down your resistance. When you resist, they show frustration and start offering "a special price just for you." Finally, when you refuse to play along, they exchange disgusted looks, looks that are the final assault of guilt, intimidation, and peer pressure.

I looked at Mohammed and said, "I don't want any jewelry." Is this your friend?" I asked, pointing to the store owner.

"Oh no, no, no!" Mohammed exclaimed.

The owner asked me if there was anything else I might be interested in buying, but I stood my ground.

"No, I don't really know anyone who wears jewelry, I don't want jewelry, and I'm not going to buy anything," I insisted. After days of having people try to scam me, I was finally losing my patience. I got up and walked past Mohammed toward the trishaw.

"Okay, I'll take you to the Hindu festival," he said, jumping into the trishaw behind me. As the driver took off, Mohammed looked at me one more time and said, "I was just trying to help." *Yeah, right!* I thought to myself. A couple of minutes later, I heard Mohammed tell the driver to take me to a Hindu temple, and then he jumped out of the trishaw and vanished. Now I was stuck with having to pay the driver.

A few blocks later, the trishaw driver stopped in front of a Hindu temple that I had visited earlier. It was dark and there was obviously no festival going on. With a straight face, the driver looked at me and said, "That will be 1,600 rupees." I laughed out loud. For that amount, I could have taken an hour trip to the airport in the solitary comfort of an air conditioned van. A more reasonable price would have been 40 rupees, perhaps 300 since I was a foreigner and foreigners are always overcharged. I told the driver that I was not going to pay 1,600 rupees for a trishaw ride.

"But that is the price!" he said.

As the driver continued to demand 1,600 rupees, I decided to borrow a technique from the scammers and launched into a guilt-inducing speech: "In December, your country was hit by a tsunami. People from all over the world have given money to help your country. I came here as a tourist to help your country. Your country desperately needs tourism. So why are you trying to cheat me? I know what Sri Lankans pay for a drive like this. For 1,600 rupees, I could take a car to the airport! Why are you doing this to your country? Your country needs tourists, and you are trying to cheat them. Why are you doing this?"

The driver looked flustered, angry, and a bit shamed. "Okay, 1,500."

"Why?" I asked. "Why are you doing this? Your country can't afford to take advantage of tourists. You need tourists! Tell me why you are so willing to cheat the people who have tried to help your country rebuild. I didn't even know the other man that was in the trishaw; he was just trying to take advantage of me too. When I got in your trishaw, I thought I was going for a short ride, but that man tricked me and left me to pay you. How can you live with yourself?"

Finally, he broke down. "Okay, okay! Pay me what you want."

"Well, since I thought this would be a 100-rupee ride, I should just pay 100, but I'm going to give you 300." I paid him the 300 rupees and got out as he muttered under his breath.

I was now stranded at a closed Hindu temple in an unfamiliar neighborhood. A family operating a little market looked at me with sympathy, but they didn't speak any English. I felt outraged and victimized. I wanted sympathy. The truth was, though, that I was furious at myself for having been conned by Mohammed; the trishaw driver had just added insult to injury.

BACK TO SINGAPORE

On my way back home to Hong Kong from Sri Lanka, I stopped off in Singapore to revisit the Sri Veeramakaliamman Temple, which had left me feeling a bit scared when I first saw it as a twenty-year-old. I wondered how it would look to me fourteen years later.

A city, an island, and a nation—Singapore is all of them in one. It is located at the tip of the Malay Peninsula south of Thailand and Malaysia. Unlike Sri Lanka, Singapore is very much part of the first world. Like Frankfurt, Tokyo, New York, and London, it is a global banking center. It is a wealthy city with one of the highest living standards in the world. The city is well-known for its law and order. Littering, chewing gum, and forgetting to flush public toilets are all criminal offenses. Smoking is strongly discouraged, and driving is regulated to prevent vehicle emissions from polluting the skies. It is so clean, so efficient, and so wholesome that some people find it boring, referring to it as a "nanny state." Nevertheless, there is no doubt that Singapore is a very healthy, safe, and clean city, possibly the best in the world as far as those factors are concerned.

The contrast with Sri Lanka is significant. Like Sri Lanka, Singapore is a multiethnic nation born out of postcolonialism. It is, though, a manmade territory, much like Hong Kong. Throughout history, it was a disregarded piece of land used primarily by the British as a trading outpost, but ultimately it was inhabited by immigrants seeking a better life and it became one of the world's most vibrant and wealthy places. Today, Singapore is inhabited by four main ethnic groups: Chinese, Malays, Hindus (mostly Tamils from Sri Lanka and India), and Eurasians. As in Sri Lanka, it is common to see Islamic mosques, Buddhist temples, Hindu temples, and Christian churches side by side. In fact, in Singapore, the important religious days for Hindus, Muslims, Buddhists, and Christians are also national holidays for everybody.

Singapore has achieved a significant amount of racial harmony. More than any other city in Asia, multiculturalism is integral to the fabric of society. Walking the streets of Singapore, I felt like I was experiencing a bit of heaven because the mix of people was so diverse and beautiful. There have been no horrific racial riots or civil wars in Singapore as there have been in Sri Lanka. Hinduism and Buddhism have remained tolerant in this small country. Why is it that Singapore has been able to develop economically out of nothing while Sri Lanka, rich in resources that the world loves, has remained underdeveloped? How is it that Singapore has managed to create such a high degree of equality between the various religious and ethnic groups given their short history of coexistence while Sri Lanka, a multicultural country for centuries, is now torn by war?

The answers are complex, but one of the most significant factors is the way that the two islands reacted to post-colonialism. Once the countries gained independence (Sri Lanka from Britain, and Singapore from Britain and Malaysia), they made choices critical to the future of their societies. In Sri Lanka, the dominant Sinhalese chose to seize power, making sure that the Sinhalese and Buddhism would dominate the island. This created a deadly division between the Hindu Tamils and the Buddhist Sinhalese.

In Singapore, on the other hand, Lee Kuan Yew, the country's ethnically Chinese founder, chose to view all of the ethnic groups and their religions as equal. If one group was going to have an economic advantage, all groups would share the same economic advantage. If one group suffered the from unemployment, all groups would suffer from unemployment. Lee Kuan Yew made sure that this multilingual, multicultural, multireligious society was as fair as possible. While perfection is not possible, Lee made the point to all Singaporeans that equality was the goal; the people believed him and joined him in pursuing that goal.

For instance, when Malay students began to lag behind Chinese and Indian students scholastically, Lee instituted community-based self-help groups that required financial investment from the Malays themselves but which was matched dollar for dollar by the government of Singapore. Working closely with Malay leaders, Lee encouraged Malay children and parents to make more of an effort in school. As a result, the success of Malay students increased dramatically.[27]

The emphasis on racial harmony and multiculturalism freed Singapore's ethnic groups to focus on succeeding economically. When certain ethnic groups needed assistance, welfare programs were created, but they required people to do their part to better themselves. Lee Kuan Yew pursued, in his words, "a fair, not a welfare, society." There are imbalances and racial tensions at times, but they are certainly not as bad as they could have been had Singapore been given less enlightened and more prejudiced leadership.

I made my way through the city, strolling along Singapore's immaculate sidewalks and through beautiful parks toward Borders bookstore. Outside of Borders, on a street that is surprisingly tranquil despite the fact that it is not far from the busy Orchard Road, I asked a Malay man why there is so much racial harmony in Singapore.

"It's because we have jobs! We're too busy to go out and start riots. You know, things are not always perfect. Sometimes, me and my Malay friends get together and we curse the government! But that's all we do, because at 7:00 AM, it's time to go back to work." Pointing toward Indonesia, just a few miles away from Singapore, he continued, "Over in Indonesia, they have riots all the time because they have no jobs."

That certainly made sense to me. World religions don't usually teach their followers to hate their neighbors, but

---

27. Kuan Yew Lee, *From Third World to First*, 210–212.

Hinduism in Sri Lanka and Singapore

economic disparities and feelings of injustice certainly have the ability to reduce people's tolerance toward one another.

Singapore had many advantages that Sri Lanka did not. Among them is the fact that Singapore is the size of a thimble. So small is the island nation that seconds after the plane took off, I could see the entire country out the window of the plane. It is much easier to organize and manage a small territory like Singapore than a much larger island like Sri Lanka. Singapore is also a nation of immigrants, people who are generally prepared to work hard to better their lot in life and who have no ancient ties to the land they now live on. And perhaps most importantly, Singapore has been blessed with wise leadership.

In the neighborhood of Little India, I made my way to the Sri Veeramakaliamman Temple, where I had once been so spooked by the temple gods. The temple is dedicated to the ferocious goddess Kali. Kali is an incarnation of Shiva's wife Parvati the Beautiful and often appears jet black, naked, and emaciated, with fangs protruding from her mouth. She has sixteen hands and is surrounded by skulls and severed bleeding heads; sometimes, she is portrayed drinking her own blood which spurts out of a wound. For Hindus, she represents the frightening, painful side of life which people must overcome. She maintains order and destroys ignorance, blessing those who strive for knowledge of God.

As I wandered around the temple, I saw people lining up to receive a blessing. The priests were men, dressed in blue, white, and orange robes that exposed the chest and shoulders. As people lined up in front of them, the priests placed *vibhuti* (white ash from burned cow dung) on the foreheads of the believers. Shiva is said to have once smeared ashes on his body, and those who worship him believe that the ashes have the power to restore the dead to life.

In the crowd, I noticed a young Chinese woman and her mother bringing an offering of fruit to the gods. Obviously, it is not just Sri Lankan and Indian Hindus who worship here. The priest took the food offerings, walked into a cove with a statue, and began chanting their prayers. Moving on, I saw Ganesh, the elephant-headed god, as well as Murugan, the four-headed child god who is worshiped in a frenzied sacred dance and who is particularly beloved by the Tamils in Sri Lanka and southern India. Finally, I stopped to look at Sri Peryiachi, a hideously frightening woman with a black face, huge fangs, six arms, and a dead body lying on her lap. Despite her appearance, Sri Peryiachi is believed to be a kind-hearted woman who punishes women that make others feel bad.

As I made my way out of the temple, I did not feel afraid as I once had. However, the sheer number of gods and the crowds of people petitioning them left me feeling sad. There is simply nothing like Christianity, which offers a mediator to God who entered into our human realm as one of us. Jesus is not a white-fanged serpent or a pink elephant; he came to us a child, a vulnerable baby. Christians do not pray or seek assistance from a distant monster from some mythological realm, but from a personal God who put on flesh and blood and lived for a time in ancient Palestine.

This God knows of our failings and failures—the kind that lead to civil wars in Sri Lanka and to the offenses that we perpetrate on others daily—and he forgives. Jesus knows of the cancers that we let fester inside of us and the damage they can do because he was the victim of our unrighteousness on the cross—yet he forgives. I cannot know what it is like to be a Hindu, but I certainly know what it is like to be a sinner, to feel enslaved by my selfishness and immaturity and longing to be set free. As I left the temple that day, I felt joy that I had found Christ—or rather, that he found me.

In the book *Finding God at Harvard*, there is a moving essay by Krister Sairsingh, a former believer in Hinduism. In his essay, he shares that, as a Hindu, the most amazing thing to him about Christianity was the concept of forgiveness.

> What astounded me most was Jesus' claim to have power to forgive sins. I understood the fundamental principles of my religion well enough to know that within the Hindu scheme of things, there is no such thing as forgiveness for one's wrong actions…Who was this Jesus who could break the bondage of karma, who said he had the power to forgive sins?[28]

In the coming decades, there will be more global conflicts in the name of religion. We will need to be wise and discerning if we want to be agents for peace instead of conflict. Many horrific things will be done; at times we will all be guilty, on some level, of allowing our selfishness to wreak havoc on our cultures, our nations, and even the ones we love. We will need patience with each other and with ourselves. Most of all, we will need forgiveness—the kind of forgiveness that can only be found in Christ Jesus.

---

28. Sairsingh, "Christ and Karma," 184–185.

4

THE MEANING OF NOTHING:
BUDDHISM IN SOUTH KOREA AND THAILAND

"If you see the Buddha, kill him!"
—Zen Buddhism saying

My friend Duk Pun and I climbed a mountain in order to visit a Buddhist monk living in a temple perched high above the city. Duk Pun, who at the time was a practicing Buddhist, wanted me to get to know more about her beliefs. I had been sharing my Christian experience with her and her family for a few months and was very willing to learn more about her faith. I had gotten to know Duk Pun through her sister-in-law Kyung Sook, whose family ran a little restaurant across the street from my apartment complex in Pusan[1], South Korea, where I was teaching English at a local language institute. Since I can barely make a peanut butter and jelly sandwich, I often relied on Kyung Sook's little restaurant to keep me alive.

My small neighborhood of Shin Mandok was in a gorgeous suburb nestled in the beautiful mountains around

---

1. The romanization of the city's name was later changed to *Busan*.

Passport of Faith

Pusan. Kyung's restaurant was on the main drag. I was at the restaurant so often that I became more than a regular; I was practically an employee. Although I could not take phone orders over the phone (my Korean was not good enough), I parked the delivery motorbikes and helped Kyung Sook close up shop at night and then walked her and her four-year-old daughter to the bus stop and waited with them. When I was sick or needed help of any kind, the Han family was always there for me, offering tremendous hospitality. Kyung became my Korean sister, and her family became my family.

The Hans were Buddhists, as are many South Koreans. Roughly one-third of South Korea's population is Christian; the remaining two-thirds of the population practice Buddhism. The Hans were nominal Buddhists—saying a prayer when necessary, honoring certain holidays, but not really thinking about their faith in any deep way. For most Buddhists, Buddhism is not something that you seek to understand at a deep level. It just *is*. Kyung Sook's sister-in-law, Duk Pun, was unusual in that regard; she had recently become more involved in Buddhism and was on a deeper spiritual quest due to the fact that she was feeling a great deal of emptiness in her life. She had begun going to one of the Buddhist centers in Pusan to meditate and to listen to a monk discuss the Buddhist life. It was around this time that we first met.

We usually met at the Hans' restaurant, where our discussions would last for hours. It was on one of our first outings together that Duk Pun and I went to this Buddhist center. I had been sharing a lot about Christianity with her and felt that it was only fair that I hear about her experiences as a Buddhist. If she had been visiting my home country, I would have invited her to church, and I'm sure she would have accepted. I accepted her invitation out of courtesy and respect, not to mention that I was deeply interested in her ideas about Buddhism.

Located in downtown Pusan, the center did not look particularly exotic. Most of the rooms were used for meetings and community programs, but in the main hall was a large gold Buddha and an altar with food presented as an offering. Scattered on the floor were mats on which people were sitting. The monk led the people through several prostrations directed at the Buddha statue. They clasped their hands together, held them in front of their face, and then slowly bowed down until their foreheads touched the mat. They repeated this a few times. Then the monk launched into a sermon-of-sorts about the Buddhist life. It was all in Korean, so I couldn't understand much of it.

When our time was finished, we headed out to a park to reflect on what had happened. Duk Pun attempted to explain what the monk had said, but she was clearly frustrated trying to do so. She felt that I should really hear it in English. So we decided to go to the temple perched on the mountain, where there were many monks, some of whom spoke English very well. That is how we found ourselves climbing up the mountain together.

All of the buildings in the temple complex were Chinese-style pagodas made of wood and painted red. In the middle of each hall were gold statues of the primary Buddha, with altars in front and numerous other *bodhisattvas* surrounding him. The complex had a very classically East Asian atmosphere of courtyards, trees, running water, and pagodas. Some of the buildings were not for worship, but for business. Inside were rooms with no furniture, just mats.

Passport of Faith

We went into one of these rooms to talk to an English-speaking monk.

As we entered the room, the monk was sitting with his legs crossed just like the Buddha statues surrounding us. He was wearing a gray robe and had his head shaved; he looked to be about forty years old. He had nothing in his "office" except white walls, the cream-colored mats we sat on, and a brand-new personal computer on the floor directly in front of him. It was a classic globalization moment. Back in 1995, I didn't have a computer, and most Americans were not yet surfing the Web or writing e-mail. This monk, however, was plugged in.[2] We sat down on the mats facing him, with the computer on the floor between us. I began to ask him about Buddhism.

The monk shared with me the basics of Buddhism and discussed his own decision to renounce the world and become a monk. He had done it to find peace and was now trying to help others attain that same sense of peace. South Korea was too secular, he thought, and he complained that the construction boom was obscuring temples and turning the whole country into an eyesore; no temple was too sacred to be spared. In his opinion, progress in South Korea meant cutting down trees, ruining views, and killing nature. He was sickened by the fact that the view of a particular temple in Pusan was going to be obstructed because of a new high-rise complex. "Nobody values nature anymore," he said.

I spent the next hour asking the monk numerous questions about Buddhism. What were the core beliefs? How had it helped him? Was he interested in converting others to Buddhism? His answers were usually vague. After fielding

---

2. South Korea is, in fact, the most Internet-wired country in the world.

my questions for a while, he became frustrated and finally said, "Buddhism can't be explained. It is too hard to explain. And Westerners don't get it." He continued by saying that it was really pointless to keep talking about it. He wasn't rude, just clearly frustrated. He expressed particular annoyance with the many Westerners who come to Asia to find spiritual enlightenment when they are incapable of truly understanding Buddhism. Over and over, he would pause and then say, "It is all just too hard to explain."

Duk Pun had told him that I was a Christian, and he said he respected Jesus and knew quite a bit about him. He did not, however, think much of Christians themselves. The monk felt that Christians fought too much and were too exclusive. He couldn't believe the nerve of Christians to claim that only they had the truth, and he was particularly angry at South Korean Christians and their poor attitude and behavior towards Buddhists. He lamented the fact that so many South Koreans had chosen to believe in Christianity.

THE BASICS OF BUDDHISM

Buddhism is indeed very difficult to explain. Most Asian practitioners do not demand an explanation, nor do they seek to find a clear, systematic theology in Buddhism—and Buddhism doesn't offer one. Like the believers of other Eastern religions, most Buddhists have very little understanding of their faith, using it as they see fit along with other folk religions or in combination with Shinto, Taoism, or shamanism. They have no problem believing in different and contradictory faiths all at the same time.

Unlike *Jesus* or *Muhammad*, *Buddha* is not a name. *Buddha*, which means "awakened one," is a title given to those who attain nirvana, a state of nothingness in which all

Passport of Faith

desires and cravings are extinguished. The founder of Buddhism was Siddartha Gautama, though he was not the first person to ever attain Buddha status in the universe, nor was he the last; he was simply the one that introduced Buddhism into *our* world.

There are hundreds of different variations on the story of Buddhism's founder, who is called Sakyamuni Buddha or simply "the Buddha" by East Asians. The basic outline of his story is that around 566 BC, in the country now known as Nepal, Siddhartha Gautama of the Sakyas was born the son of the ruler of a small state.[3] His birth was miraculous in that his mother Maya felt no pain during childbirth. A prophecy had been given to his parents that Siddartha would grow up to be either a great ruler or a religious figure. His father hoped for the former.

Siddartha was kept within the confines of his father's palace, where he could partake of any and all pleasures that his heart desired. Inside the walls of the palace, the world looked perfect. Life was blissful and Siddartha had no reason to be concerned about anything. His curiosity, however, got the better of him and he ventured beyond the walls of the palace. His first exposure to the real world was a shock. Outside the palace, Siddartha came across an old man, a diseased man, a corpse, and an ascetic. The world was not perfect; it was, in fact, a place full of disease, poverty, and death. Returning home, he was unable to find peace. The things he had seen so troubled him that he could no longer accept his sheltered life. The suffering in the world mystified him. One night, after kissing his wife and child, he left home never to return.

---

3. Some scholars place his birth around 488 BC; others choose more recent dates that span decades.

Buddhism in South Korea and Thailand

Siddartha began his spiritual journey by shaving his head, putting on the robe of a monk, and living the life of a wandering ascetic. He tried to follow the teachings of various gurus but was unsatisfied with their responses to the terrible state of the world. He practiced yoga and even tried fasting almost to the point of death. None of the teachers, the spiritual practices, or the various Hindu gods were able to resolve the problem of suffering for him. He saw that they were all trapped by the laws of karma and reincarnation; each person was doomed to live again and again with each future life determined by the moral behavior of the previous life.[4]

One day while sitting under a Bodhi tree, Siddhartha came to the realizations that would form the core of Buddhist beliefs and ultimately liberate people from the pain of suffering and the endless cycles of rebirth as taught by Hinduism. Siddhartha was now "the Buddha" because he had become an "awakened one." A Hindu deity named Mara appeared to the Buddha, tempting him to keep this liberating information secret, but Brahma descended from heaven urging him to share it with others.

The teachings of the Buddha and the practice of those teachings are known as *dharma*. The most central and well-known of these are the Four Noble Truths and the Eightfold Path. In his teaching, the Buddha made it clear that he had not created anything new, but rather that he had stumbled upon ancient knowledge that had been forgotten. He taught that anyone could liberate themselves through nirvana by following the "middle way."

---

4. For a discussion of the Hindu concepts of karma and reincarnation, see chapter 3.

Passport of Faith

Come As You Are, As You Were, As You Want to Be

What do Buddhists mean when they talk about achieving the blissful state of nirvana? It is not like the Christian idea of heaven. Nirvana refers to the state achieved when the desires of the ego have been extinguished. The Buddha believed that nirvana could not really be explained, just experienced. He taught that as soon as a person was able to detach from the things of this world, one would be immune to the pain and suffering of this world. Detachment means entering into a state of nothingness. The concept of nirvana does not explicitly suggest that life is so terrible that we should just be nothing and feel complete meaninglessness. Rather, Buddhism teaches that everything is an illusion and that our own cravings and desires make us invest too much in these meaningless things. The only way to escape the pitfalls that arise from believing in these meaningless things is to detach yourself completely. That is what is meant by nirvana.

The Four Noble Truths and the Eightfold Path point the way to detachment. The Four Noble Truths are:

1. *Life is Dukkha (suffering):* Life is filled with suffering, whether it is sickness, death, or the end of joyful moments. We cannot escape suffering.

2. *Suffering is caused by cravings:* We are creatures of need and want, but in this world, we cannot be pleased all the time. Left unsatisfied, these cravings cause suffering. Our problem is that we put too much stock in these things that are not permanent.

3. ***The cessation of cravings through nirvana:*** By detaching ourselves from the impermanent things of this world, we can extinguish our cravings and ignorance, thus liberating ourselves from the cycle of rebirth. The cravings and desires that once controlled us come to be viewed as the meaningless things that they truly are.

4. ***Follow the Eightfold Path to achieve nirvana:*** One does not need God, the Buddha, grace, or any other supernatural intervention to achieve nirvana. What is needed is (1) right understanding, (2) right resolve, (3) right speech, (4) right conduct, (5) right livelihood, (6) right effort, (7) right awareness, and (8) right concentration. This Eightfold Path calls for good behavior, nonviolence, ridding yourself of positive thoughts, and learning to control your mind to extinguish cravings.

Siddartha was twenty-nine years old when he became a bodhisattva, one who sets out in search of spiritual liberation. He worked toward enlightenment until he was thirty-five. After becoming enlightened, the Buddha traveled and shared his knowledge until his death at age eighty. No one is sure what it was that killed him, but his remains were cremated; many temples throughout Asia claim to have relics of the Buddha (e.g., the Temple of Tooth Relic in chapter 3).

Buddha himself did not leave any writings for his followers. He felt that people should not take him at his word, but rather find things out for themselves. After his death, Buddhism developed scriptures. They are very difficult to understand. These writings are nothing like the scriptures of Judaism, Islam, and Christianity. Buddhist scriptures tend to leave the reader completely mystified, but that is not a problem for Buddhism, which is not interested in presenting a clear, convincing case. In some instances, the scriptures are used for their magical ability, not for coherent explanations about Buddhism.

While Buddhism does not attempt to present a systematic theology, it does have doctrines. For instance, Buddhism teaches that there is no self or soul. Everything is dependent on something else. Nothing and no one stands alone. Unlike Christianity, though, these doctrines can be accepted or rejected by the believer. Their sole purpose is to assist the seeker in finding enlightenment; they are not meant to be statements of absolute truth. In contrast, for Christians, the belief that Jesus is the Son of God is nonnegotiable; it is difficult to call yourself a Christian and yet believe that Jesus was not divine or that Jesus was not crucified and resurrected.

The key scriptures in the Buddhist cannon are known as the *tripitaka*, "the three baskets." These are the *Sutras*, *Vinaya*, and *Abhidharma*. The *Sutras* are a collection of discourses by the Buddha that were transmitted orally. Most scholars do not believe that these are Buddha's actual words, but many Buddhist believers disagree. In the *Sutras*, the Buddha discusses many important beliefs and has discussions with *brahmins* (teachers of religious knowledge); they also tell stories of his birth, life, and death. The *Vinaya* (book of discipline) contains rules that the *sangha* (the order of monks and nuns) must follow. It also includes rules for ceremonies and rituals. The *Abhidharma* (the higher teaching) is a collection of seven treatises on metaphysics, ethics,

Buddhism in South Korea and Thailand

psychology, ceremonies, and ordination. It is probably the most difficult of the three to understand.

Three Branches of Buddhism

Two hundred years after Buddha's death, Buddhism splintered into many different sects. Today there are three main divisions:

1. Theravada Buddhism

Theravada Buddhism is mainly found in the Southeast Asian countries of Thailand, Vietnam, Laos, Cambodia, Burma (Myanmar), and Sri Lanka. It is a more conservative form of Buddhism that teaches that salvation is something to be worked out by the individual alone. In fact, it teaches that only monks and nuns are able to attain nirvana. Laypeople can only hope to win merits in this life that will help position them to become monks or nuns in the next life, thus positioning them to attain nirvana in their next life.

Theravada reveres the tripitaka, which is written in the ancient Indian language of Pali; it does not accept the extra scriptures and teachings that other forms of Buddhism accept. Theravada Buddhists believe that the Buddha was a human teacher who left his message and then passed away from this universe. Overall, it is the most legalistic and pragmatic of the branches of Buddhism.

2. Mahayana Buddhism

Mahayana is more inclusive than Theravada. In Mahayana Buddhism, anyone can hope to attain enlightenment if they have faith in the Buddha. Much

Passport of Faith

like Protestantism in Christianity, which empowered the layperson and moved away from the interpretation of truth by a central authority (the Roman Catholic Church), Mahayana made Buddhism very accessible to those unable to meet the strict rules of Theravada. Unlike Theravada, which reveres the one Buddha (Siddhartha) who lived, attained nirvana, and passed on, Mahayana Buddhism teaches that the Buddha lives in all eternity and has been reincarnated many times.

According to Mahayana Buddhists, all people possess a Buddha nature within them; by asking for assistance from a Buddha or Bodhisattva, any person can receive salvation. Bodhisattvas play an important role in Mahayana; these are beings that have done enough to attain nirvana but who choose to stay in our universe to help others attain salvation. They are similar to saints in the Roman Catholic tradition—individuals who have lived exemplary lives and who may then be able to offer assistance to those who have faith in them.[5]

Mahayana Buddhism originally used Sanskrit as its scriptural language before the scriptures were translated into Chinese and other languages. Mahayana has many additional sutras and works that are viewed as authoritative. Due to its lack of a central source of authority, Mahayana has opened the door to the creation of many different Buddhist sects, such as Zen. Mahayana forms of Buddhism are most common in Far Eastern nations, such as Japan, China, and South Korea.

---

5. It is important to distinguish between Bodhisattvas in Theravada Buddhism and in Mahayana Buddhism. In Theravada, Bodhisattva refers to historical Buddhas (from many worlds) before they attained enlightenment. In Mahayana, a Bodhisattva is one who out of compassion has chosen to postpone full enlightenment in order to help others.

Buddhism in South Korea and Thailand

One of the most popular forms of Mahayana Buddhism is known as Pure Land Buddhism, which teaches that a Buddha named Amithaba has created a Western Paradise, or heaven, where those who believe in him can reside in the next life. The smiling, obese Buddha statues with which people in the West are most familiar are images of the Amithaba Buddha, not Siddhartha. The Buddha statues found in Theravada are usually thin and represent Siddhartha, the one Buddha for our world.

3. Vajrayana Buddhism

The Dalai Lama represents the third branch of Buddhism, Vajrayana, which is centered in Tibet. This branch is better known as Esoteric, or Tantric, Buddhism. It is very mystical and relies on many secret rituals, mantras, and exercises to eliminate mental and physical obstacles to enlightenment. It is this form of Buddhism that has the monks wearing colorful robes and chanting to the accompaniment of exotic instruments. It is the most exotic of the three branches of Buddhism. The aesthetics of this form were captured very well in Martin Scorsese's film *Kundun*.

Dalai Lama is the title given to the Buddhist spiritual leader of the Tibetan people. Lamas are teachers who achieved enlightenment in a previous life. The current Dalai Lama is believed to have been reincarnated to teach the world. He was forced to leave Tibet in 1959 when China invaded Tibet, killing many of his followers. He currently lives in exile in Dharamsala, India, and travels the world to raise awareness of the occupation of Tibet by the Chinese. The people of Tibet anxiously await his return, but China has no desire to have such a powerful religious figure on Chinese soil. By enlisting Western celebrities in his cause, the Dalai Lama hopes to put pressure on the Chinese government to free Tibet and allow him to return as the people's ruler.

WESTERN-STYLE BUDDHISM

I find it ironic that so many Westerners are attracted to Eastern religions like Buddhism. They tend to demand facts, certainties, and historical accuracy to prove the claims of Christianity—things that Christianity *can* provide to a large extent. Yet these very same people seem to be comfortable with lessening the burden of proof for Hinduism, Buddhism, and quasi-Eastern New Age religions. They accept these vague faiths at face value even though they offer little guidance to the individual and make few demands; perhaps this is why they are so popular.

For many Westerners, Eastern philosophies and belief systems provide a do-it-yourself religion that still appears outwardly transcendent. You can be your own god, but appear to others as if you have tapped into some higher source. In other words, Western-style Buddhism is an Eastern faith with a Western worldview—highly individualistic and self-conscious. This is why the monk on the Korean mountain told me that it is just too hard for most Westerners to understand Buddhism. Western Buddhists inevitably infuse Judeo-Christian ideas about the importance of the individual into their Buddhist faith, and they will not abandon those ideas in their pursuit of nothingness.

Buddhism in South Korea and Thailand

Achieving Zen with Jim

One day in South Korea, I spent an afternoon with Jim, a twenty-something Canadian that had come to Korea to "achieve Zen." That day in downtown Pusan, Jim told me that he had finally gotten a handle on Zen Buddhism and was now achieving Zen. "I have total inner peace now, man! I've achieved Zen!"

In Korea, we had a name for guys like Jim: Elkin-heads. An Elkin-head was a pony-tailed, twenty-something Westerner that looked like he hadn't bathed since Buddha achieved enlightenment. Jim, the radical individual that he was, looked exactly like every other twenty-something backpacking across Korea. I try to be fair and tolerant with people of different faiths when I am engaging in a dialogue with them, but I must confess that Elkin-heads get on my nerves. I think it is because they don't bother to really learn about Buddhism or the cultures where Buddhism is practiced. I've seen too many Elkin-heads come over to East Asia, drop their cheeseburger wrappings on the grounds of a temple compound, and display the worst kind of stereotypical ugly-American behavior in their pursuit of enlightenment.

Zen is a Japanese form of Buddhism that originated in China as Ch'an Buddhism and which focuses on concentration of the mind. It is extremely popular in the West, where many books have been written on the subject. Ironically, not only is Zen rare in East Asia, but it shuns written works, scriptures, or any explanations about it. The goal of Zen is to achieve enlightenment in a flash—in an instant. You don't need to read scriptures, think about doctrines, or focus on the Buddha. You need to simply allow this flash of understanding (enlightenment) to enter your mind. Meditation is used to prepare the mind for Zen.

Passport of Faith

Zen is not achieved on your own; a teacher assists you in your pursuit. The teacher may use a variety of methods to clear the pupil's mind. These can include beatings, shouting, leading the pupil in meditation techniques, or giving the pupil *koans* to mull over. Koans are illogical riddles. There is no right or wrong answer, but our human tendency is to want to solve them or not accept them. Accepting koans helps the pupil empty the mind and stop looking for the rational, for Zen is not rational. Here are some examples of Zen koans:

> A monk asked, "How is illusion true?"
> The master answered, "Illusion is originally true."
> The monk asked, "How is illusion manifested?"
> The master answered, "Illusion is manifestation and manifestation is illusion."
>
> "What is the basic meaning of the Law of the Buddha?"
> The master said, "Filling all streams and valleys."
>
> Whenever there is any question, one's mind is confused. What's the matter?
> The Master said, "Kill, kill!"[6]

Knowing that Zen is something that is greatly misunderstood in the West, I was skeptical of Jim's approach to Zen. As Jim was telling me about his ability to detach from this world and achieve total inner peace, we crossed a busy downtown street in Pusan. Suddenly, Jim was nearly hit by a car. In the middle of his speech about inner peace and detachment, he yelled out at the driver, "Hey, man, watch

---

6. "Recorded Sayings of Ch'an," 365, 368.

where you're going!" He then kicked the side of the man's car, started swearing at him, and used his middle finger to give a certain, very un-Zen-like gesture.

If Jim had really achieved Zen, he would not have been upset at the driver. In fact, he would not have viewed the driver as separate from himself. The car is really no different than he is, nor are the tires. According to one Zen saying, "All is one, one is none, none is all." In order to really be a Zen Buddhist, Jim would need to be less concerned about himself. But Jim was a North American; every fiber of his being cries out, "I am important. I am a valuable individual. Don't tread on me." Westerners simply have a hard time believing that we are nothing and that we are only cogs in a bigger wheel. It is easy for Westerners to claim to believe the standard Buddhist teaching about everything being one, but it is very difficult for us to mean it. Western individualism and the Judeo-Christian belief that the life of an individual matters is deeply engrained in our psyche.

FEELING LIKE NOTHING

In predominantly Buddhist nations, there is a strong sense of fatalism. When things go wrong, it is accepted as fate. There is "a lack of zeal to improve life conditions," writes Buddhist professor Saeng Chandra-ngarm.[7] Buddhism is about detachment from this world because all of it is an illusion and is ultimately meaningless. Therefore, the Buddhist believer is not only meaningless, but also trapped in this meaninglessness until they can find their way out. Instead of liberating people, Buddhism seems to negate the meaning of the individual life. In contrast, Christianity

---

7. Chandra-ngarm, *Buddhism and Thai People*, 26.

emphatically insists that each person's life has meaning, that God has created each individual, and that he knows each one personally.

One clear spring day, Duk Pun and I headed to a park in Pusan that offered a beautiful panoramic view of the city, the mountains, and the ocean. On this particular day, I talked a lot about the historical evidence for the life of Jesus. Duk Pun listened very intently, enjoying this more scientific, historical approach to Christianity's claims. Her response was profound: "I don't have a hard time believing in the historical claims of Christianity. I believe Jesus could have been divine, I believe that he could have lived, and that he could have been resurrected from the dead. What I have difficulty believing is that my life has any meaning and that God knows me."

For Asians like Duk Pun, believing in the spiritual realm is easy. What is not easy for a Buddhist like herself is to believe that her individual life has significance. This contrasts greatly with Jim, the Canadian Elkin-head, and his Western interpretation of Buddhism: he was unable to stop thinking about his own self-importance.

Exotic Thailand

I have been to Thailand a number of times. It is easily one of the most exotic places that you can visit. It has temples, terraced rice fields, incredible festivals with people in colorful clothes, dense jungles, great food, and gorgeous tropical beaches. Any photograph taken in Thailand will look exotic; it is just that kind of place. Influenced by both the Chinese and Indian civilizations, Thailand has a unique feel. Furthermore, not only are the Thai people among the world's friendliest, but they are also a very beautiful people.

Buddhism in South Korea and Thailand

Thailand is known as "the land of 10,000 smiles," and it deserves the nickname. It is a wonderful place to relax.

Formerly known as Siam, Thailand is a constitutional monarchy with a population of about sixty million people. Located in Southeast Asia, it shares a border with Myanmar (Burma), Laos, Cambodia, and Malaysia. Most of the population lives in the countryside; the only large city is Bangkok, the capital. Unlike the other countries in the region, Thailand avoided colonization by foreign powers, a fact of which the Thai are very proud.

In Thailand, you can go parasailing, rafting, jungle trekking, hang gliding, mountain biking, and elephant riding. You can see golden temples, giant Buddha statues, ancient ruins, and kickboxing matches. It is a country that has geared itself to tourism, offering unusual experiences at a cheap price. All of this means that it is impossible to go to Thailand without being surrounded by young Westerners outfitted in REI gear, wearing backpacks, and carrying books with titles like *Thailand on 50 Cents a Day*. It is unnerving to say the least. Of course, whenever I go to Thailand, I am outfitted in REI gear, wear a backpack, and roam around the country carrying my copy of *Thailand on 50 Cents a Day*.

Over 90 percent of the population is Buddhist. In practice, Buddhism is often mingled with animism, demonology, and Hinduism. But Thailand is emphatically a Buddhist nation. According to Article 8 of the constitution, the monarch of Thailand must be a Buddhist.[8] The philosophy of Buddhism has been the underlying belief system of Thailand for over a thousand years and makes its presence known

---

8. The king of Thailand is greatly revered by the Thai people. When visiting Thailand, pictures of him can be seen throughout the country. Their kingdom is a source of great pride.

throughout their literature, music, drama, and architecture.[9] Outwardly, the Thai people appear to be a happy lot. In accordance with Buddhist teaching, they put a high premium on harmony and peace. They highly value politeness. It is considered very rude to even raise your voice in anger.

A Visit to the End of the Road

I set out from Bangkok to the center of Thailand. I had just spent a wonderful time in Phuket, where I visited with some friends from our Hong Kong church while they were on their honeymoon. I joked that they were the only couple in the world that wanted their pastor to accompany them on their honeymoon. Phuket is a very touristy but undeniably beautiful resort area in southern Thailand. When there, I prefer to stay at a small, secluded, conservative Muslim fishing village far away from the overdeveloped Patong area with its notorious nightlife. The Patong area is known not only for its lovely beaches but for its sex industry as well.

Sadly, Thailand has become as well-known for sex tourism as for its many wonderful places—this despite the fact that in relation to its size, the sex industry in Thailand is no bigger than that of the United States. When the AIDS epidemic first broke out, Thailand was hit especially hard.[10] In a Buddhist country with a prevailing sense of fatalism, it was difficult for the government to convince its citizens to practice safe sex. Eventually, a very extensive public awareness campaign helped Thailand turn a corner, and, like Uganda, the country became a model for dealing with AIDS. How-

---

9. Chandra-ngarm, *Buddhism and Thai People*, 1.
10. Official estimates for 2003 put the number of Thais who are HIV positive at 570,000, or 1 out of every 115 people. Some 58,000 Thais died from AIDS in 2003.

Buddhism in South Korea and Thailand

ever, the sex tourism industry continues to thrive, and more disturbingly, Thailand (like many other Southeast Asian countries) has become a hub for sex slavery networks trafficking in children.

Those who were infected with AIDS in Thailand were often shunned by their families and left to die horrible, lonely deaths. Very few people offered to help those battling the disease. Christian groups, however, quickly stepped in, responding to the need and building numerous clinics. Buddhist organizations are also now involved. Buddhism is well-known for its emphasis on compassion for all living things. I wanted to see this Buddhist compassion firsthand, so I made a trip to a Buddhist monastery in the middle of Thailand that has been turned into an AIDS clinic.

Wat Phrabaht is located in the middle of nowhere.[11] Much of Thailand is mountainous or bordered by beautiful blue sea, but in the central area of the country, the land is flatter and less scenic. There are no people or villages around in this area where a long gravel road cuts through the fields, leading toward a lone rocky hill with a stunning temple in front of it. The tall pagoda looks strangely out of place and menacing in the otherwise drab environment.

It was the middle of winter, but the temperature still managed to hit ninety-five degrees in the fierce humidity. I could not stop sweating; I looked like I had been standing under a water faucet. It felt disgusting, and it was quite embarrassing. The Thais, who are used to the humidity, don't seem to sweat very much and, I'm told, think foreigners have a strange smell about them (because of our diet). With my shirt absolutely drenched, I made my way up the

---

11. *Wat* is the Thai word for a Buddhist temple.

lonely road into Wat Phrabaht to introduce myself to the administrators.

Suddenly, I was within the compound. It didn't take long to find the administrative building. Inside the office, the administrators were friendly as I explained to them that I would like to take a tour of the facilities, spend time with some patients, and hear the story of Wat Phrabaht. They were more than happy to oblige. Wat Phrabaht, despite its simple offerings, is an expensive place to operate. Quite often, there is a shortage of caregivers, so they welcome people from around the world who come to stay and help the AIDS patients. On that day, I ran into people from France, a group from the Netherlands, and a large group from South Korea.

A young lady who looked a few years younger than myself, perhaps in her mid-twenties, was my tour guide. She introduced herself, but her name was so long (as Thai names can be) and hard to pronounce that I was unable to say it very well. It was Pat-something. I then told her my name, *Patrick*, and she was not able to pronounce my name either. We decided to call each other Pat and Pat.

Pat had been at Wat Phrabaht for a few years. A committed Buddhist, she was surprised to hear that I was a Christian. "We don't get many Christians here," she said. *That's too bad*, I thought to myself. The clinic was established in the early 1990s in response to the AIDS crisis by Dr. Alongkot Dikkapanyo, who was originally an engineer by trade. It began as a modest enterprise, but today the compound is relatively big, with more than four hundred beds, and quite impressive. The medical facilities are neither fancy nor high-tech, but the compound is clean and has a nice atmosphere.

Pat started out by taking me along a path leading to some concrete buildings. The buildings were small dormitories, she explained, where many of the patients live. Most of them are inhabited by people who are sick, but not in the final stages of the disease. The doors were closed on most of the dormitories, but a couple had their doors open and some men stepped outside to wave. Within the compound, these dormitories are segregated by sex. One row of homes is for women, and the other for men. Sexual relations between men and women is strictly prohibited on the grounds of Wat Phrabaht.

We stopped at a solitary building sitting at the intersection of two paths.

"This," she said, "is our new crematorium!"

Her enthusiasm was a bit jarring. She was thrilled to show it to me, however.

"It was made in the U.S. state of Wisconsin, and we just got it! All the latest technology!"

I soon learned why the new crematorium was so exciting. The old ones were not very efficient. There are a lot of corpses to dispose of at Wat Phrabaht. Through much of the year, five to seven people die every single day. During the winter, the number drops to one or two per day. Death is all around at Wat Phrabaht, a point that Pat made very clearly a few minutes later as we were just about to enter one of the buildings.

"Look down!" she said. As we stood outside, I looked down at a step that led into the building from outside in the courtyard.

"Just right here at this very spot," she told me, "someone died one hour ago."

"Right here?" I asked.

"Yes, right here. He just dropped dead."

I looked at the spot. It was hard to fathom that a life had just ended here sixty minutes before my arrival. Before long, the Buddhist priests would come to preside over his funeral. The body was being put into a coffin at that moment. The coffins at Wat Phrabaht are used over and over again. After the body is incinerated, the ashes are collected and sent with a letter to the family of the deceased. Most of the time, the ashes are not accepted by the families. There is still great shame for many families in Thailand if one of their own becomes infected with HIV. Wat Phrabaht takes in those that would otherwise have no place to go.

As is so common in the third world, many AIDS clinics do not have the resources or the manpower to deal with AIDS as effectively as in the first world. Wat Phrabaht is a wonderful place, but the care is not up to the standards that we expect in wealthier countries. The medicines that patients receive are free, but they generally just treat the symptoms. The hospice is always in danger of closing from a lack of funds. I was surprised to learn from Pat that there has not been much government support.

As we made our way into the hospice buildings to meet some patients, we passed some unusual works of art. On the ground below me were a series of graphic, modern sculptures. One was of a woman and her child; another was of a couple having intercourse. "All of these works of art," Pat told me, "are made with the crushed bones of people that have died here. These are made out of their remains." I looked at the sculptures again thinking that I may have misunderstood her. Looking more closely, I could see that they were indeed made from human bones. "These are sculptures showing the ways people can get infected with AIDS," she said.

Buddhism in South Korea and Thailand

We then came to an area known as the Life Museum. Inside the museum, actually a little room, were a number of corpses. The bodies of former Wat Phrabaht patients have been preserved with formaldehyde. The preserved corpses were extremely emaciated, their bony faces frozen at the moment of death. Their skin was black, reminding me of the mummy of Ramses II that I had once seen in Cairo. Among the corpses were a small child, a woman infected by her husband, and other adults who had contracted the disease. Given Thailand's culture of denial with regard to AIDS, Wat Phrabaht sees part of its missions as shocking people out of complacency—and indeed, the displays are shocking.

Perhaps these kinds of shocking displays are necessary for the Thai people. Thailand has been viewed, and is still viewed, as a nation that got its act together and became one of the world's success stories in the fight against AIDS. But there are signs that the Thai people are reverting to more dangerous patterns of sexual practice. "We have become complacent," says Thailand's senator Mechai Viravaidya (or Mr. Condom, as he is most commonly known). He believes that Thailand is regressing; because Thai people "can't see HIV anymore, [they think] that we have it kicked."[12] Part of the problem is that AIDS budgets have been slashed ever since the 1997 Asian economic crisis. And as medicines become more effective, people become complacent. Although fewer Thai men visit prostitutes than in the past, there has been an increase in extramarital affairs and in casual sex.[13]

---

12. Gorman, "Sex, AIDS and Thailand."
13. Ibid.

Passport of Faith

As we walked into one of the clinics, Pat told me that people from all walks of life come through the clinic. Sadly, there are many children; they were either infected by their mother in the womb or have been part of the sex trade and infected at a very early age. There are also quite a few Buddhist monks; some of them may have been infected as the result of their sexual behavior, but many were infected by contaminated needles used to give them tattoos. Of course, male and female prostitutes often end up at the hospice. They too are shunned by their families, even though in many cases their parents are the very ones who sent them into the sex trade.

The people in the first ward were quite sick, but they were not the sickest in the compound. They looked relatively normal and were able to smile, play games, visit, and engage in conversation. In time, though, they will get very sick and die. If they remain healthy, they do their best to help the clinic run efficiently. As I looked around, I saw many of them helping out with a variety of chores. One chore that must be done is blocking the orifices of the dead so that they do not stain the coffins, which are reused. The chores are rarely pleasant in a place like this. I thought that it must be a strange experience for the patients to assist in carrying coffins that will one day hold them. The patients are surrounded with reminders that no one gets out of there alive, yet there was no sign of open sadness.

Pat then took me to our final stop on the tour—the ward where the most severe cases are placed. These are the patients who are only days or hours away from death. As we walked in, I saw a number of patients lying on beds. They were emaciated and obviously in agony. One particular patient caught my eye, a young man who was probably about my age. He was lying on a bed in great discomfort, but he managed to smile at me. I made my way over to his bedside and got down on one knee. His flesh was very dark and blotchy. His body was now nothing more than skin and bones as he lay on one side. As he looked at me, his mouth was always open; his teeth were very nice and white; his smile was heartwarming.

I began talking to him in a gentle voice, introducing myself. I realized that he couldn't talk, but I just wanted him to hear compassion in my voice. As I looked at the white sheets on his bed, I noticed that they were covered with black specks. It took me a second to realize that these were flakes from his skin—his body was literally falling apart. I gently took his hand in mine, moving my thumb back and forth across his skin. The flesh was bumpy and brittle. There was nothing that I could say, but he seemed to enjoy the human contact. For about a half an hour, I did nothing but hold his hand and smile at him. A bit surprised, Pat patiently stood by.

When I realized that I was keeping Pat waiting, I let go of my friend's hand and said, "God bless you." It was difficult to leave his bedside because I just did not want him to face his final hours without the warm touch of another human being. I did not want him to die like this. Neither does God.

Pat and I ended the tour back in the office where we first met. She told me about her relatives living in Los Angeles. I told her briefly about my life in Hong Kong. As I got ready to say goodbye, still dripping in sweat, Pat spoke. "Tell everyone about us. We want everyone to know." I promised her that I would do my best to share their story with as many people as possible. A few minutes later, I walked down the path alone, leaving behind the lonely death that hovers over everyone in Wat Phrabaht.

THE FOOTPRINT OF BUDDHISM

After Wat Phrabaht, I felt a bit shaken. I was glad that I had gone, but sad to see the living conditions of so many as they face the final stages of this disease. Since I was in central Thailand, I made my way to Lop Buri. At Ayutthaya, also in central Thailand, I had spent several hours admiring the majestic Khmer ruins of one of Thailand's ancient capitals.[14] The complex dates back to the fourteenth century and was built on the Chao Phraya River, which cuts through the middle of the country and through Bangkok before ending up in the Gulf of Thailand. I had heard that Lop Buri was worth a stop for those that enjoyed Ayutthaya. In Lop Buri, there is another Khmer temple that is significant not just for its architecture but also for its monkeys.

I quickly discovered that Lop Buri is not a particularly scenic town. Nor is the temple, Prang Sam Yort, a particularly awe-inspiring structure, although it is made of sandstone. Without question, the monkeys are the main attraction. I was a bit worried that the monkeys might not be around on the day I chose to visit, but my fears were unfounded. The monkeys were everywhere. As I walked to the temple, I saw monkeys crawling along the top of the roof and down the walls. But it wasn't just the temple that was overrun with monkeys; it was the whole town. There were mon-

---

14. Beginning in the ninth century, the Khmer people built a civilization in Southeast Asia. All that is left are impressive ruins such as those found at Ayutthaya and in Cambodia's Angkor Wat complex. Interestingly, the Khmer followed both Hinduism *and* Buddhism; but they followed Mahayana Buddhism as opposed to the Theravada Buddhism that dominates the region now. They also practiced animism.

Buddhism in South Korea and Thailand

keys sitting in the trees, walking down the sidewalks with pedestrians, hanging from electric poles and traffic lights, and loitering outside of stores. I passed one pick-up truck whose owner had gone into a convenience store; the cab was filled with monkeys. A Taiwanese couple in front of me started throwing bread to the monkeys. Within seconds, the couple was overrun by simians. Since I was standing behind them, it looked as if the monkeys were going to come after me as well. These were not particularly cute monkeys, and having ten to twenty monkeys running in your direction is frightening. I decided to get out of town and go to a temple nearby that claimed to have one of the Buddha's footprints.

About fifteen minutes later, I found myself at Wat Phra Phuttabat. Thailand is filled with stunning temples, and this one is no different. The cab pulled up outside a pagoda-like structure; the gold-plated roof formed a pyramid reaching high into the sky. I asked the cab driver if he was a practicing Buddhist. "Not really," he responded.

"Do you believe that this is where the Buddha's footprint really is?" I inquired.

"Many people in Thailand believe that this is actually the Buddha's footprint. He came here from India to share his teachings."

"Yes, but do you believe this?

The cab driver—whose name was Monchai and who was ethnically Chinese, not Thai—took a second to respond. "I think when you see it you will understand why I do not believe it is the Buddha's footprint."

"Why?" I asked.

"Because it is big!" He gestured with his hands, indicating its size.

Passport of Faith

On the temple grounds, I made my way up to the hall that housed the footprint. An extravagant canopy of gold and jewels hung in the middle of the hall. Directly under it was an encasement about five feet long and three feet wide. Peering into the ornate encasement, I could make out a limestone footprint. If Buddha had made this imprint, he must have been an extremely big and tall man. Unlike many other manufactured relics of the Buddha throughout Asia, at least this one was the result of a natural formation. There were throngs of people wanting to see his footprint. As the cab headed away from the temple, Monochai asked me whether I thought this was the Buddha's footprint. "I don't really think so," I replied diplomatically. "But thank you for taking me to see it."

There is really no reason to believe that the Buddha (Siddartha Gautama) ever left the areas of modern-day Nepal and India. However, we do know that disciples of the Buddha are working in places like Wat Phrabaht, doing their best to show compassion. Despite the fact that I don't subscribe to Pat's belief system, I felt richer for having met her; she reminded me that I need to try, as best as I can, to walk in Christ's footsteps.

5

THE RULES FOR LONG LIFE:
CONFUCIANISM AND TAOISM IN CHINA

"The Way is not for, but from, man; if we take the Way as something superhuman, beyond man, this is not the real Way."

—Confucius

It was 1991, and our tour of southern China had to be done with two official tour guides monitoring our every move. Everyone in our small group was British, except my Father and me. They were all extremely polite, highly articulate, and tremendously witty. It was like traveling around in the Partridge Family bus with Monty Python's Flying Circus.

The tour guide who was in charge looked like a Chinese version of one of my childhood friends, Andy. The second one insisted that we call him Johnny Walker after the alcoholic drink that he consumed before every outing. Johnny fit in quite well with the Pythons. They were constantly making each other laugh. Dad and I were more at Andy's speed—amusing absolutely no one. It wasn't for a lack of trying, though. Dad attempted numerous times to add to the jocularity that abounded in the van. Dad, however, is not funny. He is brilliant, a phenomenal missionary, and the nicest guy you could ever hope to meet, but he's about as comically amusing as paying federal taxes.

Outside the van, things weren't so funny. China was coming out of a difficult period in its history and was experimenting with special economic zones in which capitalism was practiced by a privileged few. The cities were still in bad shape. The buildings looked like the ones in Cuba, old, worn, and paint peeling. People were still riding bicycles in mass numbers, and there was little sign of joy, laughter, or love on the streets of cities and villages. There was that feeling of oppression that communist countries seem to have perfected.

The countryside was poor. People were farming the land with centuries old methods. It was amazing to see peasants bent over in the rice patties working hard despite the withering heat. In factories, conditions were terrible, like an inferno. Grey industrial filth belched high into the sky above villages along polluted, muddy rivers.

The service in the restaurants, and even in the nicer hotels we stayed in, was pretty terrible. Customer service was nonexistent in China. In one restaurant, a waitress spilled the food she was carrying and the plates made a terrible noise. She just laughed and didn't seem to care a bit.

The trip ended with a two-hour train ride from Guangzhou to Hong Kong. On the way toward that democratic, ultra-capitalistic British colony, we traveled through endless rice fields and poor villages. Little red-brick houses with red-tile roofs dotted the landscape as we passed muddy rivers, water buffalo, and peasants tending the rice. These are the scenes that Westerners still visualize when thinking of China, complete with mountain peaks in the background. As we approached the border with Hong Kong, the empty

Confucianism and Taoism in China

fields on the Chinese side were a stark contrast to the golden arches of McDonald's on the Hong Kong side. The dramatic contrast captured the huge difference between the first world and the third world.

Confucian Basics

It is very possible that early Christians encountered Chinese people. During the time of the Roman Empire, the Near East was a crossroads of sorts, and people from Africa, Europe, and the Far East passed through as they traded. We know that the Chinese traded silk with the Parthians, and the histories of the Han dynasty include descriptions of Rome, which they called Ta Ts'in.[1]

Traveling great distances by land was quite possible two thousand years ago. It is not unreasonable to think that Christianity arrived in China much earlier than previously thought. A Chinese scholar recently claimed that he had discovered Christian rock carvings in China that he dates back to AD 86. We do know that Christianity has been in China longer than it has been in Northern Europe. By the end of the sixth century, the Nestorian missionaries had already arrived in China to share the Christian faith. The resistance they found, however, was considerable and would set the tone for most missionary work for the next fifteen centuries. China was a land where other faiths and the Confucian philosophy were so deeply ingrained in the culture that attempts to convert the Chinese usually failed.

Neither Christianity nor the "glory that was Rome" impressed the Chinese much, as they already had a well-developed civilization that was ancient and sophisticated.

---

1. Morton, *China*, 59–60.

Passport of Faith

The Chinese refer to their land as *Zhong Guo*, "the Middle Kingdom." They knew of the other parts of the world but found them lacking. As far as they were concerned, China was the middle of the Earth and all other people and places were barbaric.

Long before Christopher Columbus and Ferdinand Magellan sailed around the world, the Chinese eunuch Zheng He had already sailed thousands of miles with an enormous fleet of large, sophisticated ships, making it as far as East Africa.[2] The Chinese were so technologically advanced that many of Europe's supposed inventions, such as the printing press, the compass, gunpowder, porcelain, and even paper were already being used in China.[3] Europe itself was almost completely conquered by the Mongols in the thirteenth century when they made their way across Asia, destroying European armies in their path. China conquered the seas, sparked tremendous innovation, and formed a remarkably sophisticated government long before Europe did. Much of China's success was due to the philosophies that the Chinese had adopted.

Confucianism is not a religion, but rather a humanistic philosophy that has been the underpinning not only of Chinese government but of Chinese civilization. Con-

---

2. China's navigational history is fascinating. From 1405 to 1433, seven expeditions visited Taiwan, Indonesia, India, the Persian Gulf, and the African coast. Unlike Columbus and his three tiny ships in 1492, Admiral He sailed with a flotilla of three hundred ships and up to 28,000 men. The ships, which were technologically superior to those that the Europeans would later build, were filled with luxury items. The expeditions came to an abrupt halt when inward-looking Ming Dynasty emperors forbade the trips—even going so far as to make sailing the ocean a crime and killing sailors. To learn more, I recommend *When China Ruled the Seas* by Louise Levathes.

3. Landes. *Wealth and Poverty of Nations*, 55.

Confucianism and Taoism in China

fucius (Kung Fu Zi), was not a religious figure like Jesus or Mohammed. He was more concerned with political issues and had a strong desire to help rulers rule. Confucius is said to have lived between 551 BC and 470 BC, a time when China was divided into different states at war with each other. He traveled around China looking for a government position that would allow him to put his ideas into practice. His job interview skills must not have been too good, however, because he was never able to land his dream job of assisting a powerful leader. After Confucius's death, his ideas were embraced so wholeheartedly that they became state orthodoxy. The effects of his ideas are visible today in the way society is structured in places as diverse as Singapore, Japan, Vietnam, South Korea, and Taiwan.

Confucius was interested in morality, but not overly concerned with the supernatural. He believed the universe had a moral order and that human affairs needed to function in harmony with it. People and their leaders needed to behave in a civil manner for the benefit of society as a whole. Various folk religions already existed in China; this did not particularly bother Confucius. He was emphatic, however, that people focus primarily on their fellow human beings.

Confucius emphasized the importance of righteousness and loyalty. All people needed to follow certain rituals that were designed to keep order, such as paying respect to one's ancestors. He put a strong emphasis on the role of education and scholars. In some ways, he was China's first teacher. Just as the state needed order, so did people in their personal relationships. Confucius placed ruler over subjects, husband over wife, and parent over child. Rulers, however, were expected to be benevolent, otherwise Heaven, an impersonal force, would punish them and take away their mandate to rule.

Passport of Faith

A number of texts elaborated on the ideas of Confucianism, including the Five Classics: Book of Changes, Book of History or Documents, Book of Odes or Songs, Book of Rituals, and the Spring and Autumn annals. There are also the Four Books, which are post-Confucian and include sayings by Confucius and Mencius (the second most influential Confucian thinker), as well as commentary by their disciples. The Four Books (the Analects, the Great Learning, The Doctrine of the Mean, and the Book of Mencius) were published in AD 1190 by a Neo-Confucian philosopher named Zhu Xi.[4] These books then became required reading for those interested in taking the notoriously difficult civil service examinations that determined whether one would be able to serve in government administration.[5] The examination system remained in place for nine hundred years.

For centuries, Confucian philosophy served the Chinese well as they surpassed all other civilizations in technology and quality of life. As Europe came out of the Dark Ages, the Renaissance, the Protestant Reformation, and the Enlightenment produced massive advancements in Western civilization. Before long, the Europeans were knocking on China's door, eventually gaining access to the country by force.

China's reaction to Western encroachment was initially indifference, then suspicion, and finally anger and humiliation. The very thing that had made China strong—its Confucian orthodoxy—began to weaken it. History was revered, which stifled innovation. Confident in their civilization and distrustful of foreigners, the Chinese stopped

---
4. Morton, *China*, 34.
5. Ibid., 35.

creating and were soon surpassed by the West in many areas.[6]

The last Chinese dynasty, the *Qing*, collapsed in 1911 and the Chinese set out to become a modern nation-state, like England or the United States. A Chinese republic was formed, but the nation quickly dissolved into factional fighting between regional warlords. It was not until 1949, when Mao Zedong established the People's Republic of China, that the nation became relatively unified and began a concerted effort to catch up to the modern world that had left it far behind.

A NEW GOD EMERGES

China chose to return to the world stage through Marxist socialism. When the Communists took over, they made tremendous promises to the people of China. China was a poor, agrarian nation filled with a quarter of the world's people and its leaders were keen on making sure China caught up with the West. Unfortunately, the leader with the most influence was Mao Zedong. Under his leadership, China quickly became a country where people were denied their individuality and lived in fear of the state. Persecutions were routinely carried out, confessions were forced on people, and thought reform was practiced on those that didn't toe the party line.

Mao blamed Confucianism for many of China's problems, and he was happy to be rid of the old emperors, whom he felt were elitist and did not do enough for the peasants. Mao also did not particularly like religion; he expelled all foreign Christian mission agencies from the country. Ironically,

---

6. Landes, *Wealth and Poverty of Nations*, 335–356.

Passport of Faith

Mao was even more closed to criticism than the Confucians he tried to overthrow, acted more like an emperor than the emperors he criticized, and as an atheist allowed himself to be viewed as a god. He became everything that he overtly despised.

In 1956, after less than ten years in charge, the Communist party sought the help of intellectuals, inviting them to make suggestions on how to govern the nation. Confucianism places a high importance on teachers and education, but since Mao constantly challenged Confucianism and told the masses that educated people were detached from the real world of the peasants, the intellectuals were frightened to speak. Mao, however, assured them that he wanted to let "one hundred flowers bloom, one hundred schools of thought contend." Scholars responded to Mao's One-hundred Flowers campaign by submitting their criticisms of the government. Mao responded by killing and persecuting many of those that spoke up.

The Great Leap Forward campaign fared even worse. Mao, like the humanist Confucius, had great faith in human beings and thought they could accomplish anything. Mao wanted poor, agrarian China to catch up to Great Britain in steel production within fifteen years. He ordered everyone to build backyard furnaces to melt down scrap iron. The people of China dutifully obeyed, melting down everything they could, including their valuable jewelry. Instead of doing their normal jobs or going to school, men, women, and children committed themselves to melting scrap iron. The result was a disaster since very few had the facilities to produce quality steel. Millions of tons of metal and other valuables were wasted and the economy came to a standstill.

Confucianism and Taoism in China

Mao also disliked sparrows because they fed on grain, so he mobilized the people of China to constantly make noise so that the birds would drop dead from exhaustion and fright. Confucianism had embedded a deep-seated respect for authority in the Chinese psyche, so no command of Mao's went unheeded—no matter how preposterous. He later had people attack grass and flowers.

People were moved into rural communes, where they were expected to produce tremendous crop yields. The people were so frightened of failing their leader that they began to lie en masse about the amount of food they produced. A famine ensued and over thirty million people starved to death. Many of us in the West recall our parents' telling us, "Eat all your vegetables because there are starving children in China." They weren't kidding! People in China were so desperate that many resorted to eating rocks and tree bark and drinking horse urine. In some extreme cases, people ate children.

In an effort to regain some of the credibility he had lost due to his economic policies, Mao wrote an article encouraging a campaign known as the Cultural Revolution. Mao's enemies were labeled as class enemies. To root them out, Mao enlisted the young people into the Red Guard.

The children and youth of the Red Guard were allowed to travel around China on trains for free in an effort to weed out Mao's enemies. Mao turned Confucianism upside down by making teachers and other revered authorities submit to the authority of youth. Children and young people publicly accused, attacked, and sometimes killed their parents, teachers, and other adult authority figures. Nothing could be done to restrain the Red Guard because they had been given power by Mao himself, who by now had turned himself into a Chinese god. People of all ages carried a little red book called *The Quotations of Chairman Mao* and were expected to memorize it as if it were the Confucian classics or the Bible.

An entire generation of Chinese students left school to persecute adults, take over hospitals, and put themselves in positions of authority they could not possibly hold in any other society. Historic Chinese buildings, temples, and pieces of art were defaced or destroyed. The fanaticism for Mao's Red China was so extreme that in some places, a red traffic light meant "go" and green meant "stop." Numerous accidents ensued. Streets were given new revolutionary names and unacceptable books were burned. Many Chinese were beaten so badly that they remained forever maimed or paralyzed, including the son of China's future leader, Deng Xiaoping. So fanatical were the Red Guard that in some cases loyal followers literally ate their enemies to prove their contempt for them.

China had overturned Confucianism temporarily and banished religion. In its place, Mao had turned himself into a god and led an entire nation into famine and anarchy. From 1966 to 1976, tens of millions of Chinese people died and millions more took part in savage acts of brutality in the name of Mao Zedong. To this day, many middle-aged Chinese people suffer from extreme feelings of guilt for destructive actions carried out as teenagers and children.

It was not until after Mao's death in 1976 and Deng Xiaoping's clear emergence as China's leader in 1980 that China was able to move forward again at a rapid pace. Deng did not turn himself into a god. Instead, he focused on making China a nation that was tightly controlled by the government, but which experimented in free-market economics. He began to liberalize the economy by creating special economic zones where people had the right to privatize commerce and try their hand at capitalism. Those regions changed at a dramatic rate; China was soon averaging 10 percent growth in gross domestic product (GDP) per year. China was on its way to regaining its place in the world.

Cell Phones, BMWs, and Fast Food

Ten years later, I returned to China. That same two-hour train trip now took me by houses, factories, and gleaming skyscrapers. By 2001, the whole region had experienced a tremendous economic boom. At the time of my first trip, the first McDonald's had just opened in Beijing. Now there were over 250 in the city of Shanghai alone, with Pizza Hut, KFC, and even Wal-Mart not far behind in tapping into the Chinese market. Shenzen, which was a little fishing village bordering Hong Kong when Deng Xiaoping came to power, now boasted a skyline to rival Dallas, Houston, and Chicago. Some of the largest skyscrapers in the world are found in Shenzen.

The coastal cities of Fujian province were now filled with wealthy Chinese people doing business with the Taiwanese, and Shanghai had become an enormous city of never-ending construction sites and freeways. Beijing was starting to look a lot more like Los Angeles and less like Moscow. More and more Chinese people were becoming involved in manufacturing and service jobs as opposed to farming. Even more amazing was the number of Christians operating successful businesses in provinces like Zhejiang in eastern China.

Passport of Faith

Deng Xiaoping had ushered in a new day in which people were free to prosper. "To get rich is glorious," he exhorted. When asked what he thought about socialism versus capitalism for China, he responded by saying, "Black cat, white cat—as long as it catches mice." In other words, I don't care what we do, as long as we make money.

The reforms that took hold of China in the 1980s triggered major transitions in Chinese society. First, China moved from being an agricultural society to an industrial society. Foreign companies began to invest in China and set up factories employing cheap Chinese labor. People began to abandon farming and move to the city in search of better jobs. Even today, train stations in China are filled with rural workers looking for work in the city. They sit or stand around the station hoping to be selected for some kind of job.

Second, China began to decentralize. Confucianism had made it possible for China to have a strong central government, which made China into a relatively stable and prosperous empire. Under Mao, however, authoritarianism had been taken to an extreme. Deng loosened the reins and allowed elections at the local level (although only Communists were allowed to run).

Third, China began to move from being a collective society to an individualistic one. Confucianism strongly emphasizes family and obligation toward parents, but in the new China, people began to look out for themselves first and foremost. For centuries, family lineage had been vital to preserving community. Do you ever wonder why there are so many Chans and Lees in the Chinese community? These are the names of kinship groups. In Chinese history, quite often villages would consist of one large extended family.

Confucianism and Taoism in China

Lin village, for instance, would be filled with people having the last name of Lin, though not everyone was a Lin by blood. Quite often, people who moved into the village would adopt the local name for protection and community. This explains why there are so few family names in China. In the new China, family and lineage have become less important.

Fourth, China became increasingly connected to the larger world. In the days when Confucianism helped to sustain a great empire, China did not interact much with the rest of the world. In this new age of globalization, however, that kind of isolation is impossible. China now receives Western television shows, interacts with foreign companies, and purchases foreign products.[7] The Internet has become a powerful means for the Chinese to hear views from beyond their country's borders. The government tries to regulate access, but that is not entirely possible.[8]

Lastly, communism as an ideology died. Communist party leaders are now too busy driving their BMWs and vacationing in Orlando to keep up the charade. They wear business suits, carry cell phones, and send their kids to prestigious American universities. The day of living communally and believing in the government's Communist rhetoric is over. Today, Mao's little red book is sold on souvenir stands along with bootleg CDs of the latest American boy-bands.

---

7. China is extremely interested in engaging the world and becoming a global player like the United States. China's leaders routinely travel to South America, Africa, and Asia to drum up business and build credibility and alliances. They are following the U.S. model of establishing significant business interests around the world and setting themselves up as an alternative to U.S. hegemony.

8. The Chinese government even got help from Microsoft in trying to control access to the Internet within China.

Passport of Faith

Neither Mao's ideas nor androgynous pop bands have much staying power in the modern world.

One Nation Under Stress

While there are many new fat cats in China (as many as 120 million Chinese have made it into the middle class, by some estimates), there are still millions of impoverished people willing to eat the fat cats. Most of the nation (particularly away from the wealthy coasts) is not profiting from the push toward modernization. Two Chinas are being created: one wealthy, one poor. China is a place were a few own Mercedes, but most are lucky to own an ox. Some have cell phones, but others are lucky to have electricity. Some are now living in brand-new condos with satellite dishes, while others still live in caves. Some Chinese attend the West's finest universities, but most are fortunate if they make it past the sixth grade. Some are fortunate to live in China's booming cities, but most continue to live in its dying villages.

While the Western media treat China as if it were an economic giant on the verge of supplanting the United States economically, the truth is rather different. While China does have tremendous potential, it is a nation with mind-boggling problems.

Cities like Shenzen have become wealthy, but they are beset with gangs, crime, drugs, and prostitution—problems which were largely unknown during the days of strict Communist rule. The Golden Triangle area of China (on the border with Myanmar and Laos) has become a world supplier of heroin; many Chinese have themselves become addicted. Forced abortions due to China's one-child policy have left a critical shortage of women. Homosexuality is on the rise, and the United Nations is warning of a looming AIDS crisis due to intravenous drug activity, prostitution, and unsafe sex.

China's environmental problems are so severe that they are likely to affect the rest of the world. Already, Hong Kong suffers from extreme air pollution blown by the wind from mainland China. China's factories and rivers are among the most polluted in the world. Most Chinese still do not own a car, and one can only imagine what will happen to China's environment once the average Chinese family can afford the kinds of machines and appliances that Westerners depend on. Environmental degradation may well become a source of future conflict and even war.

State factories are not only polluted but bankrupt, so the government has been closing down factories that are losing money. No longer can the Chinese count on their government for cradle-to-grave support. China now has a floating population of an estimated 150 million people—migrants who are moving from the country to the city in search of jobs. It is the largest peacetime migration in human history. Many do not find jobs, so they become homeless and destitute. The disparity between rich and poor in China has reached potentially disastrous levels. Millions have yet to taste the new wealth, and street children, the homeless, the elderly, and those with AIDS are being left behind.

China also faces an alarming shortage of teachers. Most students consider themselves lucky if they have an uncertified *miniban* teacher. Conditions are so bad in some schools that children are losing their eyesight in poorly lit buildings, chalk is treated as if it were gold, and textbooks are rare. The vast majority of young people still cannot go to college.

Passport of Faith

In cities such as Shanghai, a private high school can charge $62,000 per year; most students, however, are lucky if they can afford $125 per year for public school tuition.

Even if China's gross domestic product catches up with that of the United States, that does not mean that China and the United States will be economic equals. It will take decades, if not a century, of economic stability, with few setbacks, for China's economy to develop the depth, resources, and flexibility of the U.S. economy. A five-trillion-dollar economy that is limited to a small number of sectors (e.g., toys, shoes) does not constitute a strong, balanced economy. In addition, China is still overwhelmingly a farming and manufacturing economy. In contrast, the United States has a high-tech and service-oriented economy, which employs less than 10 percent of its population in farming and manufacturing. With the threat of severe setbacks very likely, China's rise to economic power, wealth, and stability is by no means certain. And a setback in China's growth could result in conflict. Those who think that China will soon surpass the United States as the world's richest and most powerful nation are sorely mistaken.[9]

A moral vacuum has emerged in China. For centuries, Confucianism offered social guidance and Chinese religions offered spiritual guidance. When Mao Zedong and the Communists took over, they discarded Confucianism and religion, making themselves the supreme authority. But within decades, it became clear that neither Mao nor the Communist party were trustworthy. With no source of moral authority, many Chinese have become extremely

---

9. By the Chinese government's own estimates, they will not achieve parity with a first-world nation like the United States until the year 2100—if all goes well.

Confucianism and Taoism in China

individualistic, creating a society in which it's every man for himself and the only god is money. The ancient Far East has become the gun-slinging, gold-searching Wild West.

Blind Ladies and Rats

My wife Jamie and I routinely visit China to help provide social services to people who are struggling to survive in this new age of government cutbacks and radical individualism. We love the people of China and simply want to help in the best way possible. The Chinese government has an enormous challenge in trying to prevent catastrophe in this land of 1.3 billion people; as far as I can see, they are managing as best as they can. No country is facing the pressures that China is currently facing. It is easy to criticize China from afar, but lifting a half a billion people out of poverty is a herculean task.

One of the places that we visit often is a home for the blind. It is nothing more than an abandoned two-story factory without windows, electricity, or running water. The stairs threaten to collapse each time we climb up to see the blind ladies. The first thing we always see is the rats running around them and under their beds and tables.

Although their home is dark and overrun with rats, the blind ladies always offer us the only thing they can, a cup of hot water. These ladies are Christians and have been for most of their lives. Most of them were unwanted children; not only were they born female, but they were born with a physical handicap. One of the negative aspects of Confucianism is its tendency to create divisions between people, for instance, encouraging people to value males more highly than females.

Passport of Faith

When abandoned as children on the streets of China in the 1930s, the girls were rescued by Christian missionaries, who placed them in orphanages. Mao kicked the missionaries out of China in 1950, but these women remained faithful to Christianity. They endured tremendous persecution during the Cultural Revolution at the hands of the Red Guard and others for not believing wholeheartedly in Mao Zedong's teachings, but they survived with their faith intact.

These blind women have not yet escaped persecution, however. When Jamie and I and our Christian friends visit, we always buy them food. They are often cheated at the market because of their blindness; they are overcharged and robbed by the vendors. No one works in this center for the blind. Instead, the women live alone with the rats. They are fortunate if they receive their monthly stipend of $25 from the government.

The ladies radiate a joy and happiness, however, that is hard to find in the new China. Jamie and I particularly like to give them hugs and hold their hands. In a society that places so little value on those who are different, something as simple as a touch and a hug can mean a great deal. Quite often the ladies don't know how to respond, since they have gone most of their lives without receiving a hug; but there is no doubt they like it.

Each Sunday, the ladies walk sixty minutes each way through busy city streets to attend church, where they sing in the choir. When we visit them, they sing us Christian hymns, such as "Amazing Grace," in Chinese. Their walk to church can be extremely dangerous; it is literally a case of the blind leading the blind. On one occasion, a few of them fell into an open manhole, but they were unharmed. They attributed this to the amazing grace of God. In 2004,

Confucianism and Taoism in China

we were finally able to help move these ladies to a better location.

The Return of Religion

Christianity may not be new to China, but the tremendous growth now occurring definitely is. Over the course of fifteen centuries, Nestorians, Franciscans, Jesuits, and Protestants all tried to bring Christianity to China, but Christianity was always dismissed as a foreign religion. Ironically, Mao's attempt to close the door on Christianity had the opposite effect. Banning foreign mission agencies from China made Chinese Christians take full ownership of their faith. As they passed it from generation to generation, Christianity came to be viewed as Chinese, not foreign.

Throughout the history of Christianity, persecution has usually led to revival, not extinction. That is what has occurred in China. In 1949, the government listed 750,000 Protestant believers in all of China.[10] By some estimates, fifty million Chinese have been baptized since the late 1970s.[11] Although Mao Zedong is long gone, the rise of religion in China still alarms the Chinese government. Christians continue to be persecuted, but persecution seems only to strengthen their faith.

Recently, China received world attention for persecuting the Falun Gong movement, which combines aspects of Buddhism and Taoism. It is not the religion that they are practicing that alarms the Chinese government, but rather how they are organized. Founded in 1992, the Falun Gong (or Falun Dafa) has believers all over the world. Its founder, Li Hongzhi, lives in New York City. The aim of

---

10. Carroll, "Images of Church and Mission," 32.
11. Wehrfritz and Clemetson, "Jesus Is All," 36.

Passport of Faith

Falun Gong is simply to practice physical and emotional health through exercises and meditation. Members insist that they are peaceful and have no intention of threatening the Chinese government. However, the government views things differently. A 1998 demonstration outside of the government's Zhongnanhai compound in Beijing rallied over ten thousand protesters. What most frightened the Chinese government was that this rally was organized via the Internet by Li from his home in Brooklyn.

Chinese history is riddled with examples of large religions and secret societies, such as "the White Lotus" and "the Yellow Turbans" causing instability and even rebellion against the government. One of the most notable is the Taiping Rebellion, which lasted from 1850 to 1864.

At roughly the same time that the United States was engaged in its Civil War, China faced a civil war as well. The Qing Dynasty faced a messianic Christian cult led by a man who thought he was God's Chinese son, Jesus' younger brother. Hong Xiuquan was a frustrated, lower-class member of the Hakka, a Chinese ethnic minority. In an effort to better his life, he attempted to pass the notoriously difficult Confucian examinations. After numerous failures, Hong became sick and bedridden. He then had a vision that was undoubtedly influenced by some Christian pamphlets picked up from an American missionary. The vision revealed that it was his duty as God's son to establish a heavenly kingdom in the heart of China. (Conveniently, God was asking Hong to destroy the empire that was so insistent on those difficult Confucian examinations.)

Hong began to preach his message to his village and then his province. Before long, he had many followers in Guangdong and Guangxi province; they became his army.

Confucianism and Taoism in China

This "Christian" army grew so large that it nearly defeated the Chinese government and conquered all of China. Had this Christian cult won, history would certainly have been much different. But Western commercial powers were tired of losing money in China because of this internal conflict, so they came together to defeat Hong and his army once and for all. Over thirty million people lost their lives in this rebellion led by "Jesus' Chinese brother."

The memory of Hong lives on, though. Jamie and I occasionally run into people whose negative feelings about Christianity are based on this bizarre incident in Chinese history. During one particular Chinese New Year celebration, we had dinner with a family of Hakka ancestry. I asked our host about her feelings toward Christians and Christianity.

"We know all about Christians and we respect them," she said in a friendly manner. "But we stay away from it."

"Why?" I asked.

"Because of Hong," she replied. "Hong Xiuquan. Have you heard of him?"

One hundred and fifty years later, Hong's legacy continues to affect religious beliefs. It reemphasizes the need for Christian missionaries to be well-schooled in the history of the region where they serve. The current government also remembers this piece of Chinese history. Consequently, government action against the Falun Gong and against Christians has been very aggressive.

One of the legacies of Confucianism in East Asia is that the people often respond to radical authoritarianism. Whether it is the very controlled society of Japan or the incredibly regimented life in Kim Jung Il's North Korea, East Asians accept authoritarian rule better than many other cultures. The current government in China tries to take advantage of this Confucian heritage by keeping China a one-party nation governed by strong, unapologetically authoritarian leadership.

The Chinese people's propensity to obey authority is what enabled Mao's ideas to prevail for so long. That propensity may also be contributing to the rapid growth of Christianity in China, though there is reason to be concerned. While evangelical Christianity is growing quickly, Christian cults are also growing at an alarming rate. The Born Again Movement (BAM), led by Peter Xu Yongze, expects new converts to cry for three days to bring about forgiveness. Both registered and house church leaders have criticized Yongze for doctrinal aberrations. The government has identified him as a David Koresh–like figure and sentenced him to a reeducation camp. Nevertheless, his movement has three million followers and many spin-offs.[12]

Lightning from the East promotes the idea that Christ has already come again, bodily reincarnated in a woman named Lightening, and that only those who believe in this female messiah will be saved. The Disciples (Mentuhui Society) was started in 1989 by Ji Sanbao, a farmer with a strong end-time theology, who, like Hong, called for the overthrow of the government. The Lingling Cult was founded in 1985 by Hua Xueche, a man who claims to be a second Jesus and in 1990 prophesied the second coming of Christ.[13] The Bureau of Religious Affairs recently reported that 500,000 people in China are involved in such cults. It is easy to see why the clampdown has been harsh and has targeted lead-

---

12. Morgan, "Tale of China's Two Churches," 34.
13. Ibid., 30–31.

ers such as the illiterate founder of the Beiliwang (Anointed King) sect, for instance, who was executed in 1995.[14]

It is not so much religion which frightens the authoritarian Chinese government as it is religion's potential for the mass mobilization of people, which could then challenge the authority of the government. Ironically, the Chinese government is increasingly trying to incorporate aspects of religion, particularly the ethical foundation that it provides, into Chinese society; it has come to recognize that religion, particularly Christianity, has been key to the success and stability of Western civilization.

Many of those left out of China's economic boom are attracted to Christianity and to the Falun Gong. Alan Hunter and Kim Kwon Chan, in their book *Protestantism in Contemporary China*, suggest that Christianity is contributing to the psychological well-being of Chinese society. Their research shows that both Christian and Buddhist believers tend to be more positive about their lives and are neither carried away by the radical individualism of China's nouveaux riche nor the despondency and cynicism of the newly marginalized.[15] Religion stabilizes such people and provides the moral compass that is so desperately needed in China today.

The Basics of Taoism

As we have seen, Confucius was not concerned with the spiritual life but with bringing order to society. However, all people in all societies seem to want spiritual answers as well. Taoism has helped to meet that need in Chinese society. Taoism is a loose body of philosophical and religious teach-

---

14. *Bridge: Church Life in China Today*, 84, 4.
15. Hunter and Chan, *Protestantism in Contemporary China*, 235.

ings inspired by a book titled *Tao-te-ching* (Classic on the Way and Its Power). The founder of Taoism was Lao Tzu (which means "old master"), who is said to have lived at the same time as Confucius. It is very possible, though, that Lao Tzu never existed. We do know that the *Tao-te-ching* was compiled in 350 BC.

Much like Hinduism and Buddhism, many Taoist beliefs are impossible to explain. In fact, the first of the five major characteristics of Taoism is that the Tao cannot be explained. The Tao is the source of all things, it is in all things, and yet it is nonbeing and functions through nonaction. It is an object of awe and the ultimate reality behind our world. The Tao is perfectly balanced, and nature is in harmony with it, unless disturbed by human action. It is a difficult concept to explain.

A number of legends have been influential in Taoism. The Yellow Emperor Cult (fourth century BC) idealized the first emperor because he supposedly went to heaven on a dragon and became immortal. He was the father of China and brought order to the world. The Yellow Emperor was said to be the perfect student of Lao Tzu. Not only did he invent Chinese culture and gain immortality, but he became one of the stars in the sky.

Another influential myth focused on the Islands of the Immortals. These islands supposedly existed off the coast of China and were inhabited by fabulous animals and other beings. The islands were also home to the magic mushroom, which gave health, wealth, and immortality. Most Chinese explorers who tried to find the islands died or never came back. Some did find an island to the east; most likely, it was Japan (whose citizens, amusingly, do have one of the highest average life spans).

Confucianism and Taoism in China

In the West, the most popular Taoist concept is the idea of yin and yang, which explains the balance of nature. Out of the void—the primordial breath—two complementary forces exist. For Taoists, yin and yang are the balancing forces evident in nature. Examples include light and dark, hot and cold, male and female, shady and sunny, penetration and absorption.

Taoism does not value wisdom. The ultimate goal is eternal life. Central to Taoism is the idea that our longevity is threatened by worms inside of us. In order not to feed the worms, you must avoid grain and meat, practice certain respiratory and gymnastic techniques (such as Kung Fu) or take special elixirs, and use prescribed sexual techniques. The three primordial forces within Taoism are breath (*ch'i*), semen (*ching*), and spirit (*shen*). For the Taoist, life centers on respecting nature and staying physically in balance with nature. For some, the quest for immortality is literal; for others, it is symbolic of the hope for a long, healthy life.

As with other religions in East Asia, the average believer is unaware of many specific Taoist beliefs. Taoists in China today are likely to also be Buddhist or follow a folk religion. They are likely to practice each faith out of ritual only. The Chinese are pragmatic; they do what they think will benefit them in the moment. If a Taoist ritual will help them feel better or live a longer life, they will practice it, whether or not they know anything about Lao Tzu, evil worms, or magic mushrooms.

This applies to Hong Kong as well, which has been a part of the People's Republic of China since the British handed over control in 1997. Though Hong Kong is a sophisticated, modern city where consumerism is king, the ancient Chinese religions are still alive and well—

particularly for the older generation. As in Japan, many of the temples mix religions without any sense of contradiction. Confucian ancestral halls sit beside Buddhist and Taoist temples. Believers walk freely between them all, offering worship as they please to whomever they please. The Taoist temple is often constructed in a fashion similar to the Buddhist temple except that, instead of being filled with statues of the Buddha, they are filled with statues commemorating local immortals.

A couple of blocks from my home in Hong Kong is the Che Kung Taoist Temple. It is named for a general who is believed to have protected this area from the plague. General Che Kung is said to have achieved immortality. Since the Chinese concept of divinity is not as elevated as it is in Christianity, Judaism, and Islam, in China, even those who are not dead can be said to have attained divinity. This makes it easier to understand how Chairman Mao could have been viewed as a god by the people of China.

Filling the Moral Vacuum

My friend Orange is a student at a Chinese university. In China, many young people learning English take unique English names. At our church in Hong Kong (which consists almost entirely of people under the age of twenty-five), we have members with English names such as Angel, Chicken, and Apple. We even had someone visit us named Kinky. Orange is no different.[16]

As part of our work, Jamie and I assist at a leprosy center. Orange joined us on one visit as we accompanied a group of university students to deliver food to the lepers. The center,

---

16. In the same way, we have taken Chinese names. My name is Laih Paak Cheng, Laih being my surname.

which is completely unstaffed, is a series of concrete buildings far out in the Chinese countryside. The lepers live alone and grow their own food. The setting is beautiful, located beyond rice fields near some beautiful mountain peaks. The conditions at the center are not as nice, however.

Orange was not a Christian, and neither are most of the lepers. In fact, Orange was very skeptical of Christianity and quite uninterested. However, he was deeply moved by this trip of compassion to visit outcasts of Chinese society. "No one comes to visit us, except for the Christians," one of the lepers said.

Chinese society can be very hard on people who do not fit in. It is a legacy of Confucianism, which for centuries defined right and wrong, orthodox and heterodox. This heritage with its legalism and demand that rituals be followed without exception has made much of East Asia very inflexible. It has affected everything from the way that the East Asians educate their students to the way that they treat sick, diseased, or deformed people.

Self-interest and self-preservation are powerful forces in all societies, but in China they are particularly acute. Those of us that have lived in East Asia have many stories of the failure of East Asians to come to the aid of those in need of help. In traffic accidents, the injured may be left unattended for an extremely long time because people fear bad luck if they get involved with someone struck down. Even my wife was stunned by the lack of concern in a Hong Kong subway as she witnessed a man go into a violent seizure. The Chinese on the train backed away as my wife got down on the floor to cradle the man's head to keep him from cracking his skull against the metal seats.

Passport of Faith

Much of this indifference toward others comes from Confucianism. While Confucianism does teach *jen* (benevolence), it does not have anything like the concept of love—deep, *agape* love. In fact, *love* is a word rarely used in China. Confucianism's emphasis on family helped to build a system that created a stable society, but not a society particularly compassionate toward strangers. Throughout Chinese history, one's obligation primarily was to one's family. People outside of the family or kinship group did not matter.

Francis Fukuyama, professor of international political economy at Johns Hopkins University, has referred to China as a low-trust society. People do not have faith in those they do not know. Americans may think they live in a low-trust society because of crime and other problems, but in fact the United States is a very high-trust society. I trust my banker, the person that fills up my car, my doctor, and the chef at my favorite restaurant. There is also a sense that a universal ethic will cover even those people to whom we are not directly obligated. But China is a place where it is acceptable to take advantage of blind ladies at the market if you can get away with it. It is the kind of place where a store owner might lace his food with opium just to make his customers addicted to his food.[17]

In China, even the family unit is breaking down; divorces and affairs are becoming more common. The East Asian family has never been as close as many Westerners believe. Most East Asian families are not close emotionally, just closely bound together by Confucian obligations. In Japan, husbands and wives spend very little time together,

---

17. This story was documented by Pulitzer Prize–winning journalist Nicholas Kristoff. *China Wakes,* the book he co-wrote with his wife, is filled with stories that reveal the moral vacuum found in China today.

and the kids may hardly know their father. In Hong Kong, my Chinese friends admit that they don't know their parents all that well, nor do their parents know them. My Korean friends all felt deeply misunderstood by their parents. In the West, parent–child problems occur when intimacy fails to occur for any reason. This is in contrast to the East, where there is never an expectation of intimacy in the first place. My Asian friends are quite candid about this.

It is because the Chinese do not have any real concern for others that Orange was deeply moved by our trip to the leprosy center. The lepers have been abandoned by the government and by the community. Not all of them are active cases, so there is no need to run in fear. Leprosy is not highly contagious, and furthermore, there is now a treatment for the disease. For the most part, the lepers are very normal-looking people. They may have stumps for hands or other deformities, but they are not the ghoulish figures that one might imagine. Yet no one comes to visit the lepers except the Christians.

On the way home, Orange and I were riding in the back of a truck. He said to me, "I'm deeply ashamed. I'm deeply ashamed of the way China treats its people. I don't understand why we are that way." I was silent as I listened to him unload these very deep, personal thoughts. "I've never done anything like this before, but doing this makes me feel really good."

Orange was experiencing the liberating power of agape, in which we love as Christ loved us. In fact, Christ commands agape love of his followers. Not only are we to love our neighbor as ourselves, but we are to seek their highest good. Agape love is nonnegotiable. This command to love comes directly from a personal God who demonstrated his love for us. It is much more powerful, convincing, and insistent than the general, humanitarian suggestions of the Chinese faiths. In the People's Republic of China, agape is a revolutionary love.

Even though the United States is quite secular, the influence of agape is still felt. For the most part, the Christian ethic of treating others as you would want to be treated is still practiced.[18] People still hold the door open for me when I walk into a building in the United States. Though we are highly individualistic, we are also quick to think of others. It is so deeply ingrained in our culture that we don't think about it. In China, a supposedly communal society, people are so individualistic with regard to people outside of their immediate community that that they have no problem ignoring them. Increasingly, the Chinese themselves, like Orange, cannot deny it. Orange was honest and correct in recognizing that a concern for one's neighbor is missing in Chinese society.

There is a new openness toward religion in China. The government continues to persecute mass people movements, but they are increasingly aware of their need for religion to maintain civil order. Under Mao's communism, people were forced to live communally, even though they deeply resented it. (I call it agape at the barrel of a gun.) Modern China needs citizens who voluntarily choose to obey the law and be good to each other. To build a powerful economy

---

18. Confucius did tell people to treat others as they would want to be treated if they want harmonious relationships. But this is different from the nonnegotiable Christian command to love, which places love at the very center of all of Christ's teachings and is at the center of salvation itself, as opposed to Confucius's pragmatic guideline for maintaining political and societal order.

and a strong society, China will need to establish a civil society that has a high level of trust.

Getting It Right

China is trying to learn how to be nice to people. When Dad and I first went to China, we were astounded at the horrible service. Dad called it "perfunctory." We saw few people smiling or being helpful. But things are starting to change.

When Jamie and I go up to China, we occasionally stop at Do & Me Chicken, a local fast-food restaurant. It used to be the only fast-food restaurant in this town. There was no McDonald's, KFC, or Pizza Hut. Some local entrepreneur of the new China decided to create Do & Me. The food is a bit on the gross side. It is just as oily as KFC, but in a less appetizing way. My spicy chicken burger always has an egg lobbed on top of it, which drives me nuts. The imitation apple pie does not taste sweet like the apple pie at McDonald's, but rather has an unappetizing bitter taste. Do & Me would not survive in an American strip mall.

But Do & Me is getting the customer service aspect right. After a few minutes of giggling, the girls behind the counter enthusiastically come up to the counter to take my order. They look back and forth at each other with laughter as the foreigner orders their pseudo-American fast food. A chart with pictures of the food is nearby in case foreigners can't speak Chinese. The manager hovers in the background, making sure that the order gets filled right. Best of all, my Do & Me combo #5 comes with a gift. Unlike American fast food restaurants, the gifts are huge. Rather than a cheap plastic toy, you might walk away with a giant stuffed animal next to your burger.

Passport of Faith

The Chinese food in this town is much more delicious than Do & Me's fast food. However, I like stopping by Do & Me Chicken because it allows me to observe the emergence of a civil society in which individuals are valued and business and governance are conducted with higher levels of trust and honesty. China needs this kind of transparency in order to survive. Do & Me Chicken is a sign of hope.

Will China survive? With so many different groups of people falling through the cracks and a government that is overextended, it will be very difficult. If China is to survive, it will have to become a more selfless society, and faith, not just materialism, will have to undergird it.

Do & Me Chicken is promising. But my friend Orange is even more promising. Orange became a Christian. When I last spoke with him, he said that his parents were pressuring him to get a job that paid lots of money. His male friends were telling him that his girlfriend is too ugly. The message was that he needed to pursue wealth and find a prettier girlfriend. Orange told me that he disagreed with this. "I don't care about money. I want to help people." He added, "Furthermore, I accept my girlfriend and think she's pretty."

Orange looked me in the eye and asked, "Am I doing the right thing?"

"Yes," I said. "You are doing the right thing."

Agape love had waged a revolution in his heart and won. As long as China produces more people like Orange, there is hope.

6

SCATTERED SHEEP:
JUDAISM IN ISRAEL

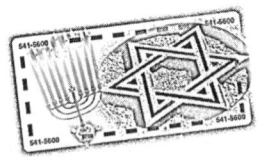

"You shall inherit their land, and I will give it to you to possess, a land flowing with milk and honey"
—Leviticus 20:24

The three monotheistic faiths of Judaism, Christianity and Islam are deeply rooted in history. In contrast to the Eastern religions, these three religions teach that God acts in history and that history must be interpreted correctly to understand the faith. Furthermore, all three faiths believe that God is still acting in history and that the world is headed toward some kind of conclusion; all three have strong apocalyptic strands in their theology.

In the traditions of each of these monotheistic faiths, God did not stay removed from and unknowable to humans, but made himself known in a moment in history and called people to him. For Christians, that moment was when God sent his Son Jesus Christ to earth to show us how to live, taking on our sins and thus forever binding us with God the Father. For Muslims, that moment was when the Prophet Mohammed began reciting the words of God (Allah) that formed the Quran. The Jews look back to the Exodus, when

Passport of Faith

God delivered the Hebrews from Egyptian slavery and led them to the Promised Land, the land where the nation of Israel is now located.

The roots of modern Judaism stretch back to Abraham, Isaac, and Jacob, who established a relationship with the one true God called YHWH.[1] God established a covenant with Abraham (then called Abram), promising to make him the father of a great nation (Genesis 12:2). Originally from Mesopotamia, Abraham was led by God to the land of Canaan (later known as Palestine and Israel), where his family flourished. Abraham's descendents became God's chosen people. From his grandson Jacob's twelve sons came the twelve tribes of Israel.[2] The word *Jew* comes from *Judahite*, meaning a member of the tribe of Judah, though it now refers generally to those who practice Judaism or who are culturally Jewish.[3]

The name *Israel* comes from Jacob, the grandson of Abraham, who was given that name after wrestling an angel in the desert (Genesis 32:28–19)[4]. Today, it is the name of

---

1. God is given many names in the Hebrew scriptures. *Yahweh* (YHWH), the personal name of God, is prominent throughout and is not spelled out in permanent written form by the Jews. Their concern is that if it is spelled out, it can be defaced, which is an offense to the Jews.

2. The twelve tribes are Reuben, Simeon, Levi, Judah, Dan, Napthali, Gad, Asher, Isacchar, Zebulun, Joseph, and Benjamin.

3. The Jews have been called a nation, a people, an ethnic group, and a culture. Each definition is problematic for some portion of the population. I have chosen to use the term to signify both those who are practicing Jews and those who are culturally Jewish. Theoretically, Jews are the descendants of the patriarchs, and one can be called a Jew if born to a Jewish mother. However, there are problems here as well. The Reform movement within Judaism is willing to also accept a person as a Jew if their father is a Jew.

4. The Jews, followers of YHWH, were also known in history as Israel. When the ancient kingdom of Israel split into two halves (north and south) after King Solomon's reign, the northern kingdom was also known as Israel.

Judaism in Israel

the country in the Middle East that was established in 1948. Citizens of the modern-day country of Israel are referred to as Israelis instead of Israelites.

The era of the patriarchs (Abraham, Isaac, and Jacob) lasted from roughly 2000 BC to 1700 BC. Due to famine, however, the tribes relocated to Egypt, where they were eventually enslaved under the Egyptian pharaohs. The story of their deliverance from slavery is known as the Exodus, which remains the pivotal moment in Jewish history. It occurred sometime around 1250 BC. Moses led the people out of slavery in Egypt toward their promised land and gave them the Ten Commandments revealed to him by YHWH. The Hebrews (which is yet another name for Israelites and Jews) rebelled against God and spent the next forty years wandering through the desert. Sometime around 1200 BC, Joshua, Moses's successor, led them into the land and conquered the city of Jericho. Over a period of time, the Israelites were able to wrest large portions of the land from the tribes living in the region.

At the time, the people of the land lived in small city-states consisting of groups such as the Canaanites, Hittites, Amorites, and Jebusites. The Israelites established their own kingdom with their first king, Saul, sometime around 1020 BC. Saul was followed by King David, who expanded the kingdom, and his son, King Solomon, who brought the kingdom to its zenith before he died around 931 BC. Establishing a king was a radical move for the Israelites, who had traditionally believed that YHWH was the only one who should be king over them.

King Solomon built the First Temple, which is also sometimes called the Solomonic Temple. The temple was God's house on earth, a very holy place. While the Israelites worshiped in other places at times, the temple made Jerusalem the center of Jewish religion. Within the temple was the most sacred room, the Holy of Holies, where the Israelites kept the Ark of the Covenant, which contained the Ten Commandments among other things. This inner sanctum was off-limits to all except the high priest, who entered it only once a year on the Day of Atonement known as Yom Kippur.

Shortly after Solomon's death, the kingdom was divided into two smaller kingdoms (Israel and Judah). Weakened by this division, both kingdoms eventually succumbed to the powerful Assyrian Empire, which not only took control of the land but destroyed the First Temple in 587 BC and deported the Jews to other regions within the empire. The Jews were once again separated from their promised land.

The land of Israel was occupied by foreign powers for the next two thousand years and was often referred to as Palestine[5] instead of Israel. The Babylonians, the Persians, the Greeks, the Romans, the Byzantines, the Arabs, the Christian Crusaders, the Turks, and the British all controlled Palestine at different times over the centuries.

Some Jews returned to their promised land in about 325 BC. They built a Second Temple, but they were never able to regain full control of the land. The Jewish religion began to take a different shape. No longer did Jewish worship exclusively center around the physical temple in Jerusalem

---

5. There is dispute about which group in history was the first to use the term *Palestine*. But it is clear that the term was used to designate a geographic area—the area of land along the Mediterranean coast of modern-day Israel. The name itself comes from the ancient Sea Peoples (including the Philistines) who settled in the Eastern Mediterranean in the first half of the twelfth century BC. Their land became known as Phillistia and was later called Palaestina in Latin.

JUDAISM IN ISRAEL

with priests offering sacrifices. Instead, the religion focused on obedience to the law (*torah*). Eventually, the Jews came to recognize the books of Mosaic law, the collected writings of the prophets, and the Deuteronomic History (Joshua–Kings) as their holy scriptures. The law was interpreted by rabbis teaching local congregations known as synagogues. In the centuries after the Babylonian exile, Jewish sects such as the Essenes and the Pharisees formed; these new groups no longer put such a great emphasis on the need for a temple.

The Jewish books of law are known as the written Torah or the Tanakh.[6] Jewish culture was an oral culture, passing on its teaching and history through storytelling instead of writing. The oral Torah developed while the Jews were in exile. Part of this oral law is the mitzvah, the 613 laws that Jews are required to observe. In the fifth century BC, another collection of Jewish law and tradition known as the Talmud developed; it consists of the Mishnah and the Gemara. This oral torah explains the scriptures and how to apply the laws.[7]

Despite the new place of the Torah after the exile, the Second Temple was completed in 515 BC, after the Persian occupiers gave permission for the Jews to rebuild it. Jesus worshiped in a third temple build by Herod the Great. It was this Herodian temple that he predicted would also be destroyed. In AD 70, roughly forty years after Jesus' death and resurrection, his prophecy was fulfilled when the Romans destroyed the temple in Jerusalem; it has never

---

6. *Torah* can also refer to the Pentateuch, the first five books of the Tanakh: Genesis, Exodus, Leviticus, Numbers, and Deuteronomy.

7. There are actually two Talmuds: the Babylonian Talmud and the Jerusalem Talmud. The Babylonian Talmud is more comprehensive and is the one most often used today.

been rebuilt. Today, in its place stands the Al Aqsa Mosque and the shining Dome of the Rock, which is the most visible landmark of modern-day Jerusalem. The only thing that remains of Herod's Temple is the Western Wall, also known as the Wailing Wall.

While some Jewish people continued to await the reconstruction of a new temple and the return of the Messiah (thought to be an ordinary man who would rise up and restore the kingdom of Israel), other Jewish thinkers spent their time debating the Torah and studying in academies of learning known as *Yeshivot*. Still others attempted to take matters into their own hands, forming militant groups with aims to reclaim the land. One of these revolutionaries was Simon bar Kochba, whom many Jews believed to be the Messiah. Bar Kochba waged a three-year war against the Roman occupiers that nearly defeated their forces. The Romans got the upper hand eventually, however, and they massacred or sold most of the rebelling Jews into slavery.[8]

For centuries afterward, the Jews were a people without a home. Many of them settled in Europe, where they faced anti-Semitism—prejudice and hatred against Jews and Judaism. Sadly, some of the worst cases of anti-Semitism came at the hands of Christians and Muslims. This hatred for Jews grew to a horrific level in Nazi Germany under Adolf Hitler; six million Jews were murdered between 1933 and 1945 in what has become known as the holocaust or *shoah*. Many Jews trying to escape persecution were turned away by countries in Europe as well as by the United States.

It was not until 1948 that Israel was restored, this time not as a kingdom but as a modern nation-state. In 1917,

---

8. Wright, *New Testament*, 166.

JUDAISM IN ISRAEL

the Balfour Declaration stated that the Jews should have a home in the land of Palestine. The declaration was approved by the United States, Britain, France, and Italy. Prior to that time, Palestine was inhabited by both Jews and Arabs and was controlled by the Ottoman Empire. World War I ended the Ottoman era and Palestine came under the protection of Great Britain. Eventually, the British allowed the United Nations to decide the Palestinian question, and in 1947 both the Jews and the Palestinian Arabs were offered separate states. The Jews accepted the offer and the state of Israel became a reality in May 1948. The Palestinian Arabs, however, rejected the offer, spawning a series of wars and uprisings lasting to the present day.

DAZED AND CONFUSED IN ISRAEL

Almost forty-one years to the day after Israel became a state, I stepped foot in the country for the first time. Israel shocks visitors who don't know what to expect. It is very much a modern, first-world nation where things function extremely well. There is a healthy middle-class and a booming economy, despite the violence that often breaks out between Israelis and Palestinians. Israel could easily pass as part of the United States. This is due, in part, to the fact that by the time I arrived in Israel in 1999, the United States had given over $74 billion dollars in aid to Israel since its establishment in 1948.[9]

I went with my wife Jamie and her family. Jamie grew up in Egypt and spent many vacations in Israel, so for her

---

9. This statistic comes from the Washington Report on Middle East Affairs (www.wrmea.com), which seeks to provide Americans with an unbiased view of U.S. relations with Middle Eastern nations. Its neutrality is disputed by some.

it was all old hat, although she always enjoys her time there immensely. She was even baptized in the Jordan River (like Jesus).

We left the airport by way of *sherut*—a shared taxi that goes from city to city or to various locations within a city. Driving along the freeway, it did not take long for the geography to change from the flat green valley around the airport. Within a few minutes, we were passing towns perched on the rocky hills that lead up to the Judean hills and valley where the holy city of Jerusalem is located.

At the time, Israel was abuzz with news of an upcoming election, one that people hoped would bring peace between Palestinians and Israelis. It was the first time I had ever heard the name Ehud Barak. His photo was very visible along that drive on posters and billboards. We heard his name repeatedly in announcements playing on the van radio. At the time, Israel's prime minister was Benjamin Netyanahu, a member of Israel's Likud party, which was very wary of negotiating with the Palestinians, particularly their leader, Yassir Arafat. Barak was a member of the One Israel party, which sought to find a peaceful settlement to the Palestinian crisis. The election would be held a week after we left Israel. Little did we know how much would change in the Middle East after that particular election. None of us realized that we were enjoying a vacation in Israel during what would be the last remaining days of relative peace in the country. A violent new chapter in the Israel-Palestine conflict was about to begin.

However, my first priority at the time was not to learn about Israeli politics but to see as many biblical sites as possible. Like so many other Christians, I felt a great desire to see the things Jesus saw and to walk where he walked. This included seeing Bethlehem, where Jesus was born; Nazareth, where he grew up; the Jordan River, where he was baptized; Golgotha, where he was crucified; and the Mount of Olives, where he ascended into heaven. Since many of the popular locations are really just traditional guesses, I never really knew if we were at the exact location where Jesus had once been.

For instance, our tour bus took us to the Mount of Beatitudes where Jesus gave the Sermon on the Mount. Located between Capernaum and Tabgha, the hill has a church built by the Byzantines to commemorate the spot. However, the New Testament does not tell us exactly where the mount was located, so we cannot be sure.

We found the same thing when we went to the Garden Tomb in Jerusalem. This is supposed to be the location where Jesus was buried before his resurrection on the third day. Just a couple of hundred feet away is a rocky hill that the overseers of the Garden Tomb claim is Golgotha (the place of the skull), where Jesus was crucified.[10] However, across town is the Church of the Holy Sepulcher, built by Emperor Constantine's mother, Queen Helena, in AD 330 to commemorate the place where Jesus was crucified and buried . Which place is the actual location of the tomb and of Golgotha?

Our delightful English tour guide in the garden insisted that the Garden Tomb and the neighboring rocky hill are the places written about in the Gospels. He shared with us that this location has been the site of veneration for centuries. However, since it was only identified in 1884 (by an Englishman, of course), one may doubt its authenticity.

---

10. Christians often use the term *Calvary* for Golgotha. *Calvary* is derived from the Latin *calva*—the scalp without hair. *Golgotha* is an Aramaic word.

Passport of Faith

The tour guide's case seemed stronger when he pointed to Golgotha. It is indeed a rocky hill that looks like a human skull. The eye sockets and nose are clearly visible. The top of the hill is flat; I could easily imagine three crosses raised there overlooking the city. For a minute, I was overcome with emotion. *Is this the place where my Lord and Savior Jesus Christ was crucified? Am I really looking at the spot where he took my sins upon himself?* I was looking for a specific piece of land where the single most important event in human history and in my life took place. It is the location of the historical act that has led to our redemption and salvation. Given the strength of my sentiments, it became very clear to me how Israelis and Palestinians, Jews and Arabs, can feel such a tight bond to this land; the land is intimately linked to all of our faiths and our individual lives.

Bethlehem offered more of the same. It's impossible to know exactly where Jesus was born. Early Christian tradition suggests that he was born in a cave. Caves were commonly used for shelter, storage, or even stables. Constantine's mother built a church on the location that tradition has most strongly identified as the place of his birth. The Church of the Nativity stands on a hill in front of the little promenade known as Manger Square.

While the locations of biblical sites left me somewhat confused, that pales in comparison to the confusion that arises when you try to get a handle on the Israeli-Palestinian crisis. Both sides present their cases to the world simplistically, yet the history of their struggle is extremely complex. Many Christians are equally divided about who is to blame for the perpetual tension in this part of the Middle East. I have many evangelical Christian friends who believe that the Palestinians are the proper owners of Palestine and that

Judaism in Israel

the state of Israel is nothing more than the creation of Western powers, who created a new colonialism after World War I. They often point out that not all Palestinians are Muslims; some are, in fact, Christians—a point that is often forgotten by pro-Israeli Christians.

At the same time, I have friends who believe that the Israelis and the Palestinians both have valid claims to the land and that the Palestinians should have accepted the two-state solution they were offered in 1947. These friends suggest that Israel claimed the land thousands of years before Islam came into existence. However, because the Jews lost the land and were later outnumbered by Arabs, a two-state solution is the most logical. They believe that neither the Israelis nor the Palestinians should be denied the right to govern themselves.

Then there are my Christian friends who believe that the land of Israel was promised to the Jews by God, and God never reneges on his word. They see Israel as not only a land that played a significant part in Jewish and Christian history but as one that will play a key role in the end times. These friends believe that God gave the land to Abraham and his son Isaac instead of to his other son, Ishmael, who is believed to be the ancestor of modern-day Arabs. They point to Genesis 16:12, which they believe is a prophecy that Arabs would always have a propensity for violence and conflict. They believe that the State of Israel has shown great restraint, considering the number of times that it has been attacked by Arab states as well by terrorist organizations and suicide bombers. They also like to remind me that the term *Palestinian* was only recently adopted by the Arabs in order to gain sympathy for their cause—despite the fact that there is no such ethnic group as Palestinian. If there are Palestinians, they say that Jews would have to be included. All of this leaves me wanting to avoid any conversation about Israel and Palestine, with Christians or anyone else.

Meanwhile, the people of this land, Palestinian and Israeli, try to live life as normally as possible. In Bethlehem, Jamie and I walked around Manger Square together and visited the little shops that sold souvenirs, food, and other goods. As we entered one empty store after another, we were greeted with looks of desperation. One Palestinian store owner told us that business was terrible. "Nobody comes here anymore. They are all too scared." We felt sad that life was so difficult for him, especially since his store was located about a hundred feet from the supposed location of Jesus' birth.

As bad as business was that day, it got a lot worse three years later when as many as four hundred Palestinian militants and their hostages holed up inside the Church of the Nativity, engaging in a shoot-out with Israeli troops. For an entire month, bullets ripped across Manger Square in Bethlehem. Jamie and I watched the images on television, horrified that such a special place had become a death trap. I couldn't help but wonder how business was for our storekeeper friend, if indeed he still had a business by then.

Not only do ordinary Palestinians suffer, but ordinary Israelis as well. One night, Jamie took me to her favorite place in Jerusalem—Ben Yehuda. She had often talked of this well-known street in Jerusalem with a nice pedestrian mall where you can sit outside and watch the young and hip hit the discos and clubs. At the time, we were young and hip, so Ben Yehuda was our kind of place.

Jamie and I tried to take a bus to Ben Yehuda, but we never did find the right bus stop. Walking through the streets of Jerusalem, we passed many Haredi Jews. Wearing the style of clothing worn by their ancestors in eighteenth- and nineteenth-century Europe, they stood out in this modern quarter of the city. The men wore long beards, wide-brimmed black hats, and black coats. I noticed that they kept their eyes lowered and never said hello or acknowledged us in any way. Much like the Amish in America, they exuded a sense of timelessness—a community set apart from the modern world.

Ben Yehuda Street was a sharp contrast. Many Jews were there, to be sure, but they looked as cool and sophisticated as anyone in the fashionable districts of modern New York City or Paris. As Jamie and I sat down to order dessert and a Coke, we couldn't help but notice the overwhelmingly young and beautiful crowd around us. Even the many Israeli soldiers patrolling the area were good-looking.

Nothing about Ben Yehuda Street looked particularly Jewish or holy. Not all modern Jews subscribe to the beliefs of the Jewish religion. In fact, the country of Israel has a large population of secular Jews. They are culturally Jewish, descendents of Jews, but they do not practice the faith. Some are even atheists. Many young Israelis (the kind who go to places like Ben Yehuda) favor peace with the Palestinians and want to give them their own state. Nevertheless, these young Israelis are often the ones targeted by suicide bombers. A mere year and a half after Jamie and I had coffee on the Ben Yehuda pedestrian mall, a suicide bomber penetrated the area, killing fourteen people and injuring nearly two hundred others. Once again, Jamie and I watched the images on CNN, horrified that the beautiful places we loved had become the scenes of such carnage and destruction. Ismail Haniya, an Islamic militant, was quoted as saying,

Passport of Faith

"The Israelis love life more than any other people, and they prefer not to die."[11] Consequently, suicide bombings became the terrorists' weapon of choice.

Like the Palestinian shopkeeper in Bethlehem, the Jewish store owners on Ben Yehuda Street would see their businesses suffer as tourists stayed away. Sadly, many of those secular Jews, particularly the young who had been in favor of peace, abandoned the quest for peace as a result of the waves of suicide bombings that followed.

A Visit to Yad Vashem

I was particularly eager to visit the Holocaust memorial museum known as Yad Vashem. When the movie *Schindler's List* came out in 1993, I was deeply moved by what I saw. Its portrayal of the Nazi extermination campaign against the Jews is unforgettable and should be required viewing for students throughout the world. I had not heard of Yad Vashem until I saw the movie, but now I wanted to go there and pay my respects.

Jamie and I took a bus one morning to the museum in southwest Jerusalem. As we walked from the bus stop into the grounds of the museum, I was struck by how beautiful the landscaping was. The museum is set on a ridge, with beautiful pine trees lining the path to the entrance. Both the weather and the scenery reminded me of areas in Marin County, California, where I lived for a time. Once inside the museum, we viewed photos, films, letters, documents, diaries, and works of art that captured the horror of Hitler's attempt to exterminate the Jews.

---

11. Friedman, *Longitudes and Attitudes*, 217.

Judaism in Israel

The part of the museum that I found most disturbing was a section titled "The Final Solution," a phrase used by the Nazis to describe the extermination process that they were carrying out. The pictures on the wall looked remarkably like the images in the movie *Schindler's List*, except that these were the actual people who had suffered and died in the concentration camps. There are no words to describe my feelings as I looked at the faces of hundreds of people living the last few days of their lives. Had Jamie and I had children at the time, I'm sure I would have found some of the pictures unbearable. For instance, children arriving at the Aushwitz-Birkenau concentration camp in Poland were often separated from their parents and immediately put to death, since they were too young to be useful as slave labor. They were told they were going to take showers, but were gassed instead and then immediately cremated—the furnaces constantly burning the corpses of dead Jews.

What disturbed me most was something unexpected. It was a blue-and-white pin-striped outfit hanging in a display case. It had been worn by some unknown victim of a Nazi death camp. As I looked at that piece of cloth, I couldn't help but think of the suffering experienced by the person who had worn that uniform. More than the photos of brutality, that one soiled garment brought the reality home to me.

We also went to the Hall of Remembrance, where an eternal flame burns next to a crypt containing the ashes of Holocaust victims. Sunlight shines through a hole in the ceiling. On the floor are the names of concentration camps where Jews were exterminated; places such as Treblinka, Aushwitz, Buchenwald, and Dachau were sites of terrible suffering and torture. Horrific medical experiments were performed on the living. Even those who survived the camps had to live through total hell.

As we left Yad Vashem, we saw a list of the number of Jews killed in various countries. In some countries, such as Germany, Hungry, Lithuania, and Holland, hundreds of thousands died. In Poland and the Soviet Union, the number murdered exceeded one million. It's hard to believe that the world stood by while this happened. Yet today, across Europe, the Middle East, and even on American university campuses, anti-Semitism is on the rise again. It is seldom discussed seriously by anyone other than Jews. Must history repeat itself?

Yad Vashem is supposed to remind us of a terrible moment in history and make us promise ourselves that it will never happen again. Anti-Semitism is increasing once again, however. Consequently, it is easy to understand why the Jews are so desperate to have their own country, Israel, a place where they are the dominant majority. But the fact remains that this is not ancient Israel and the Jews possess a country that is increasingly populated with Palestinians. If things continue as they are, the Palestinians will become the majority in the country. Since Israel was established as a democracy, this means that theoretically the Palestinians could gain control. The future of Israel is in a state of flux. Despite the tremendous success of the Jewish State, the land has never been completely theirs. Nothing symbolizes this more than the two walls.

The Two Walls of Israel

The ancient temples were located on Mt. Moriah, high above Jerusalem. Mt. Moriah is no longer as high as it once was; modern-day Jerusalem has been built up both in size and altitude. Much of ancient Jerusalem is underneath what we see today when we visit the city. All that is left of the temple is a section of retaining wall known as the Western Wall. Herod's Temple was so large in its day that it took up a quarter of the entire city of Jerusalem. N. T. Wright suggests, "It was not so much a city with a temple in it; more like a temple with a small city round it." The temple served as the center of worship, government, and finance for the Jews of that time and the high priest who oversaw the Temple was as much a political figure as a religious figure. Herod's Temple was controversial; many Jews believed that it was illegitimate because it had been built by the nefarious Herod the Great instead of by a Davidic king or a priestly figure as prophesied in the scriptures (Zephaniah, Haggai, Zechariah, and Malachi).[12]

In order to get to the wall, one must enter into the Old City of Jerusalem. While much of Jerusalem reminded me of suburban America, the old part of the city is cloistered behind large ancient walls that are five hundred years old.[13] I loved the fact that the walls significantly reflected the sunlight so that it often gave the city of Jerusalem a holy glow as we would look at the old city from a distance. And once inside those walls, it felt like we were being transported back in time—even if these are not the streets that Jesus and the ancient Israelites walked. Various gates lead you past the walls and into the old city.[14] It is a place with narrow, winding alleyways that lead to some of the holiest sites of Islam,

---

12. Wright, *New Testament*, 225–226.
13. Older walls constructed around Jerusalem were destroyed.
14. One of the gates, the Golden Gate, was closed up by Muslims centuries ago since it is believed that the Jewish Messiah will enter through that gate and they wanted to prevent that.

Passport of Faith

Christianity, and Judaism, as well as to the Arab market and shops with cheeky T-shirt vendors. As if to make it more apparent that these faiths have trouble getting along, the Old City of Jerusalem is divided into the Jewish Quarter, the Muslim Quarter, the Christian Quarter, and the Arminian Quarter—named after the groups that live there.

At the wall, it is fascinating to watch Orthodox Jews saying prayers as they move their torsos back and forth. For many Jews, it is a mournful experience to be at the wall as they pray and cry (hence the name Wailing Wall) to YHWH, wondering how long it will be before the temple and the kingdom are reestablished. In front of the wall is a large plaza where the tourists stand around staring and taking pictures while pious Jews say their prayers.

Anyone is allowed to approach the wall, provided that they cover their head with a yarmulke—a thin, round skull cap worn by Jews. A fence juts out from the wall dividing the men from the women; they are not allowed to pray together at this holy site. I picked up one of the flimsy paper yarmulkes that are provided. My family then watched as I struggled to keep it on my head. I took this problem very seriously, so I had a slight panic attack when a gust of wind came along and blew off my yarmulke. I caught it with my hand, but I was afraid that I had deeply offended every Jew in the country. Despite my best efforts, the thing wouldn't stay on my head, so I spent the entire time at the wall with one hand on my head holding down the paper yarmulke. I looked back and noticed my family laughing at me behind the fence. The moment was captured forever on video.

Many Jews believe that the Wailing Wall survived destruction because YHWH's holy presence is there. Consequently, it is very common to see people writing prayers on

Judaism in Israel

slips of paper and then inserting them into the cracks of the wall. When Pope John Paul II visited the Western Wall, it is said that on his paper he had written just one word: peace.

Later, Jamie and I headed up the pathway adjacent to the Western Wall and went through a heavily guarded security checkpoint as we made our way up the Temple Mount to the Islamic holy sites. Everywhere we looked, we saw Israeli troops with machine guns slung around their shoulders. Orthodox Jewish extremists have threatened to destroy the Islamic sites so that the Jews can rebuild the temple. Israeli authorities are always on the lookout for militant Jews that want to target the Islamic mosque and the Dome of the Rock. In the past, Jewish militants have been arrested trying to pull off the unthinkable.

I reached the top of the hill and headed inside the Dome of the Rock. Jamie chose to stay outside since she had been there many times before. On this particular day, I forgot the number one rule for tourists visiting religious sites: Always wear pants instead of shorts! As I headed in toward the famous golden dome, I was stopped by the Muslim gatekeepers. They gave me a brown gown to cover my legs with and reminded me to take off my shoes.

Inside, I marveled at the glass mosaics, ornate jewelry, and the beautiful dome—the outside of which I have seen so many times in pictures. I moved toward the middle of the edifice where a slab of rock rests. Jews believe that this is the precise location where Abraham prepared to sacrifice his son Isaac to show his devotion for YHWH.[15] Once YHWH saw that Abraham was willing to submit to his will no matter what, an angel of the Lord intervened and prevented the

---

15. Muslims, however, believe that this is where Abraham prepared to sacrifice their ancestor Ishmael, not Isaac.

sacrifice (Genesis 22:1–19). To our modern ears, this story can sound rather harsh. It's important to remember, however, that infant sacrifice was very common in the ancient world. The fact that YHWH was not the kind of God that would demand this type of cruel sacrifice was one of the many things that set the Jews apart from the other religions of the region. Ultimately, YHWH is a God of grace, not appeasement.

We Christians believe that the story of Abraham preparing to sacrifice Isaac foreshadows the life and death of Jesus. Not only is YHWH a God who will not demand those kind of tributes to gain his favor, but YHWH so loves us that he paid tribute to us by giving us his only son, Jesus! Jesus thus ends sacrificial religion for all time and replaces rituals with relationship. The beautiful story of Abraham shows the grace and mercy of YHWH that we believe is perfected through the story of Jesus Christ and available to all—Jew and non-Jew alike.

This is also why we do not weep at the Wailing Wall. We do not believe YHWH's temple has been destroyed; rather, we view Jesus as having "rebuilt" the temple. In the gospel of John (John 2:19), Jesus said that if the temple were destroyed, he would raise it up again in three days. The Jews, of course, asked him how this would be possible since it took forty-six years to build the temple. We Christians believe that Jesus was referring to himself—that he was the new temple resurrected after three days. Instead of needing a geographical location where YHWH could dwell, through Christ's death and resurrection (YHWH's sacrifice), God made his grace accessible to us anywhere through faith in Jesus Christ.

Judaism in Israel

The Western Wall, like so many other things scattered throughout Jerusalem, is interpreted so differently by the three monotheistic faiths. If ever someone needs to be reminded that all religions are not the same, they need only walk around Jerusalem.

However, another wall is being constructed in Israel that is less ambiguous in its meaning. At the time of this writing, Israel has completed a substantial portion of an electronic security fence between Israel and the Palestinian West Bank.[16]

A year after our visit, Ariel Sharon, Israeli politician and former military general, walked up the hill to the Temple Mount. His walk was considerably more controversial than ours. It was not just a leisurely stroll; rather, it was meant to signify that the Jews would never give up their claim to the Temple Mount, even if that mount was now covered by sacred Muslim holy sites. The result was Intifada II, a ferocious uprising in which Palestinians took to the streets to resist Israeli control of Palestine.[17]

---

16. The West Bank is a hotly disputed section of Israel/Palestine that stretches from Jerusalem to the Jordan River as well as roughly fifty miles north and thirty miles south of the city. Portions are controlled and governed by Israel; other areas are Israeli-controlled but governed by the Palestinians; still other sections are both governed and controlled by the Palestinians. Palestinians call the area the Occupied Territory, while the Israelis refer to it as Judea (the name of the ancient southern kingdom) and Samaria (formerly the capital of the northern kingdom of Israel).

17. The first intifada occurred in 1987, putting pressure on Israel to begin negotiations with the Palestinians. The Oslo II agreements had come about when both sides felt that the process of establishing a two-state solution had to begin in earnest. The 1990s were not without tension and violence, but they were a more stable period in Israel's recent history. When we visited in 1999, it was significantly safer than it ever has been since.

Passport of Faith

Intifada II ushered in a new wave of violence that saw Israelis use their considerable military power to enter into Palestinian territories and directly attack Palestinian command structure, infrastructure, and resistance leaders. It also led to a wave of suicide bombings that killed over a thousand Israelis and saw groups like Hamas (created out of the first intifada), the Al Aqsa Martyrs Brigade (part of the Palestinian National Liberation Movement), and Palestinian Islamic Jihad become household names throughout the world. Pedestrian malls like Ben Yehuda, pizza parlors, discos, buses, and even a university became the targets of Islamic suicide bombers—some of whom were women and children. The events of September 11, 2001, brought an even greater tension to the Middle East; for Israel, the past few years have been ones of carnage.

A security fence was first discussed in March 1995 after a suicide bomber killed twenty-one Israeli soldiers at a bus stop.[18] The fence is intended to make it more difficult for suicide bombers to cross into Israeli territory. Israel's economy is very dependent on cheap Palestinian labor as there are more than 100,000 Palestinians that work in Israel.[19] Palestinians cross the border in search of better, higher-paying jobs since Israel is a much wealthier area than Palestine. By the mid-1990s, when the fence was first considered, the per capita gross national product (GNP) of Israel was $14,000; in Palestinian areas, it was only $2,000.[20] The disparity became even greater after the dot-com bubble of the late 1990s when Israel incorporated many high-tech industries

---

18. Elizur, "Israel Banks on a Fence," 115.
19. Ibid., 112.
20. Ibid., 113.

into its economy.[21] The fence has meant that there are now huge bottlenecks at border crossings and that many Palestinians who go to Israel every day for work can no longer keep their jobs because they spend the bulk of each day waiting in line. It has also hurt the Israeli economy because companies are denied cheap labor and will have to find another way to fill those jobs.

Some think that the fence has been a wonderful tool to stop terrorist attacks; others, though, suggest that it is a racist wall put up by an apartheid state.[22] Charles Krauthammer, remembering the one thousand people killed by suicide bombers since 2000, suggested in a 2004 column that the regularity of that kind of terrorism will end because of the fence: "What has happened, however, is an end to systematic, regular, debilitating, unstoppable terror—terror as a reliable weapon. At the height of the intifada, there were nine suicide attacks in Israel killing 85 Israelis in just one month (March 2002). In the past three months there have been none."[23]

Krauthammer was correct. The security fence has reduced the number of attacks to virtually zero. A different wall in Gaza has also stopped terrorist attacks. However, in

---

21. According to the journalist Yuval Elizar, in the mid-1990s, it was Shimon Peres' desire to see the Palestinians profit from Israel's economic and technological boom by providing them with technology and helping them obtain financing from the global community. The reasons peace often breaks down in Israel-Palestine are very complicated and have as much to do with economics and resources as they do with religion.

22. Apartheid was the system used in South Africa through most of the twentieth century by the white minority to control and segregate the black majority. It ended in 1990; Nelson Mandela, a black man, was elected president in 1994.

23. Krauthammer, "Israel's Intifada Victory," A29.

this era of division and walls, there are just as many Palestinians willing to join the fight against the Israelis as before.

Many are concerned that the fence signals the end of negotiations. Rowan Williams, Archbishop of Canterbury, earlier that same year said, "The security fence stands as a terrible symbol of the fear and despair that threaten everyone in this city and country, all the communities who share this holy land…it is seen by so many as one community decisively turning its back on another, despairing of anything that looks like a shared resolution, a truly shared peace."[24]

While the fence does seem to indicate a substantial cooling off in negotiations, Rowan Williams' assessment may be a bit too simplistic and sanctimonious—which is often the case when religious figures try to become geopolitical commentators without ever having to deal with the intricate realities on the ground.

In a 2003 article in *Foreign Affairs*, journalist Yurval Elizur suggests that the wall is temporarily bringing an end to negotiations but that a cooling off period with separation may be exactly what is needed. He argues that the fence reduces violence and should convince both sides that a two-state solution is the only way forward. Economically, it might hurt the Palestinians, but it will also encourage them to finally develop their own economy instead of relying on Israel or foreign aid. Psychologically, he sees benefits as well, as the wall can provide some "breathing space" and help negotiators focus on more important issues that are often neglected, such as the equitable division of land and water and the future economic and social relationship between the

---

24. Bates, "Israel's Wall."

Judaism in Israel

two sides.[25] As terrible as the idea of a wall strikes us, it is worth considering Elizur's opinion.

Leaving for "Home"

On our last day in Israel, Jamie and I decided to take a sherut and head to Tel Aviv, Israel's largest and most secular city. When we got into the little van in Jerusalem, we were the only passengers for the first few minutes of the trip. After a short time, we picked up two twenty-something European girls that were obviously trekking around Israel on vacation. The sherut then drove us into the suburbs of Jerusalem and stopped at the home of an Orthodox Jew. The man was standing on the sidewalk in front of his home with his wife and two-year-old son. As is customary, he was wearing a black suit, a black coat, and a rimmed black hat. His wife was dressed in the conservative fashion required of Orthodox women.

As he came toward the van, the driver opened the door and pointed him toward the first set of passenger seats in the van. The Orthodox man sat down for a couple of seconds and then got up. He began to speak in a brisk manner to the driver. The driver responded in animated fashion in Hebrew. The two went back and forth with the Orthodox man pointing at the European girls. Something was clearly wrong and he did not want to sit next to them.

The driver then made all of us get out. He then put the two European girls in the second set of seats and pointed Jamie and me toward the first set of seats. The Orthodox man then began speaking again in forceful tones to the

---

25. Elizur, "Israel Banks on a Fence," 116–117.

driver. It was clear that it would not be acceptable for him to sit next to us either. I was at a loss as to what was happening. My wife whispered in my ear, "He won't sit next to a woman or be in a row with a woman." At that moment, the driver told me to get out again, apologized, and then had the European girls move to the first set of seats beside Jamie. He put me in the second set of seats with the Orthodox man. With that, the Orthodox man was satisfied, although his face showed only annoyance and sternness. He reminded me of the Orthodox Jews that we had passed while walking to Ben Yehuda Street—the ones that always looked down and never acknowledged us.

After all that tension, it took me by surprise when he looked past me and waved at his wife and child with an enormous grin and a giddy expression on his face. His wife and son waved back just as enthusiastically.

"Did you see that?" my wife asked me later. "Did you see how happy they were as a family and how happy he was as he waved? He saved all of his ebullience for his wife," she said, contrasting his ebullient demeanor with the aloof, reserved manner he displayed to us. We both immediately thought of a book I had given Jamie for her birthday that year, *A Return to Modesty*. The book was written by Wendy Shalit, a twenty-four-year-old Jewish writer. In it, she relates how stunned she was to come across the Jewish laws of *tzniut*—laws of sexual modesty. Under tzniut, men and women do not even touch before marriage. This kind of conservative behavior is often frowned upon and even ridiculed in our modern society. Yet Shalit found that people observing tzniut were not only happy but very sexually satisfied. She contrasts this with the unhappiness she found in her sexually liberated female coeds at Williams College and wonders if perhaps the Jewish faith that she had never taken very seriously isn't more substantial, relevant, and wise than she had assumed. She goes on to argue in favor of modesty as a way to preserve a sense of the erotic in a culture that is dispassionately oversexed.

In Judaism, following the prescribed laws on diet, work, and even sexuality is known as the halakha. For Orthodox Jews, the halakha must be followed at all times in order to keep the holy from being compromised by the secular. Consequently, even sitting in a van next to a woman would have been unholy for our Orthodox friend.

Beginning at birth, Jews are introduced into a world of religious observances. Male infants are circumcised on the eighth day after their birth (brit milah) and a young boy is later declared a man after declaring his allegiance to the Torah in a ceremony known as a bar mitzvah. More liberal Jewish sects celebrate a similar rite for girls known as a bat mitzvah.

By far the most important law to follow is keeping the Shabbat (Sabbath). In Genesis 2:1–3, we read that YHWH created the earth in six days and rested on the seventh day. The fourth of the Ten Commandments declares, "Remember the Sabbath day, to keep it holy" (Exodus 20:8). The Shabbat begins on Friday afternoon when two candles are lit by the mother of the household and a kosher meal (a meal prepared according to the extensive prescribed dietary laws outlined in Jewish law) is eaten by the family. A worship service is held the next day, and it is expected that Jews will genuinely make the Sabbath a day of rest and relaxation. The service at the local synagogue is conducted by a rabbi, who may not be a priest or minister (any Jewish male can preside over the rituals) but rather a recognized teacher or lawyer.[26]

Seeing the Orthodox man struggle with the seating arrangement in the van allowed us a glimpse into the customs and rituals that have served the Jews well, defining them as a community and forming a social cohesion that has enabled them to survive thousands of years of exile and persecution. At times, the Jews have been like sheep without a shepherd. These scattered sheep may not always have had a home, but they have the Torah and they have each other. That has become home.

Most Israelis come from other places, such as Eastern Europe, Russia, and America. They finally have a homeland but it is in a culture different from the ones in which they were born. The whole country of Israel, in fact, remains unsettled. It is a Jewish homeland, but it is by no means safe, with firmly established borders. There's always a sense that this home might be taken away. Moreover, many modern Jews in Israel are like sheep waiting for their shepherd, still waiting for the return of their Messiah to bring back the kingdom of Israel, to truly bring them home.

Our television screens and newspapers remind us that Israel is a constant source of geopolitical tension. Would the world be safer if the state of Israel had never been formed? In a 2005 article in *Foreign Policy*, Josef Joffe argues that the Middle East would not be any more peaceful without Israel. He points to the fact that when the colonial powers moved out, instead of pushing for a Palestinian homeland, the neighboring Arab nations immediately moved in to

---

26. The reform movement refers to the place of worship as a temple instead of a synagogue.

Judaism in Israel

claim the land for themselves. He also points to the fact that much of the violence in the Middle East is between Arabs and Arabs and that much of the hatred toward Israel is due to the fact that Arab people do not have the freedom to express anger toward their authoritarian leaders.[27] Furthermore, Israel's strength has probably served as a neutralizing force to keep Arab states from taking even more reckless military risks in the region.

It takes more than reading a few good books to begin getting a handle on the complexity of the issues that must be resolved in this region of the world. For those of us who live far from the scene, a giant dose of humility is in order, lest we make shallow and moralistic proclamations about who is right and who is wrong—Israeli or Palestinian, Arab or Jew.

We Christians believe that Jesus has already ushered in the kingdom of peace, not through a political revolution but through a revolution of the heart. Anyone who accepts Jesus Christ as Savior becomes part of God's true Israel. We believe that YHWH chose the Jews and Israel to share the good news of his grace with the world rather than building an earthly kingdom tied to one nationality. In other words, we believe that everyone can be chosen of God and that ancient Israel was called to let everyone know this truth. The more closed Judaism became, the more it needed Jesus the Messiah to reaffirm the gift of grace which is extended to anyone who will accept it. Jews disagree, of course, believing that the Messiah has not yet come.

In Tel Aviv, Jamie and I spent a leisurely day before boarding our flight to New York City, which has the larg-

---

27. Joffe, "A World without Israel," 39–40.

est population of Jews outside of Israel. We walked through neighborhoods close to the beach. We could sense the more secular atmosphere of this city. We enjoyed sitting on the beach, watching young Israelis play ball and drink bottles of Maccabee beer. That night, we sat on the sand and watched the sun set. Little did we know that the sun would also set on the peace process that next year.

7

SEARCHING FOR OSAMA:
ISLAM IN MOROCCO AND EGYPT

"September 11 was a wake up call for Muslims. It is not about East versus West. It is a conflict within Islam. We are the next target for the extremists."
—King Abdullah of Jordan

A mere eight months after the terrible attacks of September 11, Jamie and I found ourselves in the Islamic country of Morocco. We had taken a ferry from Algeciras on the southern coast of Spain to Tangier. Morocco is a beautiful country on the northern coast of Africa. While the southern part of the country is engulfed by the Sahara (a desert about the size of the United States), much of the northern and central parts are quite lush and mountainous. Many films with biblical settings are shot in Morocco because its geography is similar to Israel's. In recent years, Morocco has also become a popular spot for budget travelers. It has a reputation for being friendly, exotic, inexpensive, and, most importantly, safe. I wondered if people in this relatively peaceful Islamic nation would have sympathy for Osama bin Laden and his ilk.

I was not surprised by the terrorist attacks of September 11, 2001. Al-Qaeda's abilities were diabolically impressive that day, but the extent of their anger was not surprising. Lamin Sanneh, one of my professors at Yale University, is an internationally recognized expert on Islam. He was raised a Muslim in West Africa, but converted to Christianity as a young man. In a class on Islam, he guided our reading about Islam and its problematic relationship with the West. We learned that in Islamic nations, there is a considerable amount of hostility toward the United States, the West as a whole, and our system of government in particular, liberal democracy.[1] In the American media, we were often told that only a small group of Islamic fundamentalists[2] around the world harbored this anger, but as we learned after September 11, many nonfundamentalist Muslims feel the same frustrations that fueled the terrorists. In other words, many ordinary Muslims might have applauded or at least understood Osama bin Laden's rants and Al-Qaeda's actions. I was soon to meet one of those Muslims.

---

1. Defining democracy is notoriously complicated. By using the phrase *liberal democracy*, I mean a system of government in which the people share governance through elections and each individual has freedom, unless it is reined in by a majority of the people. It is supported by the rule of law, and it places a high value on the life of individuals, their human rights, their right to own property, and the right to support various political parties. It encourages the free flow of information and supports a free press and freedom of speech.

2. The term *fundamentalism* was coined about a hundred years ago to refer to a movement in Protestant Christianity that distanced itself from mainline churches in support of a belief in literalism, the inerrancy of Scripture, and a mistrust of biblical scholarship. The goal was to return to the fundamentals of the Christian faith. Only recently has it been used to identify militant Muslims. In referring to Al-Qaeda and other militant Muslims, I prefer the term *Islamo-fascists* since they are more interested in establishing authoritarian governments ruled by dictatorial Islamic rulers and imposing Islamic law by force. It is fascism that is the real enemy in the post-September 11 world, not Islam.

Islam in Morocco and Egypt

Although Morocco is no revolutionary Iran, Tangier did not seem particularly safe—not for religious or political reasons, but for social reasons. The city seemed to be filled almost entirely with men. Most of them seemed to enjoy leering at Jamie. We found it uncomfortable even to go to a restaurant since there would be no females present other than my wife. We had checked into a hotel located on the waterfront facing the Mediterranean Sea. It was not an expensive hotel, nor was it very good. Wanting to get away from the industrial, dingy-looking port city and see the countryside, we decided to tour the neighboring mountains and visit the beautiful Mediterranean coast.

We hired a taxi driver to take us out of the city. Hassan, a devout Muslim, took us to the northernmost point of Morocco's coastline, where we could get a panoramic view of the Mediterranean and see Spain's coastline on the other side. Since Hassan could not speak English very well, we decided to communicate in Spanish. Hassan's Spanish was excellent, and he proved to be a wonderful conversationalist.

Hassan and I were born a mere month apart in the autumn of 1970. I look quite young for my age, however, and Hassan could easily have passed for forty. Hassan and I were about the same height, and we both had mustaches, olive skin, and dark hair. In fact, in Morocco, the people assumed that I was a local. Hassan was a bit wider around the mid-section than I was, but otherwise we could have passed for brothers. I was eager to find out more about him.

Hassan took us to a lush park overlooking cliffs that dropped off into the sea below. The water along the rocks was a crisp, bright sky-blue. Hassan told us that as a boy he used to come to this particular location to swim. I tried to imagine him doing just that twenty years earlier when we were both children. The hills were covered with trees so dense that it made us forget how close we were to the world's largest desert. We drove up into the green hills, got out of the car, and walked past some goats on our way to a prospect with a view of Tangier below. We could see the minaret, the tower of the mosque where the muezzin performs the call to worship Allah five times a day. We then drove along the coast past shacks as well as the palaces of Saudi sultans and Middle Eastern royalty who find Morocco a nice place for a vacation home. We descended through the countryside to a section of the Moroccan coast where Hassan wanted to show us some caves by the sea.

When we arrived at the caves, Hassan handed us over to a friend who gave us a tour of the caves. Of course, we were quite aware that Hassan was receiving a commission for bringing us here. They both hoped Jamie and I would buy many trinkets and dole out lots of tips. Hassan let us know that he needed to excuse himself for a few minutes. He did not tell us why, but Jamie pointed out that it was shortly after lunchtime and Hassan needed to perform his afternoon prayer. A Muslim must pray five times a day—at daybreak, noon, mid-afternoon, sunset, and evening. Muslims must prostrate themselves fully on the ground as they recite their prayers, and they must face Mecca, Islam's holiest city and the location of its holiest shrine, the Kaaba. Even on ships and airplanes, devout Muslims will determine where Mecca is and pray in that direction. On our Moroccan ferry, there was a small prayer room with a carpet where the Muslims could pray while at sea. In this electronic age, there are even gizmos that can tell a Muslim where Mecca is at all times.

Islam in Morocco and Egypt

I was impressed by Hassan's piety, so I asked him about his faith. He began by giving me his take on the basics of the Islamic faith. What he told me jibed quite well with what I had learned about Islam's core beliefs.

The Basics of Islam

Islam was born out of the particular cultural milieu of seven-century Arabia. The Arabian Peninsula was a land of Bedouin tribes and traders. It was a rough environment—a desert region peopled by nomadic clans, or *hayy*, each attempting to avoid annihilation at the hands of stronger clans. Without a central authority or government, tribes served as a form of protection. If one tribe attacked another, it was not uncommon for retaliation to include the complete annihilation of the other tribe in order to gain revenge.[3] This aggressive and violent lifestyle enabled the tribes to coexist in a barren land with few resources. But constant fighting left them vulnerable to exploitation by non-Arabs, such as the Persians.[4] Hostility toward neighbors and an inclination toward militancy are problems that would plague Arabs into the twenty-first century.

Like other regions discussed in this book, Arabia was a land where the people believed in many gods and goddesses and in spirits who dwelled in trees, stones, and other inanimate objects. The city of Mecca possessed a central shrine of the gods known as the Kaaba, a cube-shaped building. Today, it is toward this precise location that Muslims face as they perform their prayers five times a day. In Muhammad's time, the Kaaba was filled with 360 idols of deities from whom the tribes would seek protection. The supreme God

---

3. Esposito, *Islam: The Straight Path*, 3.
4. Armstrong, *History of God*, 134–135.

Passport of Faith

was known as Allah, and he was the creator and sustainer of life, yet he was far removed from people and not a direct object of worship. Allah was believed to have three daughters—al-Lat, Manat, and al-Uzza. There was no belief in an afterlife.[5]

Muhammad ibn Abdullah was born around AD 570, five centuries after Jesus Christ. Both his parents were dead by the time he turned six. He was raised by his grandfather and then by his uncle Abu Talib.[6] According to Muslims, Muhammad was an ordinary man who became Allah's final prophet, so he is held in very high esteem.[7] At the age of twenty-five, he married a forty-year-old woman named Khadija and had seven children, three of whom died in infancy.

Nothing unusual happened in Muhammad's life until he was forty years old. During a retreat in a cave on Mt. Hira near Mecca in AD 610, the angel Gabriel appeared to him and commanded him to recite.[8] Muhammad was frightened, as he considered himself an ordinary man. He even became suicidal and afraid that he might be possessed by desert spirits known as *jinn* (from which we get the word *genie*).

Although Muhammad could not read or write, tradition says that he began to recite the words of Allah and continued to do so over a period of twenty-two years. The collection of these revelations is known as the Quran, which means

---

5. Esposito, *Islam: The Straight Path*, 3.
6. Guillaume, *Islam*, 24.
7. Images of Muhammad are not allowed, nor is cursing of his name. Nothing would rile a Muslim more than ridicule of Muhammad. That is why avant-garde artists in New York never desecrate Mohammed in their efforts to show the stupidity of religion.
8. Esposito, *Islam: The Straight Path*, 6–7.

Islam in Morocco and Egypt

"recite."[9] In Islam, the Quran, not Muhammad, is viewed as divine. Muslims see the Quran as Allah's divine revelation, for which Muhammad was simply Allah's messenger. Muslims treat copies of the Quran with great reverence and care. It is notably different from the way most Christians treat their Bibles, throwing them on the backseat of the car after church or even putting stickers on them.

Unlike the Bible, the Quran is not a collection of narratives, poems, laws, letters, and history. In fact, to many Westerners, the Quran can seem dull and repetitive. Its content is primarily meant to be recited. It is a small book compared to the Bible, consisting of 114 chapters (*surahs*) and six thousand verses, of which the main thrust is that there is only one God—Allah. Islam is a monotheistic faith like Judaism, Christianity, and Zoroastrianism. However, the Quran teaches that these other faiths have been corrupted. Jesus is honored as a prophet, but he is not considered to be God's final prophet. Nor do Muslims consider Jesus to be the Son of God, as surah 23.91 of the Quran makes clear: "No Son did God beget nor is there any God along with Him." Islam finds the Christian doctrine of the Trinity to be contradictory to monotheism. Further, Muslims do not believe in the resurrection of Christ.

Christian and Jewish communities flourished in seventh-century Arabia, and interaction between Arabs and believers of the two monotheistic faiths was not uncommon. The indigenous Arab religion was originally polytheistic and not very structured. Muhammad's revelation began to change that. Not only did he call the Arabs to worship the one true God, Allah, but he outlined the role of the Jewish

---
9. Ibid.

prophets, explained the relation of Islam to Christianity and Judaism, and laid down many ethical guidelines. The Quran honors the Jewish prophets and acknowledges that Moses received the Law from God. Abraham, Moses, and Jesus are all revered as men of Allah, but the Quran teaches that followers of these men have distorted the truth over time. For Muslims, the fact that Jews and Christians are disunited proves that they have misunderstood the desires of the one true God.[10]

Muhammad condemned the traditional Arab concepts of Allah. The Quran makes it clear that Allah does not have daughters, neither does he associate with other deities.[11] Not all Arabs took kindly to these new proclamations. Mecca, which is today the holiest city in Islam, had become a center of Arabian commerce and idolatry. When Muhammad shared the Quran's message in Mecca, he was rejected. In AD 621, he was asked to become a tribal counselor for a tribe living outside of Mecca in a town called Yahtrib. The town was later renamed Medina, which means "the city of the prophet," for there the people heeded his words.[12]

In Medina, Muhammad introduced a civil constitution, thereby becoming not just a religious figure, but a ruler.[13] He preached about Allah and governed the city according to Allah's laws. Thus, religious authority and civil authority were unified from Islam's inception; the effects of this would be felt for centuries afterward. The September 11 incidents occurred, in part, because Osama bin Laden and Al-Qaeda want the entire world to submit to Islamic law and they

---

10. Guillaume, *Islam*, 63.
11. Esposito, *Islam: The Straight Path*, 22.
12. Sanneh, *Piety and Power*, 43–44.
13. Ibid., 44.

Islam in Morocco and Egypt

want to destroy the nation that is so insistent on the separation of church and state, the United States of America.

In order to bring more people into Allah's will, Muhammad went to war. In AD 624, he conquered the city of Badr in a battle that would be remembered as miraculous. By AD 630, Muhammad and his followers had conquered Mecca and cleaned out the Kaaba, ensuring that only Allah would be worshiped there and no other gods.[14]

As Jamie and I rode along the beautiful coastline of Morocco, our taxi driver Hassan reminded me in Spanish that there are Five Pillars of the Islamic faith.

1. A Muslim is one who proclaims the *Shahadah* (witness or testimony): "There is no God but Allah and Muhammad is his messenger." This is stated when one converts to Islam and is repeated each day in prayer.

2. Prayer occurs five times a day for Muslims. The call to worship comes from the muezzin, who from the tower of the mosque (the minaret) proclaims loudly, almost in song, that there is no God but Allah. Believers face toward Mecca as they bow and prostrate themselves on the floor.

3. A Muslim believer is expected to give alms to the poor and pay a tax above the regular tithe. This money is supposed to go to help the poor, orphans, and widows; to free slaves and debtors; and to help spread the message of Islam.

---

14. Ibid., 45

4. Muslims are required to fast for the entire month of Ramadan, which is the ninth month of the Islamic calendar. Muslims are expected to refrain from eating from sun-up to sundown.

5. All physically able Muslims who can afford it financially are expected to make a pilgrimage to the holy city of Mecca, in present-day Saudi Arabia. Millions of Muslims from around the world flock to Mecca each year to worship and march around the Kaaba.

I asked Hassan if he had made the pilgrimage yet. He said he had not. Perhaps one day he would have enough money to make the voyage. That was his hope.

"Osama Is a Great Man"

Hassan gave a beautiful soliloquy about the importance of being true to your faith. He spoke about how he follows all of Islam's rules and lives a disciplined life. It is disgraceful, he said, when Muslims drink, chase women, or act in an unbecoming way. Islam calls for self-discipline and refraining from tawdry behavior. Hassan wanted me to know that his Islamic faith keeps him out of trouble. He doesn't waste money on liquor, prostitutes, or any of the other things that Moroccan men fall into. It saddened him to see his male friends fall prey to these vices.

He held "liberal" women in contempt. "In Morocco, many women dress in a Western way. It is not uncommon to see girls in skirts, pants, and even bikinis on the beaches in the summer," he said. For Hassan, this was immodest. He felt that Moroccan women who dressed like this were "presenting themselves as whores and disrespecting themselves and Islam." Hassan stayed clear of "modern women" who choose to dress in a Western style instead of covering their heads.

Hassan was preparing to marry his sixteen-year-old cousin. This is a common practice in Morocco and in the Middle East, and was viewed as wonderful by both families. He was building a house with the money he was making as a taxi driver. I asked if he could take other wives, as the Quran allows men to have more than one wife. "Yes," he said. "Ideally, I would like to have four wives. Right now I can't afford it, but if I could I would. Hopefully, in the future, I will be able to have four because the Quran says I can."

For Hassan, impropriety was not an option. He was emphatic that his Islamic faith not be tarnished by bad behavior. "Yes, I make a lot of sacrifices for my faith. There are many things I could do. I could make more money, have more women, drink alcohol, and do other things, but I choose not to." He then added wistfully, "Sometimes, I wish I had a lot more money. Everyone wants a lot of money. It is natural to want such a thing, to want that security. But then I remember my faith. This world is only temporary. These things, like money, are not real. I remind myself of that and then I live my life knowing that one day I will be in heaven and not on this earth. It is only temporary."

He opened the proverbial door and I walked through.

"Is it true that heaven is a wonderful place?" I asked.

"Oh, yes," he said. "You get all the desires of your heart!"

I pressed further, "Is it true that men are given virgins for sex in heaven?" I asked this question since many television interviews had shown would-be martyrs mentioning that they looked forward to this particular experience in the afterlife.

"Yes, it's true," he confirmed. "When men die they get to have sex with as many virgins as they want. You can have sex with the virgins forever! There are many available for you and this is all okay."

"All Muslim men are guaranteed this?" I asked.

"Yes. All Muslim men," he replied.

I looked at my wife Jamie, who was unable to understand our conversation. (I felt particularly grateful that she had chosen to study German in college instead of Spanish.) "What do women get when they go to heaven? Can they have sex with all the men that they want?"

Hassan laughed. "No! Of course not! They get nothing!"

I then asked him about September 11. What did my new Muslim friend Hassan think about the terrorist attacks. In particular, what was his opinion of Osama bin Laden? At this point, Hassan's pleasant demeanor changed. His voice tensed up and his gestures became much more animated. Jamie noticed his intensity rise a notch. Hassan knew that we were Americans, but he did not hold back.

"Osama bin Laden is a great man!" he exclaimed. "We are very proud of him. Osama is not intimidated by the power of the United States. He is not intimidated by Israel, either. He has proven this to the entire world!"

Hassan was on a roll, and I let him speak freely. "The best thing about September 11 is that it has proven that we Muslims can be powerful too!" The sense of powerlessness among Muslims in general, of which many Islamic experts have written, was being expressed in his words. "Osama bin

Laden made the world notice the strength of Muslims, and now everyone sees that we have power also."

He loved the fact that Osama bin Laden had Israel firmly in his sights. "The United States is being punished, and they are being punished because they are always supporting Israel. They are partners with Israel. We know what is happening. America is controlled by the Jews," he informed me.

"Actually, George W. Bush is a Jew," Hassan said. "Did you know that? I'm right, aren't I? He's a Jew!" Hassan looked at me through the rearview mirror to see if I was acknowledging the President's supposedly Semitic heritage.

The picture that came to mind of George W. Bush wearing a yarmulke, a prayer shawl, and long, curly locks was ridiculous. *George W. Bush is a Jew?* I thought. *I've never heard that one before. Conspiracy theories are alive and well in the Islamic world.* Hassan was still looking at me in the rearview mirror awaiting my response. I gave a slight nod with a strained, skeptical face.

"It's all the Jews, you know!" Hassan looked at me through the rearview mirror again and said in hushed, serious tones, "The Jews are Satan, you know? The reason that Jews are so evil is because they are the Devil."

Once again, I remained quiet, feeling that a speech on multiculturalism would probably fall flat on this particular cabbie.

I finally asked him, "What about the innocent people that died in the terrorist attacks? There were children who died and people who had nothing to do with the Jews or politics. Is it right that they were killed?"

Hassan paused. "Look, I don't like to see people die, especially innocent people," he said. "But everyone got

Passport of Faith

what they deserved because of Israel and the Palestinians."[15]

We asked Hassan to take us to Tangier's central mosque. By now, it had begun to rain. The mosque had a beautiful minaret and lovely white walls with intricate patterns in blue, but it was surprisingly small. Jamie and I ran out into the rain to look at the mosque close up and snap some pictures. We then ran across the crowded street and got back into the cab.

Our time with Hassan was finished. Obviously, the old Islamic ways and the ways of the West were colliding in even gentle Morocco.[16] Hassan was a young man my age, from a generation raised on satellite TV and pop music, yet he was choosing to place this ancient Islamic faith and its moral tenets at the center of his life. He was modern, he was pious, and he was angry. Hassan seemed to be the perfect example of the modern Muslim in the Middle East who is in touch with the Western secular world and hostile to it at the same time.

We were two American Christians in a predominantly Muslim country and this clash of civilizations left us shocked, tired, and hungry. We did the only thing we knew to do: we asked Hassan to drop us off at McDonald's.

---

15. Apparently, the death of innocent children and women was an issue for Osama bin Laden. E-mails found on Al-Qaeda computers show that bin Laden wrestled with the issue and asked Islamic religious leaders to weigh in on the subject. The e-mails were featured in a cover story in the September 2004 issue of the *Atlantic Monthly*.

16. Sadly, according to European counterterrorism officials, the majority of the would-be terrorists arrested in Europe are of Moroccan descent. In Belgium, 80 to 90 percent come from Morocco. Moroccans were also involved in the 3/11 terrorist attack in Mardrid. See "Morocco: The New Face of Terror?" *Time Asia* 165, no. 11 (March 21, 2005): 26–27.

Islam in Morocco and Egypt

Is Islam Inherently Violent and Angry?

Years of watching wars, coups, bombings, hijackings, and other forms of terrorism done in the name of Islam have left many around the world asking, Is Islam an inherently violent religion? That is a very difficult question. The politically correct reply would be, "No. How can you think such a thing! Terrible things are done in the name of religion all the time. Islam should not be singled out anymore than Christianity or any other faith." Many Western scholars have chosen to defend Islam at all costs—something they rarely do for Christianity, I might add. They argue that Islam is ultimately a peaceful faith that has been distorted and misinterpreted by a few extremists. The George W. Bush White House quickly borrowed this line to reassure Islamic nations and Muslims in America that the U.S. government would not demonize Islam. The administration suggested that depraved individuals who are making a mockery of the faith had hijacked Islam itself.

Others have raised serious questions regarding the claim that Islam is a peaceful religion. They argue that Islam does not foster an attitude of tolerance, but rather is frequently militant and violent. Samuel P. Huntington refers to "Islam's bloody borders" and shows statistically that Islamic nations have a difficult time coexisting peacefully with their neighbors. Furthermore, he demonstrates that Islamic nations have recently gone to war with each other far more than nations of any other faith.[17] Many are angered by Huntington's claim that Islamic nations are prone to war, but it has seemed to be the case in the recent past and at the time of this writing.

---

17. Huntington, *Clash of Civilizations*, 255–258.

Passport of Faith

Some Christians don't bother to look closely at this question and simply view Islam as nothing more than a false religion. For them, Islam is clearly not a religion of peace, as George W. Bush must say it is. Rather, they believe it is a demonic deception that threatens the world. Some extreme Christian believers would even argue that Islam is Satan's tool in ushering in the era of Armageddon. They say that the Muslims are simply acting out their role as the descendents of Ishmael, forever wild and prone to war, particularly against Israel. As a Christian pastor, I too believe that Islam, or any other religion, has the power to lead us away from the Savior Jesus Christ, but I do not find it useful to label any religion as demonic and then dismiss it entirely. I am not disputing the very real power of Satan and his influence in the world. But Satan has managed to do damage within the Christian church as well. If I am to share Christianity with Muslim people, then it is not productive to demonize them and their faith. Furthermore, I've given up believing that we should be very preoccupied with the end times. Practicing *agape* love should be our first priority—at all times.

Islam is currently the fastest growing religion in the world. Christianity is still the fastest growing religion through conversion, but most Muslims are born into their faith. A child born in Iran or Indonesia (two Islamic nations with very high birthrates) will most likely be born into a Muslim home, causing Islam's numbers to grow. For Muslims around the world, Islam is not a religious belief that they have consciously accepted; rather, most Muslims were born into Islam and it is deeply linked to their whole culture and identity. They haven't "accepted Allah into their hearts" in the way that evangelical Christians accept Jesus; they were just born Muslims. This is an important distinction.

Islam in Morocco and Egypt

Is Islam prone toward violence and intolerance? The answer, in my opinion, is both yes and no. To explain, it would be helpful to look at the Islamic world as it is today.

The Islamic World Today

Islam has over one billion adherents. There are peace-loving people in Islam just as there are in any other faith. In many places around the world, people are too busy trying to survive to wage militant jihad or join in a peace march. Their faith is a given in their lives. As with other faiths, there are many divisions within Islam. There are Shiites, Sufis, Wahabbites, and Sunnis, for instance. Of these groups, it is primarily the Wahabbites who have been inspiring Al-Qaeda. In countries as diverse as Lebanon, Malaysia, Egypt, and even England, many Muslims are quite secular and unconcerned with politics or religion. So, it is safe to say that being Islamic does not automatically mean being militant.

The Islamic world is not just Middle Eastern, nor are all Muslims Arab. In Nigeria, most Muslims are black Africans whose ancestors converted from tribal faiths to Islam hundreds of years ago. In Alex Haley's epic saga *Roots (*about the origin of a family of black slaves brought over from Africa in the 1700s), the lead protagonist, Kunta Kinte, was a pious Muslim who prayed to Allah and who was captured and taken to America on a slave ship.

The most influential country in the Arabic world is actually located in Africa. It is Egypt, where most people are of Egyptian descent, not Arabic. Their ancestors built the pyramids and worshipped the Sun God Ra. Today, it is Egypt, a non-Arab nation, that is the center of Islamic scholarship and the home to other Islamic institutions. It is also a thriving center of modern Middle Eastern culture.

Thousands of miles away in Southeast Asia, Malaysia looks and feels as exotic and Asian as Thailand or Vietnam. The tourism slogan is "Malaysia, Truly Asia." Yet this emerging, modern nation, whose capital city, Kuala Lumpur, currently boasts the second-tallest building in the world, is also a predominantly Islamic nation.

Some countries in the Islamic world are Islamic states, meaning that the country is governed by Islamic law (*shari'a*), not secular law. Not only is Islam the dominant faith, but it is the source of these countries' laws and government. In Islamic states, ayatollahs or mullahs (religious leaders) are as important as government officials. Iran and Afghanistan under the Taliban are two examples. Nations such as Turkey and Malaysia which have large Muslim populations are trying to remain secular states. Other countries like Indonesia and Egypt, which have been quite secular, are feeling the pressure to make the transition from secular government to Islamic state. Under Saddam Hussein, Iraq was an example of a Muslim country whose authoritarian leaders were quite secular; even Islam took a back seat to the cult of Saddam Hussein.

Other nations around the world have significant Muslim minorities, such as the Philippines and China. Islam also has a major presence in the West. England's most dominant faith is Islam; every week Christian churches in England close and mosques are built in their place. In France, the sizable Islamic population has often caused a lot of tension between the secular French people and the strongly religious Islamic immigrant communities. Tensions in suburban

Islam in Morocco and Egypt

Paris housing projects were the focus of the French film *La Haine* (Hate). Even the United States has a large Muslim population; for instance, mosques are a common sight in Michigan, particularly around Detroit and its suburbs. And within the African-American community, many have converted to Islam via the Nation of Islam, a heterodox sect of Islam popularized by Elijah Muhammad, Malcolm X, and Louis Farrakhan.

Clearly, it is dangerous to make generalizations about Islam and the way it is practiced around the globe. We would certainly not want Christianity to be judged by David Koresh and the misguided people who perished with him inside the compound in Waco, Texas. Nevertheless, there are a few facts about Islam as it currently exists in our world that deserve our attention.

The Tough Neighborhood of Islam

While it would not be fair to say that Islam teaches violence, certain cultural, political, and theological factors within Islam lend themselves to abuse by militant Muslims who use the faith to justify violence.

Recall that Islam was born out of the culture of seventh-century Arabia. At that time, the Arabian Peninsula was a violent place in which nomadic tribes struggled against the harsh desert environment and against each other. Battles were common, and those attacked exacted retribution. This eye-for-an-eye warfare prevented extinction and intimidated foes.[18] It is significant that Islam is rooted in these desert cultures where violence is still viewed as necessary and as a

---

18. Armstrong, *History of God*, 133–134.

sign of strength. The Islamic faith has been propagated primarily by believers from these cultures.[19]

Second, the founder Mohammad was not just a religious figure, but also a warrior. Lamin Sanneh describes Mohammed as Islam's St. Paul and Constantine rolled into one person, meaning that he was both a missionary and a conqueror who led his armies into battle. His example still inspires many believers within Islam.[20]

Third, in addition to the Quran, Muslims take direction from the Haddith, a supplementary collection of maxims about the Prophet and Islam that seeks to explain the basics of everyday life as a Muslim. It deals with a wide array of subjects and is very important for interpreting Islam properly. Some texts within the Haddith can be understood to support violence in the name of Allah. Those Muslims who say that the Quran preaches tolerance are countered by others who use the Haddith to justify militancy. Islam has no clear, inherent, consistent teaching against violence.

Christians who cite Islamic texts that call for making war on nonbelievers have annoyed defenders of Islam. Christians concerned about creating an atmosphere of intolerance between the two faiths argue that pro-war passages can just as easily be found in the Holy Bible. So I will not cite passage after passage. However, even if these passages are viewed as isolated texts that have been misinterpreted, Islam is clearly more comfortable using force than any other major faith. As Salman Rushdie, the Indian-born writer, said in a

---

19. To this day, backing down from a fight (cowardice) is seen as a tremendous sign of weakness in the Middle East. Bin Laden has said repeatedly that he attacked the United States because he perceived that the United States would not fight.

20. Sanneh, *Piety and Power*, 44.

Islam in Morocco and Egypt

Salon magazine interview, "[In Islam] there is an acceptance of brute force, an easy acceptance."[21]

While Islam's founder used the sword in the name of Allah, Jesus Christ called his followers to put away the sword. In Matthew 26, Peter attacked and cut off the ear of a Roman guard who was in the process of arresting Jesus. "Put your sword in its place, for all who take the sword will perish by the sword," Jesus said, before reattaching the ear of his captor (Matthew 26:52). He went on to tell Peter that he could call legions of angels to defend him if need be. He did not call upon the angels, however.

Clearly, the followers of Islam hope to establish it as "the way" on earth. This does not mean, however, that Islam is a religion of war. War is not the Muslims' ultimate goal; creating an environment where Allah's laws are obeyed is the goal. *Jihad* is a common word in newspapers today, but it does not mean "holy war," as commonly believed and claimed; rather, it translates as "striving in the cause of God."[22] There are at least two categories of jihad. The most important is jihad against oneself in an effort to resist temptation and impurity. The second type is considered less important; this jihad involves defending Islam against invaders of a Muslim country or community. Nevertheless, even this jihad of self-defense and violence calls for restraint. Many commentators and scholars have sought to point out that the violent jihad of which terrorists are so fond is a distortion of the original meaning of jihad. Sadly, the misuse of the concept seems to be happening more and more, often by Muslims themselves to terrible consequence.

---

21. Catapano, "A New York State of Mind," 2.
22. Bowker, *Oxford Dictionary of World Religions*, 501.

Passport of Faith

Critics of Christianity like to use the Crusades as an example of Christianity's oppressive and imperialistic spirit. The Crusades were a series of military expeditions carried out in the name of Christianity. It is commonly believed that the goal of the Crusades was to recapture the Holy Land, particularly Jerusalem, which was occupied by the Muslims. In reality, though, they were really more about expanding the rule of Pope Urban II and the desire for economic gain through trade.[23] There were only a few Crusades, all of which occurred between 1095 and 1299. If anything, the Crusades serve as an example of "Christian" rulers adopting an Islamic mindset in response to Islam's expansion. These rulers were expanding their empire in the name of God to purify the Holy Land. This was an aberration of the gospel. Christianity and empire don't mix well, although many have tried. The Crusades were a peculiar moment in Christian history, not one to be forgotten, but also not one to be used as a club with which to bash the Christian faith. Both Christianity and Islam deserve a more honest hearing.

Modern-Day Trends toward Violence

There have been notable examples of tolerance within Islam. When the Islamic empire was at its pinnacle, Muslim rulers were much more tolerant of other faiths than many Christian regimes of the time. They realized that persecuting Christians and Jews might very well lead to their growth. Therefore, Muslim rulers astutely promoted tolerance in the lands they conquered. Today, Istanbul's shantytowns are remarkably free of violence compared to equally poor communities around the world because of Islam's tradition

---

23. Esposito, *Islam: The Straight Path*, 58–59

Islam in Morocco and Egypt

of benevolence toward the poor. Islam can keep the peace at times.

Even so, many Muslims today, particularly in the Middle East, are enraged with the West, the United States in particular. Why is so much fiery rhetoric aimed at Americans and Westerners? A closer look at Islamic history and current pressures within the Islamic world can help us to get a clearer picture of why there is so much anger at this time. A good place to examine that question more thoroughly is Egypt.

EGYPT: A POTENTIAL EXPLOSION

The first image that comes to mind when people think of Egypt has to be the famous pyramids at Giza. Other images that follow are of the Sphinx, the Nile, mummies, and the other wonders of ancient Egypt. Egypt does indeed have an incredibly rich history—one we can even read about in the Bible. But modern Egypt is very different from ancient Egypt. Today, Egyptians speak Arabic, not Egyptian; Egypt has a president, not a pharaoh; and Egyptians no longer worship the Sun God Ra, but rather the vast majority are Muslim.

The powerful Egyptian media has enormous influence within the Islamic world. Egyptian soap operas are popular throughout the Arabic-speaking world. The Egyptian film industry produces a large number of films, which are distributed in these nations as well. While Arabic has many dialects, most people in the Middle East understand Egyptian Arabic because it is the dialect of the media.

Egypt is very Westernized in comparison to most Islamic countries, yet it has been a center of Islamic religious thought for centuries. The oldest university in the world, Al Azhar, is still open in Cairo and has many scholars whose theological opinions carry great weight in the Islamic world. Egypt has very close ties to the United States and receives large amounts of foreign aid from Washington each year. The Egyptian government recognizes Israel's right to exist, which is unusual in the Middle East. Egypt has been friendly, progressive, and accessible to the West over the past few decades. However, it is also a nation that faces numerous problems and is in danger of falling into the hands of Islamic militants.

PYRAMIDS, CAMELS, AND FAST FOOD

In April of 1996, Islamic militants opened fire on eighteen mostly German tourists visiting the Valley of the Kings in Upper Egypt. The massacre shocked the world and led to a severe decline in tourism, Egypt's main industry. However, this did not prevent my wife Jamie and me from making a trip to Egypt three years later with Jamie's mother and her brother and his wife. Jamie and her brother grew up in Egypt, where their parents and grandparents served as missionaries for the Church of God. (When visiting the United States as a child, she was often asked by ignorant people, "Do you live in a pyramid?" to which she would always respond, "Yes.")

Seeing the Great Pyramids for the first time was one of the most thrilling moments of my life. They stand high above the sand on the outskirts of Cairo. On one side, suburbs are clawing their way right up to the ancient structures, and on the other side, there is only sand as far as the eye can see. Most pictures of the pyramids are taken from the desert side with the city blocked out, thus making them appear isolated.

Islam in Morocco and Egypt

On the morning that we set out for Giza, we all piled into a car loaned to us by a local missionary. Jamie's brother Byron did the driving. In my opinion, Cairo has the second worst drivers in the world. Manila, in the Philippines, claims the top spot. In Manila, high velocity accidents are nearly impossible since cars share the road with trucks, buses, small electric carts, oxen, cows, and endless pairs of Imelda Marcos's shoes, all of which come together to form spectacular traffic jams. One may die of old age waiting in traffic, but probably not in a traffic accident. In Cairo, on the other hand, traffic is a free-for-all. In Cairo, people don't die while driving; they just dodge death every minute or so.

Staying in one's lane is virtually unheard of. Byron explained that honking the horn is not an expression of anger in Cairo. It is a normal part of driving, like using a turn signal. As one driver merges into five other cars going in various directions, the horn is used to warn the other driver that he is going to pass him, coming within an inch of taking the paint off. The other driver understands this and honks to announce that he will do the same to the car that he is approaching on a slant. It's an amazing thing to witness.

We eventually reached a brand-new highway that cuts across the city. Before long, I could see the Great Pyramids in the distance. There are actually many pyramids along the length of the Nile in Egypt. The pyramids at Giza are the most famous due to the fact that they are the finest examples of pyramid construction. Giza has three main pyramids, named after the three pharaohs buried in them: Cheops, Chephren, and Mycerinius. Nearly five thousand years after their construction, the tombs remain a source of awe and wonderment the world over.

Passport of Faith

The most surprising thing about the pyramids to me was the fact that they are very steep. Cheops' pyramid, the tallest, stands over four hundred feet tall. Its incline was impressive. Standing next to Cheops' pyramid, I felt like I was facing a giant wall going straight up into the sky. Jamie and I went inside the pyramids by way of a small passage that goes deep underground. Bending down and descending deep into the bowels of the tomb, we felt the ninety-degree weather disappear as it suddenly became quite cold.

It was at the pyramids that I rode a camel for the first and last time. A camel's knees bend in two places, not one. This means that when a camel stands up after it is mounted, it thrusts the rider backward and then forward. You must go with the flow, so to speak, and lean against the direction the camel is bending. The camel rises in a quick, jerky movement, for which I was not prepared. I panicked. Four different people were yelling at me, "Lean! Lean!," but they were all telling me to lean in different directions. I clung to my wife for dear life in an effort to keep myself from falling to an early death—trampled by a camel at the pyramids of Giza. My wife now enjoys watching and replaying the videotape of my camel trauma, freezing the frame to look at my expression of complete disdain for the evil desert creature.

The Sphinx, located on the same plateau as the three pyramids, is one of the most famous and mysterious landmarks in the world. It is a large limestone structure with the body of a lion and the face of a man. Unfortunately, due to deterioration and defacement, it now appears to have the body of an emaciated lion and a mutilated face. I had always wondered what the Sphinx is staring at. Knowing that Giza is on the edge of Cairo and merges with the desert, I always assumed that the Sphinx was staring at an endless expanse

Islam in Morocco and Egypt

of sand dunes. The truth is considerably less romantic, but symbolic. The Sphinx is staring at a Pizza Hut. This is true. I walked directly in front of the Sphinx for a couple hundred yards past the hawkers and the entrance gate and there was Pizza Hut.

A Once Great Civilization in Decline

Egypt fell to Muslim conquerors shortly after Muhammad's death in AD 632. By AD 640, caliphs began to wield power. A caliph is a successor of the Prophet Muhammad. The designation of a caliph began immediately after Muhammad's death, ushering in a period known as the Caliphate (AD 632–1258), during which the designated caliph controlled the military, judicial, and financial institutions of the Muslim community.[24] The caliph's main job was to ensure that shari'a law (Allah's law) was being followed by the Muslim community and to continue the spread of Islam. Some caliphs managed to achieve extraordinary accomplishments. Al Muizz, a later caliph, had a Greek named Gawhar build a new city that he called Al-Qahira—the city I was now visiting, Cairo.[25]

But after years of Islam's expanding and defeating "Christian" armies across Europe, Egypt was the site of a stunning defeat. In 1798, the French conqueror Napoleon arrived with a small military force and managed to conquer the whole country very quickly. Napoleon was soon routed by the British, yet another Western power.[26] This defeat in Egypt astonished all of the Middle East. After the Renais-

---

24. Ibid., 38.
25. Humphreys et al, *Egypt*, 18.
26. Lewis, "Revolt of Islam."

sance and the Enlightenment, the West continued to gain power and influence, while Islamic nations lost control of their lands.

Much of the Middle East was colonized by Western powers, just as Egypt had been. Many of the nations in the Middle East are nothing more than Western inventions, their boundaries having been drawn up after the collapse of the Ottoman Empire at the end of World War I. A large number of the inhabitants of these nations are still tribal people, and not all of them get along; yet they were forced together and made citizens of newly invented countries. The consequences of the West's creation of the modern Middle East continue to create problems for the world to this day.

Many Islamic nations sought to break away from the shackles of colonization and become modern nation-states on their own. Egypt was one such country. Under the leadership of Gamal Abd al-Nasser, the country freed itself from Britain in 1952 and embarked on major reforms in an attempt to break free from its years of humiliation. Nasser did not like the way that the United States and the Soviet Union were dividing the world between themselves during the cold war, so he aligned himself more with the developing nations of the world. He called for the Arab nations to unite.

Nasser sought to modernize Egypt by lessening the role of Islam, yet he still used religious language to rally the masses. He put Egypt on a socialist path economically, which led to financial problems. Nevertheless, Egypt became a very influential nation with a charismatic leader and a strong military. Tensions with other Arab states and Israel reached a peak. On June 5, 1967, Israel launched a preemptive strike on Egypt and destroyed their entire air force in six days, capturing the Sinai Peninsula and the Suez Canal.

Not until Egypt signed a peace treaty with Israel in 1979 did Egypt get the Sinai back. In order to do so, Egypt had to acknowledge the Jewish state's right to exist. The Camp David Accords were signed by Nasser's successor, Anwar Sadat, who was later gunned down by Islamic militants unhappy with his recognition of Israel. (This took place just weeks after my wife moved to Egypt in 1981.) Sadat was succeeded as president by Hosni Mubarak, who still holds that office today.

Although Egypt is one of the most progressive nations in the Islamic world, it remains very troubled. Many Egyptians see their civilization crumbling like the Sphinx while Pizza Hut and other Western icons threaten to overwhelm all that is held sacred in this ancient land.

At the Khan al-Khalili, Cairo's spectacular outdoor market, I spotted a picture ridiculing Bill Clinton. I asked the storeowner what he thought of Clinton and the United States. (I didn't identify myself as an American in hopes that he would open up.) He said that he loved Americans but then proceeded to list the many things that the United States had done wrong. He mentioned the U.S. bombing of a pharmaceutical factory in Sudan, and he was suspicious of America's use of power against Muslim states. The cardinal sin for him was American support for Israel. Egypt's 1967 loss to Israel is a pain from which many Egyptian's have never recovered. American support of Mubarak and other corrupt rulers in the Middle East has not been popular, either.

Muslims throughout the world have a long memory and an acute sense of history. History is important to them in a way that it is not to Westerners. Great victors and vic-

Passport of Faith

tories from eight hundred years ago are remembered as if they occurred yesterday. Painful humiliations and attacks, such as the Crusades, are not easily forgotten. It is difficult for Americans to understand this powerful link to the past. Very few American dinner-table conversations have to do with how rotten King George was to the American colonies. For modern-day Muslims, however, the great Islamic civilizations of centuries past are as real today as they were then. There is deep pride in Muslim accomplishments and fervent anger at the setbacks.

Haunted by the Past, Uncertain of the Future

Jamie and I saw a bit of this history when we went to a section of Cairo sometimes known as Medieval Cairo or Islamic Cairo. Here we were able to see the Citadel and the famous Mosque of Mohammed Ali. The Citadel is a fortress that sits high upon a hill overlooking eastern Cairo. The home of Egypt's rulers from the twelfth to the nineteenth centuries AD, the Citadel is an impressive structure. It dates back to AD 810, though it was not fortified until 1176, when Saladin wanted to protect it from Crusaders. Saladin (1138–1193) was a Kurd from Mesopotamia; he is best remembered by Muslims as the man who retook Jerusalem from the Christian Crusaders. Iraq's Saddam Hussein views himself as Saladin reincarnated, destined to conquer the West again. Unlike Saddam, however, Saladin is remembered as a very gracious warrior who spared the lives of many. This contrasted with the "Christian" generals who often butchered women and children alike. Saladin's name is revered throughout the Islamic world.

Within the Citadel is the Mohammad Ali Mosque, built from alabaster in the Ottoman style in 1830 (finished in 1857). It has two slender, 270-foot minarets, which are extremely impressive. Apparently, the residents of Cairo consider it an ugly mosque, but I found it to be quite beautiful. After taking our shoes off and making sure we were properly covered (the doorkeepers give you a green gown to wear if you are not), we went inside. The walls were covered with elaborate patterns, including passages from the Quran. Five large domes were visible overhead; the largest dome rises 170 feet. It was the first mosque I had ever visited. Our tour guide sang the call to prayer for our benefit. The sound of his voice and its echo filled the building. It was beautiful. From the arcaded courtyard, we had a smoggy, but still impressive, view across the city to the pyramids at Giza. Visible below was Cairo with buildings as far as the eye could see.

Unfortunately, recent trends have not been kind to Egypt. Egypt has a population of almost seventy million, with 95 percent living on 5 percent of the land. Cairo receives one thousand new migrants each day, and the country's population grows by one million each year.[27] It seems that biblical floods have been replaced by floods of migrants looking for work. Mubarak's government simply cannot provide for everyone, or won't because of corruption. With so many discontented people, Islamo-fascism may gain a foothold.

Not far from the Citadel is the City of the Dead. This "city" is actually a cemetery dating to the twelfth century, but it is now inhabited by people. It is an enormous shantytown where Cairo's poor share space with the dead. It is estimated that half a million people live in the tombs, which demonstrates the severity of the housing shortage in Egypt.

---

27. Weaver, *Portrait of Egypt*, 133.

Passport of Faith

Journalist Thomas Friedman has pointed out that less than ten miles away is a gated golf-course community where Egypt's wealthy can play a round of golf for $165. With an annual income of roughly $1410, just nine rounds would deplete the earnings of the average Egyptian.[28] It is the problems that arise out of this kind of disparity between the rich and the poor that threaten to make the Islamic world volatile for years to come.

In 2002, the United Nations released the first Arab Human Development Report. This study conducted by Arab scholars shows that Arab Islamic states are doing very poorly overall, even worse than most of Africa. Arab life expectancy is on the rise, but Arab women have a lower life expectancy than the world average. Women occupy only 3.5 percent of all seats in Arab parliaments, and the gross domestic product (GDP) of all Arab countries combined is less than the GDP of Spain. One in five Arabs lives on less than two dollars a day, and unemployment averages 15 percent, which means that large numbers of young people want to emigrate.[29] Islamic nations face a myriad of challenges.

BAD GOVERNMENT AND THE PROBLEM OF LIBERAL DEMOCRACY

Islamic nations, as previously mentioned, are prone to authoritarian governments. Most Islamic nations either have leaders who try to impose Islamic law or leaders who

---

28. Friedman, *Lexus and the Olive Tree*, 321.
29. U.N. Development Programme, *Arab Human Development Report 2002*. This report covered twenty-two Arabic-speaking countries, regardless of ethnicity. Thus, the use of *Arab* in this report is misleading. The countries included in statistics for this report are Algeria, Bahrain, Comoros, Djibouti, Egypt, Iraq, Jordan, Kuwait, Lebanon, Libya, Mauritania, Morocco, Oman, the Palestinian territories, Qatar, Saudi Arabia, Somalia, Sudan, Syria, Tunisia, the United Arab Emirates, and Yemen.

are comfortable with using heavy-handed tactics to stay in power. Most Islamic nations do not have democratically elected leaders. Most countries have monarchies (e.g., Jordan), religious leaders enforcing Islamic law (e.g., Iran), leaders who remain in power because of wealth from oil (e.g., Saudi Arabia), outright tyrants who rule through fear (e.g., Syria), or phony democracies (e.g., Egypt).

Of all Islamic nations, Turkey is the closest to being a stable democracy, but it too faces intense pressure from Islamists. Turkey uses secret police to keep order, and its significant Kurdish population threatens to break away from the country. It has applied to join the European Union; negotiations continue, contingent on economic and political reforms. The outlook for Turkey remains uncertain.

Liberal democracy is hard to establish in Islamic nations because there is no separation between church and state in those nations. In Islam's ideal world, Islamic law rules the land, not the people or its civil leaders. In the United States, we believe that each person has been given rights by God; each person is free to be an individual and expects government to provide freedom. In traditional Islam, there is no doctrine of human rights. Only God has rights; human beings simply have duties.[30]

Because Western-style democracy places such high value on the individual, it does not fit well with Islamic culture. Under such democracy, the individual is free to be quite secular. This secularization is very offensive to many Muslims. The privatization of religion is too extreme; in their eyes, religion is marginalized. While there is some precedent for democratic institutions in Islamic history, conservative

---

30. Lewis, "Islam and Liberal Democracy," 98.

Passport of Faith

Muslims in the Middle East tend to view democracy as Pandora's box: adopting it would lead to radical secularization.[31] The United States embodies what pious Muslims do not want their nations to become; thus, their hostility is often directed toward the United States for symbolic reasons. The United States was called the Great Satan in Iran, not because the United States is thought to be satanic, but because it is founded upon a system that separates church and state.

Misuse of Wealth

While oil enabled many Middle-Eastern nations to rise from poverty, it has also been a curse. Some Muslim nations have been able to modernize superficially by buying things without modernizing the government itself. Saudi Arabia is a classic example in that many Saudi cities are extremely modern, sleek, and clean, with futuristic-looking skylines. But on the street, the people live as though they are still in the seventh century. While women remain veiled and are prohibited from driving (much less governing), men are buying all the modern things that money can provide. Jean Sasson's much maligned account of Saudi Arabian royals describes families so wealthy that they take their planes on weekend shopping jaunts to Europe and the men fly in prostitutes from as far away as the Philippines for just a few hours of pleasure.[32] They can literally buy anything and do anything. There is no doubt that the obscene wealth in some Gulf states has led to decadence and has stifled economic

---

31. Iranian philosopher Abdul Karim Soroush is an example of a current Islamic thinker who argues that Islam can be compatible with the future. He has been a voice crying in the wilderness, but he has gained tremendous popularity in Iran.

32. Sasson, *Princess*.

Islam in Morocco and Egypt

and societal innovation. We all remember seeing pictures of the Kuwaitis' tributes to the United States after the Gulf War, including a statue of a limousine with a fist defiantly protruding out the top. The Kuwaiti way of life threatened by Saddam Hussein was one of limousines.

Bernard Lewis has pointed out that oil has allowed Arab rulers to get away with anything.[33] They can essentially buy people off. New skyscrapers are built and no one is taxed because it is not necessary. This leaves many people powerless but wealthy. It creates a problem, though, when there is still an underclass not enjoying the wealth. Many of the September 11 hijackers, for instance, were not poor themselves, but they were viewed as heroes by the poor in the less fortunate parts of Saudi Arabia. In order to maintain control, despotic governments use their oil money to build elaborate security systems.[34]

In the case of Egypt, Iran, and Iraq, the United States has given huge amounts of money to corrupt leaders in order to keep them aligned with the West. This money seldom trickled down to the general public. Instead, the money was used to keep angry poor people from overthrowing the government. In Egypt, for example, Mubarak's security forces are powerful and keep people in line by preventing opposition. This leaves many people resentful.

While it is true that the United States has supported some corrupt regimes, it is also true that there have been few good leaders within the Islamic world with whom to cooperate. Rulers such as King Abdullah of Jordan have been

---

33. Bernard Lewis, interview by Brian Lamb, *Booknotes*, C-SPAN, December 30, 2001.
34. Lewis, "Islam and Liberal Democracy," 96.

rare, and when such men do rise to power, they live with the constant threat of being overthrown.

The Problem of Israel

Muslim states are particularly frustrated by the support Israel has received from the West, especially the United States. Israel and the United States have become scapegoats for the troubles of many Islamic nations. When policies fail, Arab leaders often blame Israel and the United States. While it is true that both Israel and the United States have made many questionable moves in relation to Islamic states, much of the blame directed toward the United States has clearly been intended to divert attention from leaders who are governing poorly. No one should minimize the things that the United States has done wrong, but neither should those things be an excuse for completely avoiding introspection. In that sense, the annual U.N. Arab Human Development Report has been a step in a positive direction.

The United States is also often accused of being hostile toward Muslim nations, never bothering to defend them the way they defend Israel. But this is not the case. Most recently, the lives of U.S. troops were risked in the Balkans, where Muslims were being systematically murdered, and in Kuwait after the invasion of Iraq. In Somalia, U.S. forces tried to keep the warlord Mohammed Aidid from diverting Western aid from the poor. The result was the famous Black Hawk Down incident in which nineteen U.S. soldiers were killed and the American military withdrew. In London, I had a conversation with a Somali Muslim named Mohammed who was infinitely proud of the fact that his countrymen forced the United States to flee. I found this sad. The United States was trying to bring food to Mohammed's starving fellow citizens. Corruption and danger were so rife in Somalia that the nation descended into chaos. Mohammed's country is now a hopeless thugocracy. But for some reason, when the United States does defend Islamic nations, it is still resented. No matter what the United States has done in the past, not all of the anti-American reactions are justified.

MARGINALIZATION OF WOMEN

One of the reasons that many Islamic nations are still struggling economically is that they do not employ their women in the workforce. Depriving a nation of 50 percent of its talent is never a good idea economically. Consequently, many Islamic nations are not developing strong economies. The wealthiest Islamic states are artificially propped up by oil or foreign aid, but that does not create a healthy, dynamic economy. When the oil or foreign aid runs out, so does the nation's prosperity if they are not willing to allow women to contribute their talent.

Ironically, Mohammed did improve the status of seventh-century Arab women. Prior to his limitation on the number of wives a Muslim can have (four), Arabic men could have as many as they could afford.[35] Some Western scholars and commentators like to point out that Islam says a lot about women, more than the Bible, they say. Some Muslim feminists have tried to argue that the Quran and Islam advocate the rights of women. But this is all a bit of a stretch. There is no doubt that Mohammed viewed women as inferior beings. This was certainly not unusual, considering the harsh culture from which he came.[36]

---

35. Levy, *Social Structure of Islam*, 100.
36. Ibid., 98.

There is no age limit on when a Muslim girl can be legally married.[37] In many Islamic countries, such as Morocco, it is perfectly acceptable for older men to marry teenagers, as our cab driver Hassan was preparing to do. He was also looking forward to heaven where he would have as many *houri* (beautiful virgins) as he wanted for his pleasure, and this is indeed how heaven is described in the Quran.[38] Islam clearly has a strong tendency to place women in complete submission to the will of men, much as would have been expected in seventh-century Arabia.

In nations where Islamo-fascist regimes exist, Muslim women can suffer terribly. In *Not Without My Daughter*, Betty Mahmoody's account of her attempt to get her daughter out of revolutionary Iran, she describes Iran as a place where women's faces were routinely attacked with acid and razor blades if they were not covered. Many women in the Islamic world are marginalized.

It is important, though, that we remember that many women in the Islamic world are happy to play a more traditional role and do not necessarily want to be liberated in the sense that Western women have desired to be liberated. Many Muslim women may desire equality as human beings, but they do not necessarily desire to be part of society in the exact same way that Western women do.

MILITARY AND EDUCATION SPENDING

As mentioned previously, many Islamic nations spend a high percentage of their income on military preparedness and have an extraordinarily large percentage of their popula-

---

37. Ibid., 106.
38. Guillaume, *Islam*, 198.

Islam in Morocco and Egypt

tion in military service.[39] Quite often, very little is spent on education in comparison. Pakistan has been a prime example of this in that it is the only Islamic nation with nuclear capabilities, has a strong military culture, is led by a dictator general, and yet most of its people remain illiterate and poor. Schools are not provided for Pakistani children, and women have very few opportunities. Education is often provided by Islamic extremists who prepare students for violent jihad rather than for entering the workforce. In Afghanistan under the Taliban, women had absolutely no opportunities to go to school and the nation was so militarized that it was basically ungovernable.

Population Problems and Unemployment

Estimated at sixteen million, Cairo's population makes it one of the largest cities in the world. Yet Egypt cannot support its population with so many other factors working against it. As the U.N. report made clear, unemployment rates are high in most Arab nations and this leaves a large number of young males disenfranchised. Almost every Islamic country is experiencing a youth bulge, with around 50 percent of the population under the age of thirty. As Huntington has pointed out, young males tend to be the primary perpetrators of violence, and in the Middle East, these angry young people can easily be persuaded to become Islamic militants.[40] This is what is happening in Egypt, through groups like al-Jihad and Gama'a, which provide a social safety net for the poor when the government cannot and which then educate young males to hate the West and take up the cause of violent jihad.

---

39. Huntington, *Clash of Civilizations*, 258.
40. Huntington, "The Age of Muslim Wars."

While I have suggested that there is a strong strain of absolutism in Islam and that many factors in its history and culture encourage militants, I do not want to portray all Muslims as having these tendencies. Most Muslims are decent people. I came away from Egypt with deep admiration for its ancient history and culture. Being in an Islamic nation was a very positive experience for me, and one that was needed. As a Westerner barraged with negative images of the Islamic world for most of my life, it was enriching and liberating to see the human face of Islam. The warmth and friendliness of the Egyptians I encountered deeply moved me.

At the post office, when I was unsure of where to mail my letter, it seemed that everyone in the crowded building offered kind assistance. At the Khan al-Khalili market, I laughed hard at Ibrahim, who tried to sell me spices for fifteen minutes. After about five minutes of his best spiel, Ibrahim looked at me and said, "You don't know anything about spices, do you?" "Not one thing," I replied. Ibrahim laughed, and then spent ten more minutes trying to sell me spices with a wink and a nod. For Ibrahim the warmhearted merchant, the sale was secondary to our human exchange. In the Cairo slum of Shubra, I visited a preschool where I saw a little five-year-old girl so beautiful that I wanted to adopt her on the spot. If Egypt ever does fall to militant fundamentalists, these are the faces I will have in my memory, not the faces of angry young men burning American flags.

I greatly admire the Muslim commitment to a life of religious discipline evident in rigorous adherence to the pillars of the Islam. I also find it admirable that Islam has rejected the lies of secular humanism, which have cast a strong spell on the "Christian" West. Sadly, it seems that Judeo-Christian societies have found it much easier to cast religion

Islam in Morocco and Egypt

aside as something relatively unimportant. As Christians, we need to appreciate the Muslim respect for the sacred.

I left Egypt anxious to dialogue with Muslims and to share Christ with them. I have seen that they are human beings in need of God's grace, just as I am. Tremendous theological differences separate Islam from Christianity. There are now tremendous political differences between us as well. In fact, many things make dialogue with Muslims difficult in the post-September 11 world.

King Abdullah of Jordan is probably right. What we are witnessing is not so much a clash of civilizations as it is a war within Islam. My own sense is that our current era of globalization will be challenged and that Islamo-fascism may be part of that challenge; but the bulk of people dying from Muslim attacks in the post-September 11 world are still Muslims themselves.

Some may blame religion for the current tensions in our world, but I believe it is our only way into the future. In this new era, we need to look beyond the resources of this world for salvation. The love, peace, and grace offered by Christianity do not come from our world. These come from beyond this planet, which has limited capacity to transform humanity. Through Christ, we can overcome the man-made obstacles that plague us and the door can be opened to our neighbor.

Jesus left Christians with a Great Commission: "Go therefore and make disciples of all the nations" (Matthew 28:19). To make disciples is a greater challenge than making converts. It means more than converting the theological views of nonbelievers to the tenets of Christianity. To make disciples means to love with God's grace. Only by extending the grace that God has shown us can we hope to see

Muslims become disciples of Jesus Christ. The eternal souls of men and women are more important than the geopolitical struggles of our nations. Many will forget this amid the war, terrorism, and tragedy of our day, but Christians cannot. There is hope for Muslims because there is hope for all of us.

Appendix 1

GLOBALIZATION AND COUNTERACTION

"There is neither Jew nor Greek, there is neither slave nor free, there is neither male nor female; for you are all one in Christ Jesus."
—Galatians 3:28

My travels around the world have enabled me to deepen my appreciation of our planet's beauty and variety. Nonetheless, I am not optimistic about the continued success of globalization and democracy. Our current era of increased peace and prosperity looks extremely fragile to me. Important global changes are occurring that, I believe, will bring about a time of prolonged instability. I fear that in the future, taking the kind of journeys I have taken in this book will prove more difficult.

I believe that Samuel Huntington is correct in suggesting that we are entering a unique and difficult period in history of radical change, with issues of religion and culture at the center of many of the challenges and conflicts that will take place. It is vital that we are not only committed to our Christian beliefs, but committed to loving all people, and taking the life of the mind seriously as well. We must be well-prepared on all fronts as we face many challenging religious and cultural encounters over the next few decades.

Preparation requires that we thoroughly understand globalization and its (potential) consequences. I have divided this material into three parts. In part one, I provide some historical background on how the world arrived at this critical point, briefly describing how the current world order of nation-states was created out of the religious wars that plagued Europe in the seventeenth century. In part two, I discuss globalization and suggest that this post–cold war era (1989–) is one which is unique in human history. In part three, I argue that globalization leads to a powerful counteraction in which people or nations use nationalism, ideology, tribalism, and/or religion to resist the homogenizing and secularizing forces, as well as to deal with changes in economic and international status.

Part I: The Invention of Nations

Throughout most of history, countries as we know them today did not exist. Human society organized itself into tribes without rulers (e.g., Eskimos, Aborigines, Kalahari Bushmen) and tribes with rulers (e.g., Zulu, Maori, Visigoths). As people settled down, the establishment of cities led to city-states (e.g., Sparta, Athens, Venice), which wielded great power and exerted influence over a significant but relatively local region.[1] The emergence of the empire changed things forever.

Empires governed enormous swaths of territory. The Roman Empire, the Chinese Empire, the Inca Empire, Aztec Empire, as well as the Assyrian, Babylonian, Mongol,

---

1. Few city-states still exist. Current examples include Singapore, Monaco, and Vatican City.

GLOBALIZATION AND COUNTERACTION

Egyptian, and Ottoman Empires all wielded great influence over large regions of the world. Empires had the power to bring stability to otherwise chaotic regions. The Chinese and the Roman Empires are both well known for bringing peace to millions of people. While it is true that empires did subjugate and conquer tribes and city-states, often brutally, they brought significant security to places that had been constantly in danger or at war.[2]

The Roman Empire brought a measure of stability to the parts of Europe and the Mediterranean regions under the control of Rome. As the empire collapsed, Christianity flourished. The conversion of Emperor Constantine to Christianity in AD 312 led to the establishment of the Holy Roman Empire (Christendom) with the Edict of Milan in AD 313, uniting church and state. Over the next thousand years, as the Holy Roman Empire declined, Christianity became institutionalized within kingdoms throughout Europe. New empires arose (e.g., Spain and Portugal) that firmly kept issues of church and state together. During this age, kings and queens theoretically ruled by God's appointment.

When Christopher Columbus "discovered" the New World in 1492 for Spain, this discovery was understood to be for the glory of the king and queen of Spain, and ultimately for God. History is rarely black and white. The

---

2. In today's era of widespread liberal democracy, *empire* is a dirty word. An essay by Jonathan V. Last accurately points out that in the Star Wars films, it becomes clear that things actually worked better under the rule of the Empire than under the rule of the rebels led by Luke Skywalker. Unintentionally, George Lucas created a story that captures the efficiency and benefits of the empire, even though the heroes of his story are in a quest to subvert the Empire. Last's essay can be found online at http://www.weeklystandard.com/Content/Public/Articles/000/000/001/248ipzbt.asp?pg=1.

conquistadors of the Spanish Empire killed indigenous peoples and destroyed civilizations in a quest for gold, personal glory, to help Spain maintain an edge on its rivals, and to Christianize the world for God. But it is also true that there was almost immediately a strong push for human rights and justice based on Christian theology, led by Spaniards such as the missionary Bartolemé de las Casas, which ultimately overturned the laws of the empire. Christianity was thus both a tool of oppression and liberation.[3]

This era after the discovery of the New World, in which kingdoms and empires jostled the globe for power, arguably ushered in the first era of hyperglobalization.[4] Suddenly, with the invention of the compass and other navigational aids, small kingdoms like Portugal, Holland, Spain, and England became naval powers, able to maintain colonies and business interests on the other side of the planet. All of these competing powers claimed to be led by the same God. The rest of Europe remained feudal or in chaos.

The Protestant Reformation unleashed by Martin Luther in 1517 led to a religious divide. The invention of the printing press and its widespread use in this era of hyperglobalization both brought people together and caused division. For instance, anti-Catholic pamphlets could be easily printed and spread throughout Europe. The numer-

---

3. The destruction of the Aztecs by the Spanish is lamentable, but the Aztec Empire itself subjugated tribes, demanding taxes and using captured slaves as human sacrifices. The Aztec Empire followed in the footsteps of the Toltec Empire of Meso-America, which was also fond of trade and war.

4. Globalization is always occurring to some extent, but I use the term *hyperglobalization* to refer to periods of dynamic change that lead to new inventions, new technology, expansive cultural and economic changes, and the ability to travel and communicate over great distances at great speed and scale.

ous rapid changes and conflicts of this era left Europe at war with itself. Christendom collapsed as the Roman Empire had before it.

It was out of the chaos of religious wars that church and state became separated in the West. Ironically, it was a religious figure, Cardinal Richeliu of France, who argued in favor of raison-d'etat, suggesting that a nation not allow its interests be dictated by God or allegiance to the Pope, but rather that a country should only be concerned with its own self-interest. In 1648, the Treaty of Westphalia, which ended the Thirty Years War, ushered in a new system of secular government: the nation-state.

Creating Law and Order

Understanding the creation of the nation-state is vital to understanding the challenges that face the world order after September 11, 2001. Nation-states (i.e., countries) are sovereign in and of themselves and have fixed geographical boundaries. Unlike tribes without rulers, tribes with rulers, city-states, or large empires, these nation-states exist apart from the authority of specific leaders such as God, emperors, popes, tribal chiefs, or any one particular ruler.[5] Instead, nation-states follow their own law within a particular territory and are governed by a bureaucracy or government bigger than any one person. The government legitimizes the leader.

The immediate goal of nation-states was to put an end to the religious wars plaguing Europe and ultimately to avoid perpetual imperialism on one hand and total chaos on the other. Nation-states, it was hoped, would provide law

---

5. Creveld, *Rise and Decline*, 127.

and order. No longer was it acceptable to conquer neighboring lands in the name of God. The new fixed boundaries and a nation-state's right to exist (sovereignty) were to be respected. Should any country violate the sovereignty of a nation in an effort to establish an empire, the other sovereign states would join together to thwart the attack and keep the peace. This was known as the balance of power system.

The establishment of the modern nation-state did temporarily bring about a greater respect for the territory of other rulers and governments. One of the great successes of this era was the creation of the United States of America (1776), which was populated by immigrants fleeing the religious wars and chaos of Europe. America's founders asked that the nation-state do more than just simply keep the peace; they asked that the government guarantee its citizens the freedom to pursue life, liberty, and happiness. This radical move elevated the ordinary citizen's interests above those of the nation-state. Keeping order was not enough. The American forefathers wanted to create a nation-state that would forever protect citizens from tyranny. In essence, they wanted to destroy the old order and chaos found in Christendom.

The founding fathers of the United States emphatically wanted to separate church and state. As students of history, they wanted to avoid Europe's past mistakes by constructing a republic that would avoid mixing religion with politics. However, the separation of church and state was not to protect the state but to protect the church.[6] They did not want to see a repeat of the previous era in which entire kingdoms were subjected to religious rule, nor did they think it would be good for religion to be under state con-

---

6. Dr. Lamin Sanneh pointed this out in a class on West African Christianity at Yale University.

trol. When the founding fathers used the language of God, they were referring to the ultimate value of human life that would undergird the value system of the republic, providing a foundation for human rights, democracy, and freedom. They did not intend that the country should be governed by God in daily matters; they did not want to establish a theocracy. Theocracies do not work well because people quickly sicken of religion and rebel, as has happened in Iran under Islamic theocracy. The separation of church and state seems to strengthen the church, which may be why Christianity is more widely practiced in the United States than in Europe, which has many negative political memories of the church.

Of course, imperialism did not entirely go away. In the Mexican-American War (1846–48), the United States went to war against Mexico and eventually took portions of California, Nevada, New Mexico, Arizona, Utah, Colorado, and Texas. By force, the American nation-state grew. However, the idealism of the founding fathers did not die; the United States did eventually seek to spread freedom and democracy throughout the world and at home, albeit in an imperfect manner.

Unlike the United States, France accentuated ethnicity when it became the first nation-state to mobilize its citizens on the basis of nationalism. In 1789, France consisted of eighty provinces, each with its own laws, traditions, and local customs. Many people in France could not even speak French.[7] By forming a centralized bureaucracy, creating a military, establishing national laws, holding patriotic festivals, designing a flag, and requiring that everyone speak French, France brought the diverse cultures under the

---

7. Creveld, *Rise and Decline,* 197

authority of the nation-state.[8] Ultimately, it was the birth of patriotism for one's country rather than loyalty to one's clan, village, or king. The birth of nationalism would soon bring chaos again.

A Return to Chaos

A second era of hyperglobalization, launched by the Industrial Revolution in the nineteenth century, unleashed rapid change and instability. New technology, better transportation, migration, economic growth, and the pressures that followed threatened local cultures, tribes, families, villages, and religions. As people began to feel rootless, patriotism gave way to nationalism.[9]

The balance of power was now challenged by newly technologically enhanced nation-states. Suddenly, war could be waged on a much bigger scale and cause much more destruction. The German nation-state quickly became too powerful to contain within the existing balance of power and ultimately engulfed Europe in two world wars. As discussed in chapter 2 on Japan, governments have at times used nationalism to mobilize people because it can bond people together, just as religion, culture, tribe, or family would. In the case of World Wars I and II, many nation-states had to join together to confront the challenge of German nationalism and restore peace and order.

After the defeat of the Axis (Germany, Italy, and Japan), nation-states divided by ideology instead of nationalism. This too was the result of hyperglobalization. The Industrial Revolution and the spread of capitalism had led to the Marxist critiques which inspired communist leaders such as

---

8. Ibid., 198
9. Ibid., 201

Globalization and Counteraction

Castro, Lenin, and Mao. The end of World War II ushered in a period known as the cold war; the world was divided between the capitalist West (the first world) and the anticapitalist communist East (the second world). The remaining countries of the world were known as the third world.

Nation-States During the Cold War

The cold war was both a blessing and a curse. It was a curse in that thousands of nuclear missiles were developed and positioned to strike. And the two global superpower nation-states (the United States and the Soviet Union) supported low-intensity conflicts around the world in places like Angola, El Salvador, Nicaragua, and Afghanistan in an effort to expand their spheres of influence. This resulted in the deaths of millions of people.

However, the cold war was a blessing in that it probably saved millions of lives. It created strong international alliances that kept the peace. After World War II, the nations of Western Europe were, for the most part, disarmed and the United States became their primary source of military power. The larger threat of Soviet invasion or nuclear annihilation encouraged cooperation between the world's major nations, creating an era of peace for much of the world.

The low-intensity conflicts waged to expand spheres of influence devastated some countries (e.g., Afghanistan and Vietnam), but other third-world nations (e.g., South Korea, Costa Rica, Singapore) benefited, economically and otherwise, from the attention the first world paid them. For instance, Singapore's Lee Kuan Yew has argued that the Vietnam War was not a mistake since it convinced other East Asian rivals that the United States would send troops to the region. He felt that the war helped to keep the peace.

Passport of Faith

My native country of Costa Rica was able to do away with its military because of its strong alliance with the United States. The threat of U.S. force buffered Costa Rica from the war and economic decline that plagued much of Central America during the cold war.

The ideological divisions of the cold war also kept religious and cultural differences from flaring up. For instance, the Soviet Union was an invented nation-state—a series of republics spanning eleven time zones. Within the USSR were many ethnic groups and nationalities (Georgians, Kazakhs, Lithuanians, and Latvians, to name a few). Under the authoritarian communist nation-state, ethnic rivalries were kept at bay.

The End of the Cold War and the Beginning of Chaos

In 1989, Eastern Europe abandoned communism and threw off Soviet tyranny. In 1991, due to economic mismanagement, the Soviet nation-state itself collapsed into many smaller nation-states. It didn't take long for chaos to rear its ugly head again. The remnants, the new smaller nation-states, divided along ethnic lines instead of ideology. The Kazakh region became Kazakhstan, the Georgian region became Georgia, the Lithuanian region became Lithuania, and so on. Yugoslavia also divided into several nation-states along ethnic lines, which led to war. Bosnia, Serbia, Croatia, and Kosovo became known throughout the world as the region descended into the kind of ethnic and religious wars that raison d'etat, the balance of power, and the cold war had tried to avoid. History was repeating itself.

Suddenly, the Europeans, who had often tired of the United States being the world's policeman, were begging the United States for military intervention. The cold war era

Globalization and Counteraction

had formed strong alliances in Europe between the nation-states, but high levels of trust between the governments were a direct result of the fact that they no longer had strong militaries and faced a common, more threatening enemy in the Soviet Union. Western Europe did not need to fear itself because all the countries had mostly disarmed. During the cold war, backed by U.S. power, this seemed logical. But now, Europe was faced with new nation-states who were weak, volatile, and prone to ethnic and religious warfare. This was precisely the kind of chaos that Western Europe believed it had left behind.[10]

For the United States, the wars in the former Yugoslavia did not seem particularly threatening. The Soviet Union had collapsed. From the American point of view, the world had just become safe for capitalism and democracy. Unlike Europe, with its history of roughly equal powers struggling to live peacefully side by side, the United States was a mas-

---

10. Europe had good reason to feel like they left this chaos behind. Under the umbrella of American military power, European nation-states found a new way to relate to each other: the European Union. They created a suprastructure (EU) that would attempt to make the wisest decisions consensually for all the nation-states. This is why Europe and the United States do not see eye to eye in the post–September 11 world. Europe believes that multilateralism works best. The United States believe that Europe's cooperation is greatly due to dependence on U.S. military power and shared values (having come out of so many wars and having created the nation-state system) and that power is necessary to maintain order. Americans are also not willing to view their country as subordinate to some larger global organization. This is because Americans view the individual citizen as being greater than the nation-state. It is the other way around in Europe—although even there, many resent the EU's power over local governments. Western Europe and the United States have very different histories and very different responsibilities. Under the Soviet threat, these differences were minimized. In the post–September 11 era, these differences have become much more evident. From the European perspective, the nation-state was created for order; Americans believe it was created for freedom.

Passport of Faith

sive country geographically located thousands of miles away from any other military power.

The 1990s launched a new age of hyperglobalization led by the United States, making it the undisputed global power. There was a sense that this new era of hyperglobalization could only lead to good things. A new era of peace was upon us; some called it *pax americana*. With billions of people watching the same television shows, eating the same cheeseburgers, and listening to the same hip-hop music, people soon began talking about a borderless world. At the very least, it seemed that a period of unprecedented prosperity and global exchange had arrived without many problems. That view of globalization died on September 11, 2001. It soon became clear that this new era would bring challenges as well as benefits.

PART II: THE CHALLENGE OF OUR CURRENT ERA OF HYPERGLOBALIZATION

The world is changing at a rapid pace. In recent decades, we have seen the birth of the Internet, the shrinking of the microchip, the establishment of new nation-states, the growth of immigration, the creation of mega-cities, the integration of world financial markets, and the practicality of satellite technology. At the same time, these rapid changes are responsible for new challenges and dilemmas in the medical, environmental, financial, political, and social spheres. The cloning of people, the homogenization of cultures, global stock market crashes, the disintegration of nation-states, environmental degradation, and the rise of transnational terrorism all remind us that globalization brings benefits as well as challenges. Globalization always demands radical change and adaptation.

Globalization and Counteraction

Consider two scenarios that would not have been possible a mere ten years ago.

Scenario one:

After attending afternoon prayers at a mosque where the imam preached on the terrible materialism of Americans, a fifteen-year-old boy in Iran visits an Internet café in Tehran to listen to the latest banned music from the West. Although he lives in a closed Islamic nation that frowns upon Western music, he and his friends regularly swap downloaded songs on their mp3 players. At the café, he finds pictures of Britney Spears on a Web site for Arabic-speaking fans of the pop chanteuse. The site also allows him to hear the latest news, watch her most recent videos, and chat in real time with his Arabic-speaking, Britney Spears–loving friends in places as diverse as Detroit, Montreal, Kuala Lumpur, Jakarta, and Paris. Leaving the cyber café, he picks up a bootlegged copy of Britney's latest film (not yet in theatres) and passes his school (which lacks textbooks that accurately describe the outside world) on his way back to a modest home that does not have consistent electricity and water but which does have a satellite dish.

Scenario two:

After skipping school on a freezing day in the former Soviet Republic of Estonia, a fifteen-year-old girl hooks up with her twenty-one-year-old boyfriend in the capital city of Tallinn. Riding in his new car and listening to Britney Spears on the CD player, they drive to the docks and board a ferry bound for Finland. Using a fake passport bought by her boyfriend, she is on her way to a wedding and honeymoon in Amsterdam. Due to Holland's lax immigration laws, she is not questioned at the border. At her new apartment, her "boyfriend" suddenly leaves her and two men enter and mercilessly beat her. After two weeks of beating and training, she is escorted by two Israelis (recent immigrants from Russia who are now part of the Israel–New York mafia) to Mexico, where she joins girls from Eastern Europe, Southeast Asia, and Central America in a brothel. A few months later, she is smuggled across the U.S. border in the back of a truck and locked into a basement in New Jersey, where she is given food, water, and MTV. She is forced to work seven days a week. From her window, she can see the Manhattan skyline, where MTV's studios are located and where her idol Britney Spears occasionally shows up on *TRL Live*. She has finally made it to America, the country that she has heard so much about, but she is there illegally and will never be allowed to leave the house.

These realistic scenarios are loosely based on recent newspaper exposés. In our new borderless world, the world suddenly seems accessible to billions who once felt excluded. There is the hope that globalization will bring the Iranian boy, not just satellite TV and downloaded songs, but a global education that will provide him with new opportunities, freedom, and a better life. Unlike the poorly educated mullahs and the isolated teachers at his high school, perhaps he will have the global worldview and skills that will enable him to reap the benefits of globalization.

However, there is a dark side to this cross-cultural exchange, technological boom, and economic windfall. In East Asia, the pursuit of this new wealth and the attempt to control population growth has led to an imbalance in the ratio of men to women. An easing of travel restrictions, lax

Globalization and Counteraction

immigration policies, an increase in migrant workers, and rapid communication via e-mail and cell phones have aided the development of a transnational sex slave industry. From the jungles of Myanmar to the suburbs of Moscow, people have found a way to exploit globalization and women at the same time, luring young girls into slavery across national borders.

Periods of innovation and new technology always bring good and bad. What makes this era so different from any other? It is the speed and the scale of the global changes. These two factors, when combined with unprecedented demographic, political, and environmental challenges, lead me to believe that this era is significantly different from previous eras.

What Is Globalization? A Closer Look

There is no precise definition of globalization. In general, we are talking about an accelerated interconnecting of the world's economic, cultural, technological, and political spheres. *Globalization* is a relatively new term, but already hundreds of books have been written about the subject. The process is not new, but recent changes in technology, geopolitics, and economics have made this an era of *hyper*-globalization.

The precise beginning of this era of globalization is hard to pin down. The 1970s and 1980s led to the rise of speculative markets and the development of the microchip, both of which had powerful economic effects. Combined with the demise of the Soviet bloc, these set the stage for the free markets that led to the hyperglobalization of the 1990s. Capitalism and democracy began to spread at an astonishing rate. From Eastern Europe to Latin America, to Africa and Asia, new democracies emerged, each trying desperately to get plugged into the global economic system. The speed and scale of this transition can hardly be understated.

Technological change: An increasingly capitalistic China is producing citizens in the smallest villages that know how to operate a cell phone better than longtime residents of the first world. Poor people in Central America have received life-saving operations from doctors working in coordination with doctors in the United States by video on the Internet. Those once left out of the academic world can now earn degrees online through Internet universities such as the University of Phoenix. Satellite technology is now able to identify diseased areas of African rivers so that a multicultural team of pilots can spray the area and help stop river blindness. Unfortunately, a disillusioned young man in Indonesia (or Iowa) can become part of an online community of terrorists and learn how to make a bomb on the Internet, provided he can read.

Cultural change: Media conglomerates are exporting their wares across the globe. The film *Titanic* did very well in Iran. In fact, Hollywood makes most of its money from overseas distribution. This is true of the music industry as well. Shortly after gangsta rap reached its peak in 1993, dressing like an African American inner-city gang member became all the rage in places as incongruous as Australia and Japan. Kids in Sydney and Tokyo were talking about their "g-ness." Although these kids lives were far different from those of American rappers, a new hip-hop subculture was created and transported globally. The effect has been powerful. Young people in different countries now have more in common with each other than with their parents. Often, their parents and grandparents cannot let go of the hostility of the past. For instance, older Japanese and Koreans generations are wary of each other. Their grandchildren, however, not only have a lot in common with each other but travel with ease to each other's countries and go club-hopping. Today, it is not traditional rock 'n' roll but hip-hop that is the most popular music in the world.

Political change: In the traditionally democratic West, groups such as Netherlands-based Greenpeace unite people in causes that transcend borders. In countries such as Hungary, the Czech Republic, and Bulgaria, democracy and capitalism are being practiced after years of authoritarian rule. Many of their citizens recall hearing news from the outside world on radios via the BBC. Today, people in oppressed countries, such as Iran, sidestep their authoritarian governments simply by tuning into CNN or passing around bootleg CDs. Even a country as well-protected as the United States is vulnerable to cyber-attacks and transnational terrorists, who share information and rage with each other. Alliances are formed to strengthen nations (NATO, ASEAN, EU). In the European Union, member countries share leadership, with a different political leader becoming the temporary head every few months. The global map looks completely different than it did a hundred years ago, or even twenty years ago. Although the spread of democracy is encouraging, we also have to face the reality that democracy is very difficult. It is by no means guaranteed that new democracies will survive the challenges ahead.

Economic change: Over 50 percent of all Americans now own some form of stocks. No longer is the stock market for big-time traders; anyone can make stock purchases online. In the predominantly Islamic nation of Malaysia, investors read about the latest ups and downs in other markets in real time and then make purchases. The Chinese government buys U.S. dollars, Americans in Kansas invest in Japanese mutual funds, and places like Santiago, Chile; Mumbai (Bombay), India; and Shanghai, China, open up their own stock markets. The democratization of information means that everyone knows what everyone else is doing in real time. In the late 1990s, this resulted in the collapse of Thailand's market. Global investors knew that Thailand was not being transparent about its monetary reserves, so they bailed out of the Thai market. Combined with Indonesia's financial problems, this unleashed a chain reaction that led to an Asian recession. The good news is that more people can participate in the markets. The bad news is that when something goes wrong in one area—such as a property bubble in the United States or Australia—it can have detrimental economic effects in other countries. The world economy is now radically interconnected.

Has This Happened Before?

This is not the first time that the world has rapidly interacted in the economic, cultural, technological, and political spheres. To some extent, global exchange is always occurring. In 1 Kings 10, we read that King Solomon's kingdom was plugged into the wider world. Merchants and explorers traveled by land and sea throughout the known world, and his kingdom regularly imported from Lebanon, Egypt, and Kue[11] (vv. 15, 17, 28). People in foreign lands also knew of Solomon's kingdom; the Queen of Sheba even made a special trip to Jerusalem in order to challenge his renowned wisdom (vv. 1–13).

---

11. Located in modern Turkey.

Globalization and Counteraction

By the time of Jesus, the world was increasingly interconnected across large swaths of Europe, Asia, and Africa. The Roman Empire established roads, communication, law, order, and trade around the Mediterranean and into Europe, North Africa, and the Near East. On the other side of the world, the Chinese already had a flourishing empire that was arguably more sophisticated than the Roman one and which routinely sent traders and spies across Asia's landmass to interact with Rome.

It is easy for us to have the impression that travel was difficult in those days. However, many people were traveling great distances by land and sea. Small ships hugged the coastline along the Mediterranean and beyond, ultimately reaching Africa and South Asia. While very few of us would ever dream of walking across a continent, long-distance walking was practiced by many traders and explorers; no route was as famous as the Silk Road, which led to highly significant cultural, economic, religious, and technological exchanges between the East and the West.

Though China's Zheng He or Scandinavia's Leif Erickson may actually have been among the first long-distance ocean navigators, it was the age of European exploration, led by Columbus, Vespucci, Balboa, Magellan, Cortez, and Pizarro, that opened the door to massive cultural exchange, exploitation, invention, and conflict. That era of significant globalization (1492–1648) introduced the compass, clipper ships, gunpowder, microscopes, and telescopes, as well as widespread use of the printing press. It also saw the dissolution of empires closely linked to the Christian church and the formation of nation-states. It was a period characterized by religious wars and great instability.

Passport of Faith

The period surrounding the Industrial Revolution (beginning in the eighteenth century and culminating with World War I) was another period of rapid change and interconnection. When the Krakatoa volcano in Indonesia erupted in a massive explosion in 1883, the sound could be heard as far away as Africa and the waves measured in England. The earth itself reminded people of their interconnection, but due to the newly invented electric telegraph, news of the explosion appeared in London newspapers within a few hours.[12]

That era of globalization was propelled by new forms of transportation: the train, automobile, and airplane. Massive machines were created that could do the work of hundreds of men. New industries were born and others died. Just as significant were the ideas that the rise of capitalism wrought. Most notably, Karl Marx's anticapitalist critiques had profound geopolitical effects. As discussed in chapter 1, Charles Darwin, Sigmund Freud, and Friedrich Nietzsche's analysis of the world situation also left a deep impression on the global psyche. This period of hyperglobalization ended with two world wars, leaving the world deeply polarized during the cold war. Periods of hyperglobalization tend to end in such massive global shifts.

Part III: Counteractions to Globalization

Each period of hyperglobalization demands a radical amount of change and adaptation. New world orders form that seemingly connect the world together. In these periods, however, people and governments turned to religion, nationalism, and ideology to help them cope with change.

---

12. Winchester, *Krakatoa*, 182.

Globalization and Counteraction

Culture and religion inevitably come to the forefront during periods when the world appears to be homogenizing. This can create a counteraction to globalization. The attacks of September 11 were an example of that kind of counteraction.

On September 11, 2001, hijackers crashed two airliners into New York's Twin Towers, symbols of American (global) capitalism. The nation suddenly found itself at war with a transnational terrorist group fueled by anticapitalist ideology. Al-Qaeda has no nation-state and no army, but for those very reasons, they are a dangerous foe for the United States and other Western nation-states. A global network of terrorists cannot be rounded up by attacking any one nation, and ballistic missiles have little effect on people who are willing to die detonating a nuclear device or unleashing biological or chemical agents. At very little cost, Al-Qaeda was able to cause billions of dollars worth of damage to the U.S. economy and fundamentally alter the world geopolitically. Samuel Huntington may be wrong about a future clash between a monolithic Islamic bloc and the West, but he was indisputably right about a challenger rising up to take on the West—a challenger that is not motivated by secular ideology but that uses (misuses) religious ideology to express its grievances.

The significance of the September 11 attacks lies in what has happened since. Since that day, the United States (and much of the world) has spent hundreds of billions of dollars on security and military enterprises. Furthermore, it exposed a deep divide in the way that nations of the world view the new world order. It was the most significant global event since World War II. During the Cuban missile crisis (which brought the world to the edge of nuclear war), the lines were clearly drawn and both sides were ultimately afraid of war.[13] After September 11, the old lines ceased to exist and debates raged about what the new lines should look like given that transnational terrorists had become more powerful, unwilling to negotiate, and very willing to die for their cause along with thousands of innocents.

Why did the three thousand deaths in New York garner such attention when hundreds of thousands have perished in a single conflict in Africa? Is this the racism of global media? No, the primary reason that September 11, 2001, is so key is because it was a strike against the world's financial center. It was not the *what*, but the *where*, *why*, and *how* of the attacks that were so significant.

The Where: The attacks took place in New York City, which is the financial hub of an economically interdependent world. Had New York City been destroyed, the U.S. economy would have suffered some, but the effects on the economy of countries such as Brazil, Chile, or China could have been devastating. The nations of the world are very dependent on the transactions that occur in and around the U.S. economy. A collapse in the U.S. economy means a collapse in the global economy. Almost everyone who depends on a nation-state for their well-being would be hurt. Those who live in premodern societies (e.g., Kalahari Bushmen) might not even notice.

The Why: Osama bin Laden and Ayman al-Zawahiri opposed the presence of the U.S. military on the holy Mus-

---

13. The singer Billy Bragg was right in his song "Do You Think that the Russians Want War?" During the cold war, the Soviet Union feared war, having lost so much in previous wars. Osama bin Laden and Al-Qaeda, however, openly invite war to the death. They are not responsible for either citizens or a nation-state, and they glorify martyrs; consequently, they are more dangerous.

GLOBALIZATION AND COUNTERACTION

lim soil of Saudi Arabia. As discussed in chapter 3, issues of land are what inspire militant terrorism. These two men have made it clear that their attacks grew bolder because they perceived weakness and a hesitancy to retaliate on the part of the United States. Further, Islamo-fascism is an anti-globalization movement. Bin Laden and other Islamic terrorists are disciples of Sayid Qutb's philosophy, which argues that Islam must make a complete break from modern systems like capitalism. Bin Laden and al-Zawahiri are also interested in restoring the Islamic Caliphate (see chapter 7) and creating an Islamic empire, thereby rejecting the nation-state concept in favor of the kind of theocracies that the nation-state system was supposed to end. People like Osama bin Laden are not happy with the expansion of liberal democracy in the post–cold war era. The September 11 attacks were a strong message to the world that some people are willing to die to destroy that system.

The How: Al-Qaeda used readily available modern technology (airplanes) against the West. Unable to produce much themselves, they literally hijacked technology and used it against the West. The attacks served as a reminder that despite all the wonderful benefits that technology wrought in the 1990s, technology can be used for ill purposes as well. The hijackers also took advantage of America's relatively open borders and lax immigration policy. It is these kinds of borders and immigration policies that have greatly benefited the global economy (especially Europe).

The hijackers were people who refused to assimilate into a nation-state because of their interpretation of the Islamic faith. This is precisely the kind of faith and ideology that has caused chaos in previous periods of hyperglobalization. The average citizen watching the attacks on television probably did not make these connections, but key government leaders around the world certainly did, as evidenced by the massive, unprecedented coordination between countries just hours after the attacks. This was no ordinary terrorist bombing. This was an attack against the modus operandi of the West and those nations seeking to join the first world.

One final significant fact about the September 11 attacks is that the terrorist camps were in Afghanistan, a failed nation-state. In general, the job of a nation-state is to protect its citizens, provide law and order, maintain well-established geographical boundaries, and create an atmosphere where civil society can emerge. Prior to September 11, Afghanistan was not able to do that. Afghanistan has a long history as a poor, war-ravaged country whose society has been stuck in perpetual warfare. At the end of the war with the Soviet Union in the late 1980s, many tribes continued to fight each other. In one television report I saw, an Afghan man said, "I wouldn't even know what to do if I weren't fighting." A culture of war had developed and the country was really just a territory occupied by warring tribes and drug lords. The official "government" of Afghanistan was the Taliban regime, which was theocratic, wanting everyone in Afghanistan to live under strict Islamic law. It is no surprise that Osama bin Laden and Al-Qaeda fit right in.

The September 11 attacks showed the world that failed-states could be dangerous. Countries such as North Korea, Somalia, Yemen, and Afghanistan could harbor terrorists, allowing them to build a significant infrastructure with which to launch attacks. Further, it is easy to hide and easy to smuggle weapons of mass destruction into a failed-state. To truly be effective, terrorists need to be able to hide laboratories and equipment for their attacks without having to constantly be on the run. One of the most dangerous threats today is that terrorists could take over a failed-state.

Who Will Fuel the Counteraction?

September 11 did not mark the beginning of the problem. Rather, hyperglobalization and the radical amount of change that it requires was on an inevitable collision course with certain cultures of the world resistant to the kind of sweeping change globalization brings. In this case, Osama bin Laden and his followers objected, not only to the presence of U.S. forces in Saudi Arabia, but to the powerful secularizing force of the marketplace that was reaching their part of the world at tremendous speed. The key word is *secularizing*, considering Wahabbi Islam's disdain of the Western-style separation of church and state and the "secular" U.S. troops that were on Islamic soil.

I am not arguing that Al-Qaeda and Osama bin Laden are going to be the source of the world's future economic and geopolitical problems. It could be that Osama bin Laden and Al-Qaeda have run their course. Rather, I am suggesting that bin Laden and Al-Qaeda are emblematic of the kind of culture of resistance that can rise and gain the support of many in periods of hyperglobalization.

It need not be Islamic terrorism that unleashes a counteraction to globalization. Although terrorism will most likely be a pressing problem for the next few decades, it could be that poor economic choices by global powers (Europe, the United States, or China) may lead to instability. The United States has already made billions of dollars worth of adjustments in response to the Al-Qaeda attacks and is now more financially vulnerable than it was in the high-flying 1990s. Since our current era is one of economic interdependence, with the United States as the primary engine of growth, ultimately, the whole world is more economically vulnerable. At the time of this writing, the global economy is very much dependent on the U.S consumer and on cheap goods made in China. If indebted U.S. consumers reduce their spending, there would be an adverse effect on the Chinese economy, which would spread to other regions as well. A global recession or even depression could result.

The financial success of globalization is much more fragile than market experts would lead us to believe. Morgan Stanley's chief analyst, Stanley Roach, is one well-respected financial expert who has been honest about the precarious nature of our global economy: "America's income-short, consumer-led recovery is the aberration—not the norm—in this Brave New World. It is all about ever-declining personal savings rates, ever-widening current account deficits, mounting debt burdens, and increasingly wealth-dependent consumers. It personifies what I believe is one of the most precarious macro models that has ever existed for a major economic power."[14]

It could also be that the counteraction is fueled by an energy crisis—oil shortages, a continued rise in prices, or the collapse of a few key nation-states that produce oil. This would have dramatically destabilizing effects on the world. Perhaps the United States would survive (driving far fewer SUVs) and new technologies could be created within a decade to make up for the shortage in oil, but this would probably not be enough to help developing and third world countries. India and China, especially, have become highly

---

14. Roach, "Big Squeeze."

dependent on oil and have high expectations that their economic rise will continue uninterrupted.

Water shortages and conflict over valuable pieces of land can also be a source of instability. We live in a period of history in which expectations throughout the world are very high—an "irrational exuberance," to quote Alan Greenspan. If anything comes along to dampen those hopes, it could open the door to antiglobalization movements.

It is tempting to take a Baconian attitude toward all these changes, believing that with all of our technology and knowledge, human beings will be able to avoid the mistakes of the past. That attitude dangerously ignores the lessons of the past and does not deal honestly with humanity's propensity to sin. I have no doubt that we will see some incredible inventions and ward off some potentially catastrophic events. Nonetheless, globalization is beyond our human control. It will, and already has, unleashed unforeseen consequences that we must now deal with. The arrogance and consequent despair that can set in around the world at a time like this needs to be addressed and corrected by Christians with agape love if at all possible.

Is Globalization Bad?

There have been a number of excellent books arguing that, overall, globalization is a good thing for the people of the world. Most notable are Martin Wolf's *Why Globalization Works* and Jagdish Bhagwati's *In Defense of Globalization*. I do not wish to join the neo-Marxist antiglobalization movement which views globalization as the source for oppression of women, exploitation of the poor, declining wages and labor standards, environmental degradation, and corporate fascism. The antiglobalization movement in the West is currently an incoherent hodge-podge of groups consisting of environmentalists, neo-Marxists, and labor activists who paint in broad strokes and have a poor understanding of economics and global cultures.

In my short lifetime and in my own travels, I have seen countries change dramatically for the better because of globalization. Ireland has gone from being a sleepy, impoverished European backwater to having a vibrant economy. The changes that have occurred in Thailand since I first visited in 1991 are stunning; a whole new middle class has emerged there. I also see it in China's Guangdong province. The sweatshops that I first saw in 1991 continue to exist in 2005, but more and more sweatshop workers are graduating to better jobs or moving to factories that treat their employees better. Those that do not move on are making more money and have more options than the generation before globalization. I have no doubts that economic globalization produces more benefits than pitfalls. Free markets, with trade across borders, seem to consistently work better than any other economic system.

However, in previous periods of hyperglobalization, the quest for global commerce led to shaky alliances, imperial overstretch, great power rivalries, an increase in terrorism, and anticapitalist movements,[15] all of which are occurring now. The last era of hyperglobalization ended with two world wars and the abandonment of capitalism by much of the world. Had Karl Marx been more patient with the development that occurred in the opening decades of the last period of globalization, perhaps countries such as the Soviet Union and China would have made better economic choices.

---

15. Ferguson, "Sinking Globalization."

Globalization and Counteraction

Globalization means change—rapid change—and inevitably there will be a significant number of discontented people. It does not take much to start a truly global revolution against globalization. German nationalism rose out of an era of rapid change. A sense of discontent about the exploitation of workers in that era led Russia to wage the October Revolution of 1917. Geopolitical instability during the First World War with Germany disrupted global trade, and the humiliation of Germany that followed paved the way for Hitler's nationalistic fascism. These were not simple chain reactions, but rather a series of key shifts that lead to disruption in globalization.

Who will fuel the counteraction? It will most likely be a combination of many different actors. No one country will be the cause, and no group of countries will be able to stop it. The world is imperfect and in a constant state of flux. The chances are slim that we will see a war between large nations, but I believe the chances are very good that we will see more countries, like Sri Lanka, deprived of the benefits of globalization because of internal civil conflicts.

A New Divide Between Rich and Poor?

In essence, we are caught in a trap. Globalization brings increased wealth, higher living standards, and longer life expectancies to billions of people. However, globalization is dependent on people creating nation-states and forming developed Western-style economies. Most people in the world want to be plugged-in to the globalized world. Russia, India, and the United Arab Emirates are three very different nation-states that have made radical changes recently in an effort to get plugged-in and develop economically. From

China to Chile, many people are enjoying this era of hyper-globalization.

But poorly governed regions can cause huge problems for the rest of the world. The entire planet has suffered because Colombia and Mexico have drug networks too powerful for their governments to control. Even after the liberation of Afghanistan, opium is still being grown throughout that country. Ethnic conflicts have the ability to spread and cause refugee crises and famines, as is currently happening in Darfur, Sudan. Poorer nations may run into problems of water scarcity, and disease may break out on a large scale. Nations with poor health infrastructures (such as the Democratic Republic of Congo) may have a hard time containing diseases, which in our era of globalization can spread rapidly. The 2003 SARS outbreak occurred in Hong Kong, a modern, first-world city, yet the virus still spread rapidly.

The temptation will be for Western nations and other newly plugged-in nations to keep their distance. It will be expensive for governments to meet their own needs and try to rebuild failed-states. This will particularly be the case for the world's wealthiest nations, which have aging populations and declining work forces. My fear is that the world will become even more divided between the wealthy and the poor—not necessarily because the wealthy are selfish, but because the enormity of the problems facing the underdeveloped world will be overwhelming.

I believe that there is a very strong chance that traditionally wealthy nations like Japan, the United States, and Germany may see an overall decline in their wealth, having peaked at the end of the twentieth century. If so, trying to share the wealth with poorer nations will be very difficult. Further, if disease, war, terrorism, and criminal activity

Globalization and Counteraction

continue to spread from failed-states, Western societies may build tremendous barriers between themselves and the rest of the world.

As it stands now, public opinion globally is divided over the War on Terror and the preventive attack on Iraq. Some believe that the United States should not have acted outside of the United Nations and should not have invaded a sovereign state—albeit one that Saddam was rapidly losing control of. Others believe that in an era when terrorists are seeking to use failed-states, the United States acted appropriately by taking preventive measures in an effort to deny terrorists a potential staging area.

Regardless of whether one is for or against American action in Iraq, a new method of dealing with failed-states (and the third world in general) is going to emerge from this. It will require more military power than Europe and the unilateralists would like, and it will require more patient diplomacy and multilateralism than the Americans would like.[16] The two sides, in effect, are currently playing good cop, bad cop. Europe takes the more politically correct and diplomatic approach toward the new antiglobalization challenges, and the United States takes the more aggressive, policing actions required. Both sides look far apart, but in actuality, they are both fighting to protect global order and the global marketplace.

The United States sees a world in which failed-states and terrorism are on the brink of upsetting the entire world order, and it is the only nation-state in the world that has a large enough reach to deal with the most difficult issues the world

---

16. The United Nations is already discussing the need for preventive action (as opposed to just preemptive action), which means that future attacks on dangerous failed-states may be sanctioned by the U.N.

faces. France and the other European nations see a world in which a peaceful Europe (in which European nation-states view cooperation as more important than national interest) is being challenged by terrorism and unassimilated immigrants from failed-states. Their job is to continue promoting the benefits of an interconnected, transnational government. The United States and Europe need each other, but both win votes by playing against each other to their very different, respective audiences. The United States has the more thankless job. Military power is exactly what everyone wants to get away from during this era of hyperglobalization. The catch is that commerce hates chaos and chaos is what anti-capitalist movements and failed-states produce. Thus, we are caught in a trap. For better or worse, the future will be dictated by how the wealthy nations of the world react to protect their interests.

It is important to note that, overall, the world is plagued by fewer wars today than ever in human history. The creation of the nation-state system, the cold war, suprastructures like the EU, and the dominance of U.S. military power have all played a part of the process of making the world a place where fewer major wars take place. There is every reason to think that we can avoid another large-scale global war between nations like World Wars I and II. However, the twentieth century has been called the bloodiest century in human history because, as discussed in chapter 3, conflicts between nations have diminished while conflicts within nations remain bloody. It is these kinds of conflicts and divisions that will pose a challenge for peace in the future.

As Christians, we need to be ready to respond to the challenges of this new, dangerous era. Appendix 2 outlines seven commitments to help Christians prepare themselves.

Appendix 2

7 Commitments to Help Us Become Global Christians

> "We demolish arguments and every pretension that sets itself up against the knowledge of God, and we take captive every thought to make it obedient to Christ."
> —2 Corinthians 10:5 NIV

If, as I have described in Appendix 1, globalization is unleashing forces that will change this world dramatically and create many challenges and potential conflict, what can we as Christians do? A lot, I hope. As I have said repeatedly in this book, religion can be a powerful force for good. Christianity has the power to transform individual lives and societies. While I do not believe that true global peace on earth is attainable until the return of Jesus Christ, we can be agents for peace, and we can definitely be agents for spreading *agape* love around the world instead of hatred. Here are seven challenges that will enable us to be a force for good in these complicated times and transform us into global Christians.

1. A Commitment to Tithe 10 Percent

This first commitment may be unexpected, but it might be the most important. In *The State of Christian Giv-*

ing through 2001, John and Sylvia Ronsvalle report that the more we Christians make in the United States, the less we give. Many evangelical Christians did quite well during the hyperglobalization-fueled affluence of the 1990s, but by 2001, giving had dropped to 3.17 percent of income for members of mainline Christian denominations and 4.27 percent for evangelical Christians.[1] In 2002, George Barna reported that only 6 percent of born-again adults tithe. This is scandalous! Tithing is a basic Christian discipline that should be taught to children from an early age and that all Christian adults should be doing. Tithing teaches us that all that we have belongs to God and that we cannot place our hope in material things.

In an age of extreme wealth and extreme poverty, it is vital that Christians do not fall prey to the excessive materialism of our societies. For those of us that live in the wealthier nations of the world, wealth is a wonderful blessing. However, we must remember that the secularizing force of the marketplace is something that not only affects nations just being introduced to modernity, but it continually threatens the values of every Christian. Jesus Christ warned us to "take heed and beware of covetousness for one's life does not consist in the abundance of the things he possesses" (Luke 12:15). In the same passage, he tells us,

> Do not seek what you should eat or what you should drink, nor have an anxious mind. *For all these things the nations of the world seek after,* and your father knows that you need these things. But seek the kingdom of God, and all these things shall be added to you. Do

---

1. Ronsvalle and Ronsvalle, *State of Church Giving,* 12.

7 Commitments

not fear, little flock, for it is your Father's good pleasure to give you the kingdom. Sell what you have and give alms; provide yourselves money bags which do not grow old, a treasure in the Heavens that does not fail, where no thief approaches nor moth destroys. For where your treasures is, there your heart will be also. (vv. 29–34)

In today's world, more and more nations are choosing the capitalist system of free markets and trade. At the moment, there is no other economic system that seems to work as well, or is as popular. We are part of a capitalist society. That does not mean, however, that Christians need to let that system dictate our values. As Christians, it is our obligation to filter everything through God's Word. I do not believe that God is against capitalism, but he is strongly against our succumbing to a spirit of materialism and viewing other human beings simply as a commodity or as consumers. We have to be alert that we do not fall prey to this temptation or radical materialism which not only can corrupt societies but the individual soul as well. We can allow the nations of the world to seek economic stability, but followers of Christ must seek to expand the kingdom of God first and foremost.

Supposing the world's economies continue to grow at a very healthy rate (which I believe they will not), the World Bank believes it may be possible to cut the number of people living on less than a dollar a day from 1.2 billion in 1990 to 622 million people by 2015. This would be quite an accomplishment, but the World Bank study *Global Economic Prospects 2004* warns that progress is highly uneven across and within countries. A lot of the growth comes from China and India (whose modernization processes are still extremely fragile). The report singles out Cambodia, Laos, and Papua New Guinea as examples of places that lag far behind.[2]

The uneven distribution of wealth in developing countries worries me very much. Many of the world's newly emerging economies (e.g., China, India, Malaysia) have this problem. The vast majority of the wealth is concentrated in certain areas. In Thailand, a country that now has a significant middle class as a result of globalization, much of that wealth is centered in the capital city of Bangkok. In rural Thailand, people are still so poor that they cannot afford the most basic medicines. Some have chosen to be involved in the sex trade for money; others are preyed upon. In India, New Delhi and Bangalore are doing well because of the information technology boom, but Calcutta is still awash in poverty. In China, the east coast, particularly the cities, has seen standards of living rise dramatically, but for many regions, life is as it was a hundred years ago.

Amy Chua, of the Yale Law School, suggests an even more challenging problem in her book *World on Fire: How Exporting Free Market Democracy Breeds Ethnic Hatred and Global Instability*. In many cases, the wealth is being generated by an ethnic minority. For instance, in Malaysia, the Chinese minority is responsible for 70 percent of the country's market capitalization.[3] In South Africa, whites still own 80 percent of South Africa's land and account for 90 percent of the country's commercial agricultural productions.[4] Throughout the 1990s, six of Russia's seven wealthiest oli-

---

2. World Bank, *Global Economic Prospects 2004*, 22.
3. Chua, *World on Fire*, 36.
4. Ibid., 99.

7 Commitments

garchs were Jewish.[5] And in Brazil *latifundio* owners are primarily white and own most of the land despite only making up .05 percent of the population.[6] The problem is evident in West Africa with the Lebanese, in East Africa with the Indians, and throughout Latin America with the lighter skinned upper class.

Chua warns that when minorities are the primary engine of economic growth under free-market democracy, there is almost always a backlash against the markets, against democracy, and against the minorities themselves.[7] This is precisely the kind of unintended consequences unleashed by hyperglobalization that I discussed in Part II of Appendix 1.

Inevitably, there will be great divisions between the wealthy and the poor. But as Christians, we need to take on some of this burden in our own lives and in our own churches. With disparities this large and conflicts so possible, there's simply no excuse for American churches to ignore teaching the spiritual discipline of tithing. We cannot let our spiritual identities be molded by the secularizing force of the marketplace. Neither can we avoid the hard topics such as tithing because we don't want to offend people coming to our church. We don't want to cultivate consumers, but rather disciples.

I realize that some Christians do not believe that the Bible asks us to give 10 percent or even to give a tithe at all, but Christ's words are clear that we are not to have a spirit of materialism. A tithe of 10 percent would help us begin to break the spirit of materialism that has so many Christians

---

5. Ibid., 78.
6. Ibid., 66.
7. Ibid., 10.

in its grip. Ultimately, our congregations will be spiritually strengthened if we give. It is tragic to think about the degree to which local churches have been limited by the lack of tithing. It is even more tragic to think of work that could have been done around the world if the 45 percent of Americans that identify themselves as born again had invested 10 percent in projects around the world during this period of economic growth.[8]

If being selfless and Christ-like is not enough motivation, consider this: the problems on the other side of the world are our problems now too. That is one of the consequences of profiting from globalization; we are richer, but we are also now in this all together. We need to be global Christians.

As Christians give money toward needs in the third world, we can certainly demand higher levels of accountability that the money is well-spent and actually produces positive results. A lot of foreign aid around the world has been wasted (lost to corruption, given to leaders or governments that will not reform, or invested in institutions that the locals are not equipped to run). We will need to try to think strategically and invest in projects that develop the people and develop local institutions. Providing quality education for young people like I met in Sri Lanka (chapter 3), for instance, is one of the best investments we can make. Education that enables people in the third world to better manage institutions within their country can have a powerful effect on underdeveloped and developing nations.

---

8. *Princeton Religion Research Report 2002*: Describing Self as Born-Again or Evangelical. Available at http://www.wheaton.edu/isae/Gallup-Bar-graph.html.

7 Commitments

2. A Commitment to Stop Demonizing the First World

Now, more than ever, the people of the third world will need to respect the people of the first world. A substantial amount of aid in many different fields (e.g., delivering water, stopping disease, investment opportunities) will need to be given. It will be up to the first world to find better ways of doing that. Organizations such as the World Bank and economic ideas such as the Washington Consensus[9] are debated, modified, and open to criticism and change.

Christians in the third world will need to cooperate with Christians and missionaries from the first world as well. Of course, first-world Christians will need to make sure that they do not impose their culture (as opposed to Christ's culture) or their spirit of materialism on people in the third world, but issues of classic imperialism are less and less relevant now than before.

We need to drop the anti-colonialist mindset. It is true that wealthy Christians from the first world have profited from the third world through globalization, but the opposite is also true, because that is the nature of globalization and free markets. We need to cooperate at higher levels of mutual respect in the future. We must forget the different worlds from which we come and remember that we form one Body.

---

9. The *Washington Consensus* is a term used to describe the economic advice given to countries that want to develop economically; a kind of bitter pill that must be swallowed to lead to development. This includes privatization, fiscal discipline, tax reforms, trade liberalization, an inflow of foreign direct investment, deregulation, securing property rights, interest rate liberalization, a competitive exchange rate, and a redirection of public expenditures. Some view this economic formula as imperialistic and/or unfair. It is being critiqued and challenged, which is my point. Many in wealthy countries are interested in helping the poorer countries of the world and are always seeking ways to be more fair.

Passport of Faith

First-world nations have exploited other nations for gain, built colonialist empires, and spread a spirit of materialism around the world. But it needs to be acknowledged that the wealthy nations of the world have also brought a lot of good to the people of the underdeveloped world. Key inventions like the automobile, telephone, and airplane have enabled poorer nations to develop economically and create food supplies that once were not possible. Vaccines have been created that have saved millions of lives, and agencies such as the World Health Organization have prevented the spread of diseases like ebola. Organizations such as Greenpeace have brought international awareness to environmental issues which often threaten the underdeveloped world far more than the first world. Groups like Amnesty International have spread the Western concept of human rights throughout the world and put pressure on tyrannical governments to stop abuse of citizens. The formation of organizations such as the United Nations, the European Union, and NATO established an era of diplomacy that would have previously been unthinkable. An incredible number of people from the developing world have benefited from first-world educations. An even greater number of people have been able to immigrate—often from failed-states and persecution—to first world nations with very few questions asked.

The ironically anti-intellectual and unnecessary dualistic view of much of the intelligentsia in the first world is that wealthy nations are suspect. Perhaps this is done out of guilt, but many minorities and people in the third world have been quick to latch on to this in order to gain social, economic, and intellectual standing. There is no doubt that Western imperialism needed to be critiqued. But we live in one world now, and it is a world where people outside of

7 Commitments

the West increasingly have the freedom to make decisions. More often than not, they send their kids to schools in the West, they court Western corporations, they desire Western-style nation-states, and they are greatly benefiting from the economic policies and the geopolitical order that the West provides through its systems of government and military. Furthermore, the "West" is increasingly non-white. With China and India now attempting to practice free-market economics, the supposedly oppressive white, Western way of doing things is no longer either white or Western.

Lastly, it needs to be understood that human systems are imperfect. Since the Treaty of Westphalia (see Appendix 1), nation-states have been slowly finding a way to govern that is ultimately more peaceful and more stable. It is working, despite the chaos that erupts at times. The balance of power system of the seventeenth century, the bipolar system of the twentieth century, and the multilateral, interdependent system of the twenty-first century are all vast improvements over the chaos that used to reign, and these improvements have been generated from the West. Despite the setbacks of colonialism, slavery, and other ills, substantial progress has been made. This is undeniable. This is the macro picture that is so often missing from our dialogues, which focus on the micro picture.

I do not mean to minimize the evils that Western nations have perpetrated on the non-Western world in the name of imperialism. Neither have I forgotten the many reprehensible dictators supported by the West during the cold war (e.g., Somoza, Mobotu, Pinochet). During that bipolar era, however, non-Western communist nations and nonaligned nations did not have stellar humanitarian records either.

The first world, the United States in particular, is also guilty of using a disproportionate amount of the world's resources. The amount of waste in the United States is extreme. But here too, the non-Western world is increasingly guilty. Within ten to fifteen years, the amount of energy and oil that China will need to run its economy will put tremendous strain on the world.

One of the best things about the West is that its Christian heritage has left it with a remarkable ability for self-introspection. We are quite open about our ills. Throughout Europe and in North America, there is a much stronger desire to critique oneself and to rectify the ills of the past than can be found in the vast majority of the non–Judeo-Christian world. That is something that is very obvious to me living in East Asia. In East Asia, with its face-saving culture, grievances from the last world war still have not been resolved. The third world needs to acknowledge that the West has been very introspective and has even exported many of the ideas (such as human rights) and global organizations (such as Greenpeace) that challenge the West on behalf of the third world.

3. A Commitment to Embrace World Christianity

While it is important that Christians interact with non-Christians in a peaceful and loving manner as the world enters into a period of global conflict, it will be just as important for Christians to learn to dialogue with other Christians in this new era.

Many in North America and Europe are ignorant of the fact that Christianity has undergone a dramatic shift in the past century. Every few hundred years, the gravitational center of Christianity seems to shift. The faith was born in the

7 Commitments

Near East and quickly spread around the Mediterranean, eventually finding its center in Rome. The Protestant Reformation shifted the center of gravity to Northern Europe, eventually making its way across the ocean to North America.

For most of the twentieth century, the United States was the world's most vocal Christianized nation. American Christians had the money and resources to send missionaries, build seminaries and universities, produce books, and create television channels that beamed the American Christian message around the world. In a sense, America became the global spokesman for Christianity. Christians in America have viewed themselves as part of a Christian nation responsible for introducing Christianity to the four corners of the Earth. Indeed, the effort by American Christians to spread the gospel and charity around the world has been primarily a powerful force for good from which millions around the world have benefited.

Another shift, however, is taking place, and North Americans and Europeans have been slow to recognize this. For the past few decades, nations in the third world have been embracing Christianity at a tremendous rate. Meanwhile, the United States and Canada have experienced unspectacular Christian growth and Europe has seen a massive decline in the number of believers. While churches in Great Britain are closing every week, Christianity in nations as diverse as South Korea, India, and Mongolia is experiencing unbelievable growth. Brazil currently has a larger evangelical population than the United States; the evangelical church in Brazil grew 71 percent from 1991 to 2000.[10] With China's

---

10. Neves, "Two Brazils."

current exponential growth, the evangelical movement there may outnumber the United States in a decade or so. Meanwhile, Africa, which in 1900 only had 10 million Christians, is now a continent of 500 million people with over 309 million of those professing Christianity.[11] This is the emergence of World Christianity.

Many in North American and Europe are still under the impression that Christianity is in overall decline and that continents like Africa are places of darkness where the gospel has not yet been widely preached. I recall a conversation with a certain American pastor who simply did not believe me when I said that Africa was a continent with more Christians than the United States. He had grown up with the image of Africa as a place where missionaries labored for decades to get anyone to accept the Christian message. This pastor literally did not believe me and asked me for proof. This is an example of how deeply entrenched it is in the American Christian psyche that we are the primary movers and shakers of the Christian faith.

Many will be quick to question the spiritual depth and orthodoxy of the Christian movement in Africa. Nevertheless, the growth of Christianity in Africa has been phenomenal and has led to many vibrant congregations, a number of which now send missionaries to foreign countries such as the United States. Cities like Chicago and Los Angeles have a considerable number of Christians from Africa who are concerned about the spiritual environment in the United States.

South Korea too has become a sending nation, the second largest in the world. Nations such as the Philippines

---

11. Siewert, Welliver, and Valdez, *Mission Handbook*.

7 Commitments

and India are also sending missionaries as far away as South America. When I returned to Costa Rica for a visit in 2003, I met a couple who wanted to be missionaries to China.

The Pentecostal faith has been key in fueling this dramatic revival around the world. It is my belief that the emphasis on the Spirit manifesting itself strikes a deep chord of familiarity in cultures around the world that have always viewed the world as spiritual. As I mentioned in chapter 1, atheism's negation of the spiritual world is really antithetical to the beliefs of most people around the world. A world without God and spirits does not resonate with most people. I do not think that it is an accident that Christian movements and denominations that take spiritual manifestations in worship very seriously are growing much quicker than Christian denominations that are more restrained in their worship. Roman Catholicism is having a hard time competing in Latin America with the zealous and dramatic presence of Pentecostalism. Growing Catholic congregations tend to be more charismatic in their approach.

As we contemplate the emergence of World Christianity, I offer a few suggestions and critiques for both liberal Protestants and conservative evangelical Christians. I write this as a Hispanic from a third-world nation who has attained U.S. citizenship and who lives in East Asia. I have been educated by both liberal Protestants and conservative Protestants. I believe this unique vantage point gives me a deep appreciation for all sides, and I do not mean to alienate either side with these observations and criticisms. I am not interested in taking either side to task but rather preparing us for dialogue.

Passport of Faith

Liberal Protestantism and World Christianity

Just as we Christians in the West must learn to dialogue with people of other faiths in this new age, we must also learn to dialogue with our Christian brothers and sisters in these new, emerging Christian powerhouses. There are some differences between World Christians and North American and European Christians. As mentioned before, World Christians seem to be more inherently comfortable with a charismatic approach to the faith. For them, the world has always been very spiritual and connecting to that world is neither difficult nor strange.

World Christians also tend to be more conservative than Western Christians. While many Christians in the West debate issues such as abortion and homosexuality, World Christians are more likely to find these topics to be completely non-issues. For them, these debates are only further proof of the secularization and moral relativism that has infiltrated the Western church. For most World Christians, believing in moral absolutes and Christian orthodoxy are nonnegotiable. They find no intellectual shame in believing in absolute truth. These are painful realizations for some liberal Protestants to accept.

Liberal Protestantism has been slow to grasp the important changes that are taking place in World Christianity. One of the sad ironies of the liberalism in some seminaries and divinity schools is that they claim to be interested in listening to the voice of the marginalized and the oppressed, when, in fact, they remain woefully ignorant of Christian believers in non-Western nations. While these seminaries and divinity schools continue to hire experts on subjects such as feminist theology, Latina studies, and various liberation theologies in an effort to provide a multicultural

7 Commitments

education, most World Christians find liberal Protestantism to be watered-down, elitist, and irrelevant.

At supposedly open-minded seminaries, it is possible to take a course on Korean liberation theology (*minjung*), yet never once while living in South Korea did I meet a Christian who remotely knew what that meant. I did, however, meet plenty of Koreans who were extremely committed to the conservative tenets of evangelical Protestantism—more so than American conservative evangelicals themselves.

In my travels in Latin America, the only Christians I met who were knowledgeable about liberation theology were educated in Western seminaries. Never are they a part of any big Christian movement or growing church. "It's all about church growth and Pentecostalism," said Ricardo, my Costa Rican uncle, when I inquired about the state of the local churches. I know of a group of seminary students studying at a prominent liberal seminary who went to Cuba expecting to find people who shared their interest in liberation theology only to find that the Cuban Christians were deeply evangelical, conservative, and pro-American. When I go back to Costa Rica, it is not Gutierrez's *Liberation Theology* that is in the bookstores but Benny Hinn's *Good Morning, Holy Spirit*.

Further, none of the Christian women in ministry that I know in Asia or Latin America are interested in feminism, nor do they particularly subscribe to Western notions of feminist oppression and liberation. In Latin America, the women I know are extremely comfortable in their roles as women. It is not an issue of being dominant or submissive; they are much more interested in just doing the will of God, as naïve as that may sound to the some.

Passport of Faith

Much like Che Guevara trying to rally the Congolese to wage a Marxist war, many liberal seminaries and divinity schools are peddling a theology that very few believe in or are willing to fight for. Many of these liberal Protestant professors think they are waging a campaign to foster tolerance, justice, and peace in the Christian world by lifting up the voices of the oppressed non-Western people. But they don't realize that they are actually ignoring the real revolution of the non-Western people in favor of clinging to their own 1960s Western ideas of tolerance, justice, and peace.

When divinity schools and seminaries claim to be interested in non-Western people but refuse to teach courses on World Christianity or refuse to hire professors that represent evangelical, Pentecostal, and other conservative points of view, they are committing a form of bigotry. I question an academic institution's interest in pluralism and diversity if it is unwilling to listen to the voice of World Christians, even if that voice is extremely conservative.

The life of the mind need not die if World Christianity is given a forum to speak in liberal seminaries and divinity schools. I believe God expects us to use our intellectual capacities. If liberal religious institutions equate intellectual vigor and credibility with the ideas of German, American, and a very selective sample of "third-world" liberal theologies, then we have a problem. I encourage faculty members and students at liberal seminaries to take a close look at Christian movements around the world and introduce themselves to World Christianity. Forget the politics and priorities of the American countercultural revolution of the 1960s, and set aside prejudices against the Moral Majority and fundamentalists in order to hear the emerging voice of Christians from the third world. To not do this would be to

7 Commitments

miss one of the greatest events ever to occur in the history of Christianity.

Conservative Protestantism and World Christianity

On the other side of the coin, conservatives may feel reassured that World Christian trends in theology are moving in their favor. There may be a sense of satisfaction that the liberalism and moral relativism that they so despise within liberal Protestantism is going to be drowned out by the conservative voices of World Christianity. However, conservatives and evangelicals also need to do some soul searching as World Christianity emerges.

For a long period of time, evangelicals, in particular, have enjoyed a tremendous amount of influence, power, and wealth. A tour that I took of James Dobson's Focus on the Family campus in Colorado Springs left me speechless as I saw all of the wealth and technology they have to transmit their message. Men like Jerry Falwell and Oral Roberts have been able to build little empires and have a tremendous effect on domestic politics. Even internationally, when Falwell speaks, many of his words are transmitted as far away as China and Iran and reactions are immediate. In Hong Kong, my friends know about Falwell's Teletubby comments, and in Iran, mullahs preached against Falwell's characterization of Muhammad as a terrorist. Although evangelicals have been much maligned in American universities and in the press, the twentieth century was very good to conservative, Western, evangelical Christians.

The target of their message—the third world—is now about to take the stage however. Are conservative Christians ready? These new World Christians will come from more humble circumstances and environments. They will come

Passport of Faith

from the *favelahs* of Brazil and the slums of Kinshasa; they will be persecuted Christians from faraway lands and peasants from the Chinese countryside. And their message for us will be important. They may challenge Western Christianity's comfort with wealth. The prosperity gospel may not resonate very well with those that have learned from tough experience that we are spirits just visiting a material world. They may challenge us and argue that we are too far removed from suffering and too distant from the cross.

There will be a need for a new attitude of humility among conservative Christians as well. American Christians have lived very comfortable lives free from danger, affording us the luxury to focus on things like connecting our spiritual life to our finances so that we can flourish economically. This is something that the vast majority of the world simply cannot do. They may still live in pre-Westphalian societies where chaos reigns and governments offer no protection. We need to be sensitive to this fact and we need to give out of agape love—not for a desire to become wealthy ourselves, but to do good and to break the spirit of mammon. We need to expand the kingdom of God, not the kingdom of Christian television or the kingdom of our megachurch. Those are not always the same.

Another challenge for conservatives will be having patience and tolerance for some of the new ideas that World Christianity introduces theologically. Quite often, Christian movements can dabble in heterodoxy and syncretism. In Africa, some Christian movements combine aspects of African religions into their theology and ceremony. While some contextualization always occurs as Christianity is practiced in varying cultures, it is not good if orthodoxy is breached. Numerous cults in China and Africa have flour-

7 Commitments

ished and frightened many Christians. While it is important that orthodoxy be preached, it is also important to know that many of these movements do not survive or in time become orthodox as believers search the Scriptures. Most likely, China, Latin America, and Africa will have orthodox churches that are just a bit spicier than Western Christian movements.

Lastly, conservative Christians might be surprised that World Christians often do not share their political point of view. In some cases, such as in China, there seems to be a great deal of sympathy for the politics of American evangelicals. In other cases, such as in Brazil, even conservative Pentecostal Christians may side with the more liberal, even Marxist, political party. World Christians will be operating in local cultures that are very different from ours. If, for instance, they have lived under the yoke of communist tyranny, they may be more politically conservative. However, there may be many Christians living in manufacturing economies where unions and Marxist ideas still seem valid. Never underestimate the complexity of this era, which is why we must be very careful in our assessments in this new era. We need to have a broad view and be global Christians.

4. A Challenge to Respond to Christian Persecution

World Christians will quickly be the dominant force in Christianity as the center of gravity shifts away from North America to the Southern Hemisphere and East Asia. They will face many challenges, the greatest probably being persecution. Perhaps the most indicting comment that one can say about the current Christian movement is that we have been deathly silent on the issue of persecuted Christians. The twentieth century saw Christians persecuted in massive numbers while most North American Christians slept. In the past few years, it has gotten better as organizations such as Voice of the Martyrs have raised awareness.

However, we Western Christians simply did not do enough. Christian children have been tortured in the Sudan, Chinese Christians in Indonesia have been burnt alive, and many Korean Christians are locked away, languishing in the demonically evil prison system of North Korea while we have, at times, waged battles against very insignificant things. If Jews had been tortured and killed at the levels that Christians have been in the past few decades, there would have been a great outcry and demand for justice by the Jewish community. Although scattered around the world, Jews are far more connected to each other than Christians have been. Just as we have been oblivious to the rise of World Christianity, we have been oblivious to the rise of the persecution of our Christian brothers and sisters.

Unfortunately, as new fault lines develop geopolitically, religious conflict will increase and Christians will be in the line of fire. Sadly, some Christians will retaliate, fueling conflict. Overall, I'm optimistic that the vast majority of Christians will not engage in violence toward others as a response to heightened tensions. Part of the problem is that the World Christian church will grow so quickly that some may try to shut it down through war, oppression, and torture. However, throughout history, persecution has always meant greater Christian growth. World Christians face challenges, and we must all be prepared to support them in difficult times.

Finally, we must do all we can to prevent Christian-on-Christian violence. This includes violence between Protestants and against Roman Catholics or against Ortho-

7 Commitments

dox believers. From Latin America to the Balkans, there are areas where Christians live in tension with other Christians. We must keep our eyes on these fault lines. We must be global Christians.

5. A Challenge to Not Be McMissionaries

In this era of hyperglobalization, it is vital that we make sure that the missionaries we send out from North America have a global vision before going out into the field. Christian agencies and organizations will need to make sure that they have equipped their missionaries with as broad of a view of the world as possible so that we are not just agents of cultural transmission.

It is important to understand that despite the fact that the age of empires is over in the pre-Westphalian sense (or in the colonizing sense of the British Empire one hundred years ago), our global order of nation-states is always somewhat imperialistic. The United States, Europe, and increasingly China, for instance, make strategic decisions to defend their economic interests and national security. That means that they seek to expand their influence internationally in a number of ways, not always nefarious but neither are they necessarily ethical. Even Europe with its post-Westphalian multilateralism still requires future members to basically become like them—and by expanding their borders they "colonize" new territories. So those Christians living in economically prosperous countries do live in empires, so to speak. But this does not mean that we have to be agents for this kind of subtle colonization. As long as we do our best to let the Holy Spirit transmit Christ through us—rather than transmitting some of the warped cultural values that we inevitably have—we can avoid becoming McMissionaries.

Passport of Faith

In order to keep us from this, an awareness of key issues in our regions will be critical. Geopolitical realities and the role of religion seems to be ignored, not only by many missionaries, but by many students of missiology whose studies tend to focus on issues of contextualization, biblical understandings of mission, statistics, or biographies. Missiology has closely aligned itself with cultural anthropology, and this has served us well. However, we need to broaden our horizons and engage other academic disciplines. Although there are reasons for the division between missiology and some of the other social sciences (for instance, the challenge of finding a clear demarcation between normative and scientific approaches in studies), I believe that other disciplines need to be taken into account at this critical juncture in history, including economics, sociology, psychology, anthropology, and especially political science.[12]

Clearly issues regarding the impact of religion on nations in light of globalization are critical and need to be examined at this particular time in global history by people involved in the missionary enterprise. The missionary movement can be a powerful force for peace and stability as well as economic betterment. We need to take the transforming power of agape seriously and make sure we are agents for positive change. This is particularly so in light of the tremendous growth of World Christianity in many of these underdeveloped or transitioning parts of the world. We need to be able to truly assess what we can do and where we are needed.

---

12. I owe Robert L. Montgomery a debt of gratitude for helping me to identify the tension between the social sciences and missiology through his essay "Mission Studies: Both Mine and Minefield for the Social Sciences," which he sent to me in the course of our dialogue on numerous issues.

7 Commitments

As we get a broader vision of where Christianity stands in the world, it will help us to be more culturally sensitive in a more credible and less reactionary way, as well as more useful to those we serve.[13]

I particularly think that missionaries need to have a strong grasp on the issues that are facing their particular region (e.g., the economic development; the relief efforts; the ethnic, political, or ideological tensions) and this is something that should be focused on during the training process before the missionary hits the field. I am not advocating that every missionary become a scholar on globalization. I realize that many who choose to be missionaries do not do so because they want to be experts on global issues but because they simply want to share Jesus Christ with people in foreign lands. Certainly, what matters most is a heart that is Spirit-led. It is indisputably the most important quality a missionary can possess. But I do think that we are being sent out "as lambs among wolves" (Luke 10:3) and that agencies and organizations have the responsibility to make sure that their missionaries are very well-equipped to deal with both the challenges and the exciting possibilities that this era offers us.

Some may want to argue that World Christianity will be sending out so many missionaries into the world that North American agencies should focus more on their own nations or close up shop altogether. I, for one, feel that there is still

---

13. I think the work of the Council on Faith & International Affairs is a prime example of what I am talking about. The mission of the CFIA is to serve scholars and practitioners active at the nexus of faith and international affairs by providing new resources for professional development and by encouraging holistic engagement in global issues through critical reflection, practical action, collaborative scholarship, and interfaith dialogue.

a great need for Western missionaries around the world—perhaps now more than ever. We are called by Christ to "go into all the world and preach the gospel" (Mark 16:15), and as long as there are people with servant hearts willing to travel great distances to share the gospel, we should allow it. There is something special about cross-cultural ministry. When we work with overseas Christians or go to distant lands to share the gospel, it connects the global church in a profound spiritual way and it reminds us that we are all of the same blood—not divided, but rather God's children. Something profound occurs when we connect with people cross-culturally. Christ modeled that for us (reaching out to Samaritans and Romans), and I am thoroughly convinced that his will was for us to always be involved in international missionary work. Furthermore, World Christianity still needs assistance from Western Christians in a number of areas, including theologically as many movements struggle with heterodoxy. But it is vital that our missionaries be equipped to deal with the kinds of difficult and volatile issues that arise in the post–September 11 world.

We need to allow World Christians to critique our churches, our mission agencies, and our theology. At the same time, they should critique us in a manner that is fair, honest, and relevant. It should not be rehashing of old charges and caricatures of Western missionaries, but honest dialogue about the state of the world today. Both Western Christians and World Christians "fall short of the glory of God." Let's always keep that in mind and become global Christians.

7 COMMITMENTS

6. A CHALLENGE TO GET INVOLVED IN GLOBAL DIPLOMACY AND CRISIS RESOLUTION

Why should we ask that missionaries and Christians be more informed about the world at a level greater than we have in the past? Because in this new era of hyperglobalization, what happens in one corner of the globe affects us all for better or for worse. We've all heard of the butterfly effect: a flap of butterfly wings affects the wind currents thousands of miles away. Whether scientifically true or not, many small things have big effects in this new era. As I have argued in this book, religious, ethnic or ideological rivalries could flare up and create many problems for the world. Small divisions can have big implications.

Whenever I hear people argue that this new era of globalization is full of safeguards and that nations have too much to lose by allowing conflict, I think of Tip O'Neil's famous comment that "all politics is local." Small divisions, local politics, and other micro issues have always had the power to affect nations and even encourage them to act against their own best interests. In the future, some significant countries will make poor choices in both the first world and the third world. Consequently, Christians need to be an active force for diplomacy and crisis resolution. As Barry Rubin has written,

> For several decades, the prevailing school of thought underlying U.S. foreign policy has assumed that religion would be a declining factor in the life of states and in international affairs. However, experience has shown and projections indicate that the exact opposite is increasingly true. To neglect religious institutions and

thinking would be to render incomprehensible some of the key issues and crises in the world today.[14]

Christianity, with its magnificent theology that has produced movements and ideas of freedom that have benefited the world immeasurably, will be able to play a part in diffusing tensions around the world. Christian people and organizations may do this by alleviating poverty, providing social services, mediating conflict, helping to establish businesses, treating diseases, transferring technology free of charge, providing education online, and fostering dialogue, to name just a few things. Christianity—and agape love—can be a force for peace.

Yes, these are the things we always do in the Christian movement. Certainly, there are groups that alleviate suffering and meet the spiritual needs of people living in troubled areas (e.g., Samaritan's Purse). But what I am asking is that we take a more calculated approach, expecting to be a powerful force on the world stage with our coordinated efforts. Let us intentionally get involved in this world and be a force for stability and order as Christians once were in the Roman Empire and as they are now in China. Let us realize that there is a powerful God supporting us that is ready to act in mighty ways. We need to be global Christians.

Looking back at history, Christianity has been at the forefront of anticolonialism efforts, antislavery movements, anti-occupation movements, civil rights movements, human rights movements, and democracy movements. The influence of Christianity in diplomatic affairs has occurred on both a small scale and a large scale. On the smaller but

---

14. Rubin, "Religion and International Affairs," 33.

7 COMMITMENTS

still significant scale, the Moravian church helped to mediate a conflict between the Sandinistas and the indigenous East Coast people of Nicaragua, and the Lutheran church was involved in opening the door for civil opposition in East Germany prior to the collapse of the Berlin Wall in 1989.[15]

On the larger scale, we remember the remarkable role that John Paul II, Roman Catholicism, and Solidarity played in Poland's liberation from Soviet tyranny. And we can all recall the remarkable peaceful transition that occurred in South Africa when the South African Dutch Reformed Church reversed its stand on apartheid. And we were all inspired by the work of Bishop Desmond Tutu and the Truth and Reconciliation Committee, which found a way to deal in a civil manner with the human rights violations under apartheid. There is power when we attempt to be peacemakers.

Let us not be unrealistic, however. In this current world order (as in all previous systems of rule—tribal, empire, or nation-state), people are still going to demand that their rulers provide them with security. It is a basic requirement for all successful nation-states. No successful state can operate without any military or strong alliances backed up by force. We have moved a long way since the Treaty of Westphalia, but we are not at a place yet where nations can get rid of all military protection (even if it comes from a distant power like the United States) or take the use of military force off the table. Even the United Nations attempts to diffuse crises and intervene when peace is elusive by using military means.

---

15. See Johnston and Sampson's *Religion, the Missing Dimension of Statecraft* and Johnston's *Faith-Based Diplomacy: Trumping Realpolitik*.

We may not want force and military to be the first option, but the threat of force and the willingness to use force has to exist in societies with interests of this magnitude and actors of varying levels of morality. (The nations of the world are not as predictable or as regulated as an Amish or a Mennonite community.)

This will especially be the case in an era of asymmetrical warfare when terrorists (who are accountable to no one and for whom traditional means of diplomacy simply do not work) threaten to use weapons of mass destruction against people in the first world and the third world alike and when heavily armed criminal gangs and terrorists operate in failed-states. For those who dream of a world without armies, they will be sadly disappointed by the coming decades.

7. A Challenge to Reclaim Community

Ironically, despite the fact that we have never been as connected to so many people in history as we are now, what is increasingly being lost in our current era of hyperglobalization is community. The Internet, laptop computers, cell phones, and a myriad of other technologies have provided us with new methods to get things done. Instead of saving us time, however, we inevitably end up busier than ever before. The illusion that we are now more connected makes it easier for us to let other things pass: dinners as a family, fellowship with neighbors, time with our church. We all may have many activities to keep us busy throughout the week, but we may not have any meaningful human exchanges.

A sense of community is an important part of human existence. A stronger, more intimate sense of community will be needed to counteract the secularizing force of the marketplace, the spirit of radical materialism, and the despair of

7 Commitments

economic hardship, as well as the false sense of connectedness that this era of hyperglobalization often offers us.

Even though our Western cultures (and others as well) may be ready to give up intimacy in exchange for technology and convenience, the Christian communities within our cultures can resist this tendency. Thus far, many of our churches have taken on some of the trappings of this technological and materialistic age without subjecting those trappings to a healthy biblical critique. More than ever, we need to be introspective and filter the values of our culture through God's Word. Many of our churches are very good at providing activities, but we are not always as good at fostering an intimate community that knows how to share and, most importantly, how to repent.

Community within our churches is more than activities and projects. Community includes a culture of accountability, holiness, and discipleship. I have been struck by the intimacy found in our church in Hong Kong. The brothers and sisters in our church honestly and frequently share their deepest needs with each other. They pursue holiness together and support each other in success and failure. Their lives revolve around the church in a way that I think is missing in the United States. Most importantly, they do not just pursue church growth and evangelism, but rather they make sure that they create disciples above all. In Hong Kong, our church teaches that we want to grow spiritually and communally first! Numerical growth will be the result of our faith community which will make us a people set apart—a genuine agape community. We find it is the mature community that leads to growth.

On the other hand, at numerous churches around the world in recent years, particularly in the United States, I have also been struck by the low expectations that pastors have for their parishioners, which then leads to a low level of commitment and spiritual formation. Unwittingly and unintentionally, we are creating a generation of Christians that view themselves primarily as consumers when they go to church instead of as disciples greatly in need of spiritual formation and accountability to a godly family. These people are completely losing the ability to view church as anything but a place (one of many) that exists to meet their needs.

The seeker-sensitive church growth movement may be trying to bring unchurched people into church, but few of these people ever learn that the church should be a living, breathing community of faith where it is expected that God and our brothers and sisters will challenge us, expect much from us, correct us, and empower us by giving us places to serve others. A new Christian joining a church should be joining an unusually selfless community, not a selfish one. But when church leadership begins with the premise that the church is here to make you more comfortable and serve you, fewer Christians view the church as their family and their primary place of service and refinement. Church has now become one of many activities (soccer, karate, working out, golf) that take place throughout the week; it has become a club that provides activity focusing on spiritual things, thus making us feel morally satisfied. That is very different from viewing the church and the church family as the center of our lives that empowers us to serve God, the church, and the world.

To be frank, the bar is low in most churches; pastors are increasingly afraid to make demands upon the congregation. It is no accident that parishioners no longer view the pastor as their shepherd, the one God has given to them to

7 Commitments

lead them along their spiritual journey, but rather view the pastor as "the preacher person." The authority and the sacred role of the pastor is being replaced; the pastor has become the CEO of an organization and a person who gives spiritual suggestions that you are free to accept or reject.

The hope of many leaders is that by demanding less and making church more comfortable, we can avoid looking like the judgmental, legalistic churches of the past that turned people off to religion. This may fill seats, but make no mistake about it, an agape-filled, spirit-filled community that is pleasing to God comes at a price. It takes fearless teaching; intentional, purposeful direction; and modeling by example. A community dedicated to God and spiritual refinement has high standards of moral behavior, high expectations regarding commitment to the church (and to the people that make up the church), and a willingness to routinely mentor and challenge the believer so that they develop a repentant heart, which is a heart that will mature. This does not need to lead to legalism (just as high standards in parenting do not need to result in a rebellious or dispirited child); rather, it can lead people to a high degree of intimacy within the church, a sense of security in a hostile world, a sense that they are truly cared for, and an intensification of their relationship with God and their brothers and sisters. Last, it fosters deep meaning in the life of the believer.

To paraphrase Martin Luther King, Jr., the church needs to be less of a thermometer and more of a thermostat. We need to be a people set apart, not to cause division, but to clearly reflect that we are a community committed to setting our minds on higher things. We want to be in the world but not of the world. As Christians, we must remember the words of Paul: "Do not be conformed to this world, but be transformed by the renewing of your mind, that you may prove what is that good and acceptable and perfect will of God" (Romans 12:2).

If we can get our sense of community in order—which means pursuing holiness, embracing repentance, creating disciples, and seeking the Holy Spirit in all that we do—our very existence will do the evangelism for us in this coming era.

Bibliography

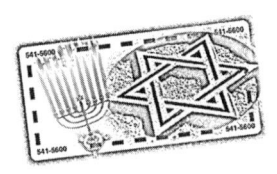

Armstrong, Karen. *A History of God: The 4000 year Quest of Judaism, Christianity and Islam.* New York: Ballantine Books, 1993.

Bates, Stephen. "Israel's Wall a Symbol of Fear—Archbishop." *Guardian Unlimited*, January 28, 2004. http://www.guardian.co.uk/uk_news/story/0,3604,1132696,00.html.

Bellah, Robert N. *Tokugawa Religion: The Values of Pre-Industrial Japan.* Boston: Beacon Press, 1957.

Bix, Herbert P. *Hirohito and the Making of Modern Japan.* New York: Perennial Press, 2000.

Bose, Sumantra. *States, Nations, Sovereignty: Sri Lanka, India and the Tamil Eelam Movement.* New Delhi: Sage Publications, 1994.

Bowker, John, ed. *Oxford Dictionary of World Religions.* Oxford: Oxford University Press, 1997.

Brekke, Torkel. *Makers of Modern Indian Religion in the Late Nineteenth Century.* Oxford: Oxford University Press, 2002.

Carroll, Janet. "Images of Church and Mission: The China Case." *Missiology* 23, no. 1 (January 1995): 31–42.

Catapano, Peter. "A New York State of Mind." *Salon*, October 1, 2002, 2.

Chandra-ngarm, Saeng. *Buddhism and Thai People*. Chiang Mai, Thailand: Ming Muang Printing Press, 2000.

Chiyozaki, Hideo. "The Japanese Emperor System: Historical Origins and Development." In *The Japanese Emperor System: The Inescapable Missiological Issue*, edited by Robert Lee, 80–109. Tokyo: Tokyo Mission Research Institute, 1990.

Chua, Amy. *World on Fire: How Exporting Free Market Democracy Breeds Ethnic Hatred and Global Instability*. New York: Doubleday Press, 2003.

Creveld, Martin Van. *The Rise and Decline of the Nation State*. Cambridge: Cambridge University Press, 1999.

Elizur, Yuval. "Israel Banks on a Fence." *Foreign Affairs* 82, no. 2 (March–April 2003): 106–119.

Ellis, Joseph J. *American Sphinx: The Character of Thomas Jefferson*. New York: Vintage Books, 1998.

Ellis, Royston. *Sri Lanka: The Bradt Travel Guide*. Chalfont St. Peter, UK: Bradt Travel Guides, 2001.

Esposito, John L. *Islam: The Straight Path*. Oxford: Oxford University Press, 1998.

Ferguson, Niall. "Sinking Globalization." *Foreign Affairs,* March–April 2005, 64–77.

Flood, Gavin. *An Introduction to Hinduism*. Cambridge, UK: Cambridge University Press, 1996.

Friedman, Thomas L. *Longitudes and Attitudes: Exploring the World After September 11*. New York: Farrar, Straus and Giroux, 2002.

———. *The Lexus and the Olive Tree: Understanding Globalization*. New York: Anchor Books, 2000.

Fujita, Neil S. "'Conic' Christianity and 'Donut' Japan." *Missiology* 22, no. 1 (1994): 43–53.

Glasser, Susan B. "Martyrs in Iraq Mostly Saudis." *Washington Post*, May 15, 2005, sec. A.

Gopal, Krishan. *Nationalism in Sri Lanka: Genesis and Evolution*. Dehli: Kalinga Publications, 2000.

Gorman, Christine. "Sex, AIDS and Thailand." *Time Asia*, July 19, 2004. http://www.time.com/time/asia/magazine/article/0,13673,501040719-662826,00.html.

Bibliography

Guillaume, Alfred. *Islam*. London: Penguin Books, 1990.

Hane, Mikiso. *Modern Japan: A Historical Survey*. Boulder, CO: Westview Press, 1986.

Homer-Dixon, Thomas. *The Ingenuity Gap: Facing the Economic, Environmental, and Other Challenges of an Increasingly Complex and Unpredictable World*. New York: Vintage Press, 2002.

Human Rights Watch. "Children's Rights" In *World Report 2001*. New York: Human Rights Watch. http://www.hrw.org/wr2k1/children/index.html.

———. "Asia: Sri Lanka." In *World Report 2002*. New York: Human Rights Watch. http://www.hrw.org/wr2k2/asia10.html.

Humphreys, Andrew, et al. *Egypt: Lonely Planet Guide*. Hawthorne, Australia: Lonely Planet Publications, 1996.

Hunter, Alan, and Kim-Kwong Chan. *Protestantism in Contemporary China*. Cambridge: Cambridge University Press, 1993.

Huntington, Samuel P. "The Age of Muslim Wars." *Newsweek* 138, no. 25 (December 17, 2001): 42–47.

———. *The Clash of Civilizations and the Remaking of the World Order*. New York: Simon & Schuster, 1996.

Ishihara, Shintaro. *The Japan That Can Say No: Why Japan Will Be First Among Equals*. Translated by Frank Baldwin. New York: Simon & Schuster, 1989.

Joffe, Josef. "A World without Israel." *Foreign Policy*, January–February 2005, 36–42.

Johnston, Douglas. *Faith-Based Diplomacy: Trumping Realpolitik*. Oxford: Oxford University Press, 2003.

Johnston, Douglas, and Cynthia Sampson, eds. *Religion, the Missing Dimension of Statecraft*. Oxford: Oxford University Press, 1994.

Krauthammer, Charles. "Israel's Infatada Victory." *Washington Post*, June 18, 2004, A29.

Kristoff, Nicholas, and Sheryl WuDunn. *Chinas Wakes: The Struggle for the Soul of a Rising Power*. London: Nicholas Brealey Publishing, 1995.

Landes, David S. *The Wealth and Poverty of Nations: Why Some Are So Rich and Some So Poor*. New York: W & W Norton & Co., 1999.

Lee, Kuan Yew. *From Third World to First: The Singapore Story: 1965–2000*. New York: HarperCollins, 2000.

Lee, Robert. "The Japanese Emperor System: Identity and Modernization." In *The Japanese Emperor System: The Inescapable Missiological Issue*, edited by Robert Lee, 110–138. Tokyo: Tokyo Mission Research Institute, 1990.

Levathes, Louise. *When China Ruled the Seas: The Treasure Fleet of the Dragon Throne, 1405–1433*. New York: Oxford University Press, 1997.

Levy, Reuben. *The Social Structure of Islam*. Cambridge: Cambridge University Press, 1995.

Lewis, Bernard. "Islam and Liberal Democracy." *Atlantic Monthly*, February 1993, 98.

———. "The Revolt of Islam." *New Yorker*, November 19, 2001. http://www.newyorker.com/fact/content/?011119fa_FACT2.

Lundell, Peter N. "Behind Japan's Resistant Web: Understanding the Problem of Nihonkyo." *Missiology* 23, no. 4 (1995): 401–412.

Morgan, Timothy C. "A Tale of China's Two Churches." *Christianity Today* 42, no. 8 (July 1998): 30–39.

Morton, Andrew. *China: Its History and Culture*. New York: McGraw-Hill, 1995.

Neves, Franscesco. "Two Brazils." *Brazzil Magazine*, May 2002.

Pape, Robert A. "Blowing Up an Assumption." *New York Times*, May 18, 2005. http://www.nytimes.com/2005/05/18/opinion/18pape.html.

"Recorded Sayings of Ch'an Master Pen-Chi (840–901) of Ts'ao-shan." In *Sources of Chinese Tradition*, Vol. 1, compiled by W. Theodore de Bary, Wing-Tsit Chan, and Burton Watson. New York: Columbia University Press, 1960.

Roach, Stephen. "The Big Squeeze," Global Economic Forum. morganstanley.com, April 4, 2005. http://www.morganstanley.com/GEFdata/digests/20050404-mon.html.

Ronsvalle, John L., and Sylvia Ronsvalle. *The State of Church Giving Through 2001*. Champaign, IL: Empty Tomb, 2003.

Ross, Andrew C. *A Vision Betrayed: The Jesuits in Japan and China, 1542–1742*. Maryknoll, NY: Orbis Press, 1994.

Bibliography

Rubin, Barry. "Religion and International Affairs." In *Religion, the Missing Dimension of Statecraft*, edited by Douglas Johnston and Cynthia Sampson, 20–34. Oxford: Oxford University Press, 1994.

Sairsingh, Krister. "Christ and Karma: A Hindu Quest for the Holy." In *Finding God at Harvard: Spiritual Journeys of Thinking Christians*, edited by Kelly Monroe, 179–190. Grand Rapids: Zondervan, 1996.

Sanneh, Lamin. *Piety and Power: Muslims and Christians in West Africa*. Maryknoll, NY: Orbis Books, 1996.

Sasson, Jean P. *Princess: A True Story of Life behind the Veil in Saudi Arabia*. New York: Morrow, 1992.

Seneviratne, H. L. "Religion and Conflict: The Case of Buddhism in Sri Lanka." In *Faith-Based Diplomacy: Trumping Realpolitik*, edited by Douglas Johnston, 76–90. Oxford: Oxford University Press, 2003.

Siewert, John A., Dotsey Welliver, and Edna G. Valdez, eds. *Mission Handbook,* 18th ed. Monvrovia, CA: MARC Publications, 2000.

Smith, Patrick. *Japan: A Reinterpretation*. New York: Vintage Books, 1999.

Tateo, Shimizu. "Gathering Thunder Clouds of Crime." *Japan Quarterly* 48, no. 4 (2001): 55–61.

Tylor, Edward Burnett. *Primitive Culture*, Vol. 2. New York: Harper, 1911.

UNICEF and Coalition to Stop the Use of Child Soldiers. "Child Soldiers: A Global Issue." In *Guide to the Optional Protocol on the Involvement of Children in Armed Conflict*. New York: UNICEF, 2003. http://web.amnesty.org/pages/childsoldiers-background-eng.

United Nations Development Programme. *Arab Human Development Report 2002*. New York: United Nations Development Programme, 2002.

Weaver, Mary Anne. *A Portrait of Egypt: A Journey through the World of Militant Islam*. New York: Farrar, Straus and Giroux, 2000.

Wehrfritz, George, and Lynette Clemetson. "Jesus Is All the World to Me." *Newsweek,* June 29, 1988, 36.

White, Tom. *Missiles over Cuba: The Tom White Story*. Diamond Bar, CA: Uplift Books, 1981.

Winchester, Simon. *Krakatoa: The Day the World Exploded, August 27, 1883.* New York: HarperCollins, 2003.

World Bank. *Global Economic Prospects 2004.* Washington, DC: World Bank, 2003.

Wright, N. T. *The New Testament and the People of God.* Minneapolis: Augsburg Fortress Publishers, 1996.